MODERN LEGAL STUDIES

COUNCIL HOUSING

by

DAVID C. HOATH, LL.B.

Solicitor of the Supreme Court
Senior Lecturer in Law at the University of Sheffield

SECOND EDITION

LONDON
SWEET & MAXWELL
1982

First Edition	1978
Second Impression	1979
Second Edition	1982

Published in 1982 by
Sweet & Maxwell Limited of
11 New Fetter Lane, London.
Printed in Great Britain by
J. W. Arrowsmith Ltd.,
London and Bristol.

British Library Cataloguing in Publication Data

Hoath, David C.
 Council Housing.—2nd ed.—(Modern Legal Studies)
 1. Public housing—Law and Legislation—England
 I. Title   II. Series
 344.204'63635   KD1179

 ISBN 0–421–27610–X
 ISBN 0–421–27620–7 Pbk

MODERN LEGAL STUDIES

COUNCIL HOUSING

AUSTRALIA
The Law Book Company Ltd.
Sydney : Melbourne : Brisbane

CANADA AND U.S.A.
The Carswell Company Ltd.
Agincourt, Ontario

INDIA
N.M. Tripathi Private Ltd.
Bombay
and
Eastern Law House Private Ltd.
Calcutta and Delhi
M.P.P. House
Bangalore

ISRAEL
Steimatzky's Agency Ltd.
Jerusalem : Tel Aviv : Haifa

MALAYSIA : SINGAPORE : BRUNEI
Malayan Law Journal (Pte.) Ltd.
Singapore

NEW ZEALAND
Sweet & Maxwell (N.Z.) Ltd.
Auckland

PAKISTAN
Pakistan Law House
Karachi

PREFACE

The basic aim of the second edition of this book remains as stated in the preface to the first edition: namely, to discuss the law and practice relating to council housing largely from the viewpoint of the tenant and the potential tenant rather than that of the local authority (there are other publications which are specifically geared to the needs of housing officers). Since the first edition was written, however, the Housing Act 1980 has made some very significant changes in the legal protection of council tenants, so that the production of this new edition has proved to be much more than a mere "spring-cleaning" exercise. While the relevant provisions of the 1980 Act have (hopefully) been given sufficient treatment, I have tried to avoid anything approaching a section-by-section commentary on the Act (several such annotations having already been produced): thus detailed attention is also focused on important topics which have remained relatively untouched by the Act, particularly allocations, repairs, and rents.

Council housing remains an area which does not lend itself to convenient legal pigeon-holing. While "Landlord and Tenant Law" might seem the most appropriate generic label, some of the material involves aspects of Administrative Law, Conveyancing, Family Law, Local Government Law, Real Property Law, Welfare Law, and even "Consumer Law" (*cf., e.g. Soonest mended* (National Consumer Council, 1979), Chapter 3; for an excursus with transatlantic overtones on the theme of the tenant as a "consumer," see D. Tiplady (1981) 44 M.L.R. 129, 139–146).

By definition, this book is a "Legal Study." However, this edition was written at a time when the traditional virtues of our council housing system were coming under sustained attack on a variety of fronts, so that it seemed particularly important also to draw attention (albeit briefly) to some of the relevant social, economic and political factors; I hope that the introduction of these wider issues has made the discussion of the law more intelligible and interesting.

The book is designed primarily for student use. Law students are most likely to meet this subject in courses on Landlord and Tenant Law, Housing Law, or Welfare Law; some iconoclastic Land Law courses may also embrace it. I would hope that students in other disciplines than law may find the book useful too: in particular, it may help in a small way to meet the calls for more legal training to be given to social workers (see, *e.g.* the Report of the Central Council for Education and Training in Social Work on *Legal Studies in Social Work Education*, 1974, and A. Phillips (1979) 42 M.L.R. 29). Council housing can also be very relevant to the work of practising lawyers, even in such traditional fields as conveyancing and divorce. In addition, the book may prove of practical use to Citizens' Advice Bureaux (who have been justifiably described by the Court of Appeal as "skilled advisers," though in a somewhat unfortunate context: see *Riley* v. *Tesco Stores Ltd. and Greater London Citizens' Advice Bureau Service Ltd.* [1980] J.S.W.L. 250), and to other information-giving agencies. Although it was not my primary purpose to produce a handbook for staff in local authorities or for local councillors, I was heartened to learn by way of correspondence received from these quarters that the first edition had proved to be of some value in what were, prior to the 1980 legislation, the corridors of local government power; I trust that, despite the intervening cut-backs, funds might somehow be found for the purchase of this edition too!

I would like to thank Professor Patrick McAuslan of the University of Warwick, the general editor of the Modern Legal Studies series, for the interest which he showed in my original proposal. I have learned much from those whom I have been supposed to teach, not only at the

University of Sheffield but also on training courses designed for practitioners of several varieties. I have also benefited considerably from discussions with several of my colleagues on those aspects of the book which overlapped with their areas of expertise: particular patience was shown by Professor Graham Battersby and John Mesher. I am grateful to Mrs. Jean Hopewell for producing a typescript which looked infinitely more attractive than the raw material with which she was supplied. Finally, I owe a great debt to my wife and children for tolerating conduct which was more than usually boorish during the gestation period of this second edition.

The law is stated as at October 1, 1981, although some later developments have been squeezed in at proof stage.

The University of Sheffield   David Hoath

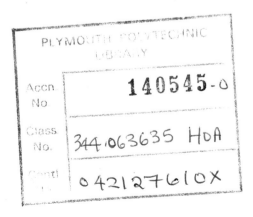

CONTENTS

OTHER BOOKS IN THE SERIES

TABLE OF CASES

TABLE OF STATUTES

ABBREVIATIONS

Apart from the standard abbreviations for citation of legal literature, the following abbreviations have been used (primarily in references to the authorship of publications):

C.H.A.C.	Central Housing Advisory Committee
C.H.A.S.	Catholic Housing Aid Society
C.I.P.F.A.	Chartered Institute of Public Finance and Accountancy
C.P.A.G.	Child Poverty Action Group
C.R.E.	Commission for Racial Equality
C.U.R.S.	Centre for Urban and Regional Studies (University of Birmingham)
D.H.S.S.	Department of Health and Social Security
D.o.E.	Department of the Environment
H.D.D.	Housing Development Directorate
H.E.O.	Housing Emergency Office
H.S.A.G.	Housing Services Advisory Group
M.H.L.G.	Ministry of Housing and Local Government
P.H.A.S.	Public Health Advisory Service
S.C.A.T.	Services to Community Action and Tenants
S.H.A.C.	Shelter Housing Action Centre

Chapter 1

INTRODUCTION

1. *The Importance of Council Housing*

The use of council housing as a viable means of accommodating low-income families began in earnest immediately after the First World War, primarily because the introduction of rent control legislation in 1915 had meant that private enterprise could no longer be relied on to provide working-class housing. Over the next 60 years, the ways in which successive governments saw the role of council housing often differed considerably, as did the type and quality of the housing which local authorities erected[1]; but council housing gradually grew, to such an extent indeed that it eventually far outstripped the privately rented sector. The D.o.E. has recorded that although in 1975 the total number of rented dwellings in England and Wales was similar to that of 30 years previously, the balance between the two rented sectors had completely changed: in 1945 there were about 8.5 million rented dwellings, of which 7.1 million were privately owned and 1.3 million were council owned, while by 1975 there were 8.1 million rented dwellings, of which 2.9 million were privately owned and 5.2 million were council owned (Consultation Paper on *The Review of the Rent Acts*, 1977, p. 3). It appears that this country has a greater proportion of its housing stock rented from public authorities than any comparable nation.[2]

However, the Housing Act 1980 contains the potential for effecting dramatic changes in our council housing system, by pruning it back and entrenching owner-occupation as the form of housing tenure most devoutly to be wished on the population as a whole. On introducing this measure to the House of Commons,[3] the Minister stated that "for those who rent or wish to rent" it laid the basis for "perhaps as profound a social revolution as any in our history" (*Hansard* (Commons) January 15, 1980, Vol. 976, col. 1443); although Mr Heseltine was predicting a benign form of revolution, it is certainly arguable that recent housing policies were a significant factor in the 1981 inner-city riots (see, *e.g. The Times*, July 21, 1981).

One commentator on the 1980 Act has written that "[t]he government have understood the purpose of public housing in its historical context, have stopped the growth of public housing which has threatened its original role, and have, as it were, put it back in its place" (A. Arden, *The Housing Act 1980*, Current Law Statutes Reprints, 1980, Introduction, p.x.); while another has described this Act as "[t]he beginning of the end for council housing" (S. Schifferes, *Roof*, January 1980, at p. 10). Many fear that the Act's provisions relating to the right to buy council housing and its recasting of the housing subsidies system, when coupled with a massive general reduction in housing expenditure[4] (including in particular a decline in new council housebuilding rates[5] and in the maintenance of the existing council housing stock), could well result in local authority housing eventually becoming nothing more than a series of "sink" estates for those who have been unable or unwilling to become owner-occupiers. It has also been strenuously asserted that owner-occupation is not necessarily an inherently superior form of housing tenure to renting from a public (or private) landlord, or one into which those on low incomes should be forced indiscriminately.[6]

The rapidity with which governments and their housing policies have changed in recent years suggests that predictions of the 1980 Act sounding the death-knell of council housing in its present form may prove to have been unduly alarmist, although there will doubtless be some rough times ahead for those hoping to become council tenants, and for existing council tenants who fail to buy their way into the "great property-owning democracy." The attempt in the 1980 Act to revive the privately rented sector by the use of "shortholds"[7] has not so far proved to be conspicuously successful[8]; and notwithstanding all the various attempts in recent years to thrust owner-occupation further "down-market,"[9] it remains difficult to disagree with the contention that "[c]ouncil housing is the only system operating in this country which can offer secure homes of a reasonable standard to people on the basis of their need rather than on their ability to pay" (M. Cutting, *Landlord: Private or Public?*, C.H.A.S. Occasional Paper, 1977, pp. 34–35)[10].

Thus, despite the manifold problems which currently beset our system of council housing, the following chapters have not been written by way of a pathological investigation of a dying tenure,[11] but rather in the expectation that the system will continue to play a valuable role in alleviating this country's housing problems.

Two further introductory matters will now be discussed, concerning the relationship between council tenants and their landlords, and that between councils and the central government.

2.   *The Nature of the Relationship between a Council and its Tenants*

In a chapter headed "Serfs or Citizens," Colin Ward wrote in 1974 that the council tenant's relationship with his landlord was "only a contractual one in the sense that a serf in the middle ages was a party to a contract with the lord of the manor" (*Tenants Take Over*, p. 14). However, as indicated in the first edition of the present work, the position of the council tenant even before the Housing Act 1980 was in fact far from being one of exclusive dependence upon the administrative decisions taken by the housing department, since there was a coherent body of law which offered some (though admittedly rather patchy) protection. There was also a widespread view that council tenants were in practice "substantially safe-guarded by normal democratic processes and the assumption of a responsible and accountable landlord" (see the H.S.A.G. Report on *Tenancy Agreements*, 1977, para. 16).[12] Nevertheless, it was becoming increasingly illogical to have an elaborate system of statutory protection for tenants in the fast-diminishing privately rented sector, from which tenants in the expanding public sector remained excluded; and reports from the local government "ombudsmen" (following their creation by Pt. III of the Local Government Act 1974) confirmed that councils could not always be relied upon to act as angelic landlords.

A statutory "public sector tenants' charter" was eventually introduced by the Housing Act 1980, which as will be seen concentrates on the individual rights of tenants rather than on collective rights. It will further be seen that this protection differs significantly from that given to private sector tenants under the Rent Act 1977: this is partly because the relationship between a council and its tenants involves not merely that of landlord and tenant, but also the more nebulous connection between local authority and citizen.[13]

However, the recognition by Parliament of council tenants' "rights" has not necessarily been matched by an instant change of emphasis in the approach of all housing managers and their staff towards tenants. Housing management is still something of a "Cinderella" profession: there is no statutory obligation on local authorities even to appoint housing managers (as opposed to, *e.g.* chief education officers, directors of social services, and chief financial officers: *cf.* the Local Government Act 1972, ss. 112(4), 151), and the training given to officers in housing departments has frequently been criticised for its inadequacy.[14]

Furthermore, as regards those aspects of council housing on which the 1980 Act has made little direct impact (particularly allocations and rent-fixing), the general judicial reluctance to interfere with the decisions of council officers on what are perceived to be matters of housing management[15] may well continue; and even when the new "tenants' charter" rights arising from the 1980 Act are in issue, it is relevant to bear in mind that the track-record of the judges in enforcing private tenants' rights under successive Rent Acts has not on the whole been very encouraging.[16]

3. *The Nature of the Relationship between a Council and the Central Government*

The separate relationship between a council and the central government, involving particularly financial constraints but also guidance by way of circulars and reports, can indirectly but very significantly affect the ways in which the authority's tenants (and potential tenants) are treated. The combined effects of the Housing Act 1980 and the Local Government, Planning and Land Act 1980, have been considerably to strengthen central government's control over the ways in which local authorities carry out their functions, especially those relating to housing. Although some previous controls have been relaxed, the all-important controls over authorities' purse-strings have been tightened, and these may have a marked effect, not merely on the building of new council houses and the maintenance of the existing stock, but also on council house rents. Moreover, as mentioned earlier, the imposition of the statutory "right to buy" has severely limited authorities' ability to keep their better stock within the public sector at all. It has been argued, indeed, that the "tenants' charter" provisions in the Housing Act 1980 (and also the legal duties towards the homeless imposed by the Housing (Homeless Persons) Act 1977) may be "as much to do with [the] struggles between central and local government as with concern for the creation of rights for individual tenants" (M. Partington, *Landlord and Tenant*, 2nd ed., 1980, p. 468); more specifically, we shall see in the next chapter that it has been suggested, as one reason why the statutory definition of the key concept of the "secure" council tenancy has so few loopholes for councils to exploit, that the government intended to maximise the numbers of tenants qualifying for the "right to buy" as a method of further eroding local government autonomy: viewed in this somewhat uncharitable light, the conferring of this valuable benefit on individual tenants is merely a by-product of the "central–local" power struggle.

Although this book is mainly concerned with the relationship between a council and its tenants, it is important not to lose sight of the considerable power possessed by central government to influence council housing matters.

Notes

[1] For accounts of the development of council housing, see, *e.g.*: A. Murie, P. Niner and C. Watson, *Housing Policy and the Housing System* (1976), pp. 92–101; *Whatever Happened to Council Housing?* (National Community Development Project, 1976), pp. 9–32; the 1977 Green Paper on *Housing Policy*, Cmnd. 6851, Technical Volume, Pt. I. Chap. 1; S. Merrett, *State Housing in Britain* (1979), Chaps. 1–2.

[2] See, *e.g.*: J.S. Fuerst (ed.), *Public Housing in Europe and America* (1974); *Housing Policy, op. cit.*, Technical Volume, Pt. III, Chap. 11; L. McDowell, *Roof*, March 1979, at p. 45.

[3] According to the parliamentary correspondent of *The Times*, Mr. Heseltine unveiled the Bill to a "sceptical Commons" as "almost certainly the greatest thing since the Garden of Eden"! (*The Times*, January 16, 1980).

[4] Although the government planned in 1981 that general public expenditure should be cut by 5 per cent. between 1979–80 and 1983–84, the projected cut for housing expenditure over this period was to be no less than 53 per cent. (see *The Government's Expenditure Plans 1981–82 to 1983–84*, Cmnd. 8175).

[5] The number of new council housing "starts" in 1980 (around 54,000) was the lowest since 1924 (see *Hansard* (Lords) May 13, 1981, Vol. 420, col. 562).

[6] See, *e.g.* V. Karn, *Roof*, January 1981, at pp. 13–14, J. Kemeny, *The Myth of Home Ownership–Private versus Public Choices in Housing Tenures* (1981).

[7] See ss. 51–55.

[8] See *Hansard* (Commons) June 4, 1981, Vol. 5, cols. *411–412*.

[9] See, *e.g.*: the Housing (Financial Provisions) Act 1958, s. 43 ("low-start" council mortgages); the Housing Subsidies Act 1967, Pt. II ("option mortgage" scheme); the Leasehold Reform Act 1967 (leasehold enfranchisement in the private sector); the Home Purchase Assistance and Housing Corporation Guarantee Act 1978 (special savings schemes for first-time buyers of low-priced properties); the Housing Act 1980, ss. 1–27 (public sector "right to buy"); see also ss. 93, 108, 110 (11)–(12) and 111 of the 1980 Act.

[10] For further spirited defences of council housing, see, *e.g.*: H. Aughton (1972) 136 L.G. Rev. 169, 397 (but *cp.* A. Sherman (1972) 136 L.G. Rev. 114, 312); V. Karn, *loc. cit.*; *A Future for Public Housing*, the Labour Party, 1981.

[11] This word is used throughout in its non-technical sense.

[12] Yet this Report also emphasised that "[t]he relationship between public sector landlords and their tenants must undergo a fundamental change" (*op. cit.*, at para. 9), and the D.o.E. produced several other publications designed to help to bring this change about by non-statutory means (see, *e.g. Getting tenants involved*, 1977, and *The Client Role in Public Sector Housebuilding*, H.S.A.G., 1978).

[13] The general interaction between private and public law concepts where property rights are in dispute can raise some very thorny and fundamental issues (by way of analogy, see, *e.g.* G. Samuel (1981) 97 L.Q.R. 19, discussing *Cinnamond* v. *British Airports Authority* [1980] 2 All E.R. 368, (C.A.)).

[14] See, *e.g.*: *Training for Housing Work*, H.S.A.G., 1977; V. Karn, *Roof*, November 1977, at p. 177; *Housing Training–findings and recommendations from the study by the City University*, D.o.E., 1978; C. Legg, M. Brion and M. Bieber, *Roof*, May 1978, at p. 84.

[15] See, *e.g.*: Harman J. in *Summerfield* v. *Hampstead B.C.* [1957] 1 All E.R. 221, at 223, 226; Stamp L.J. in *R.* v. *Bristol Corp., ex p. Hendy* [1974] 1 All E.R. 1047, 1049, (C.A.); Dunn J. in *Brent* v. *Brent* [1974] 2 All E.R. 1211, 1215–1216. But *cf.* Lord Salmon in *Liverpool C.C.* v. *Irwin* [1976] 2 All E.R. 39, 49, (H.L.).

[16] See, *e.g.*: M. Cutting (1976) LAG Bul. 101; A. Arden, *Roof*, May 1979, at p. 78; P. Robson and P. Watchman [1980] Conv. 27; A. Nicol (1981) 44 M.L.R. 21. For a more broadly based indictment of an alleged lack of judicial impartiality concerning legislation affecting matters of housing and property, see J.A.G. Griffith, *The Politics of the Judiciary*, Chap. 5; and for proposals for a specialist "housing court", see, *e.g.* A. Arden (1977) LAG Bul. 127, S. Wilcox and G. Randall, *Roof*, March 1980, at p. 42.

Chapter 2

"SECURE" TENANCIES AND THEIR TERMS

1. *The Definition of a "Secure" Tenancy*

(a) *General*

Section 28 of the Housing Act 1980 introduces the key concept of the "secure" public sector tenancy: from this concept flow the "tenants' charter" rights in the 1980 Act, so that it is a vital preliminary exercise clearly to identify which council tenants hold under "secure" tenancies and which do not. We shall see that the vast majority of council tenancies are in fact "secure," since the exempt categories have been very tightly drafted; a cynic could conclude that this "may have more to do with the intention to maximise the number of people qualifying for the 'right to buy' than with the charter itself" (*The Tenants' Charter*, Shelter, 1981, p. 7).

In one of the consultation papers which preceded the formulation of the "public tenants' charter" in the 1980 Act, the D.o.E. stated that it would be "desirable to introduce a self-contained legislative code rather than attempt to extend the existing Rent Acts which are already exceedingly complicated and which are largely concerned with matters (*e.g.* rent-fixing) which would be inappropriate to the public sector" (*Housing Management: Tenants' Rights: Security of Tenure for Public Sector Tenants*, para. 3). The 1980 Act itself reflects this aspiration, so that although several provisions have been "borrowed" from the Rent Act 1977 (such as certain of the grounds for possession), the statutory protection for council tenants is best regarded as *sui generis*. Thus, as will be seen in Chapter 7, the 1980 Act eschews the difficult Rent Act distinction between a protected (contractual) tenancy and a statutory tenancy (*cf.* the Rent Act 1977, ss. 2–3). Instead, sections 29 and 32 of the 1980 Act provide for the continuance of the contractual tenancy until the date fixed by the court for possession, and ensure that fixed-term tenancies are in general continued automatically as periodic tenancies. Further, the Court of Appeal has decided that the "tenants' charter" provisions in the 1980 Act were motivated by very different considerations from those underlying the early Rent Acts: the first Rent Acts were designed to deal with the urgent need to accommodate returning servicemen after the end of the Great War, whereas the relevant provisions of the 1980 Act were not introduced to meet any such emergency, but were designed with the social aim of giving public sector tenants similar statutory security to that long enjoyed by tenants in the private sector: *L.B. of Hammersmith & Fulham* v. *Harrison* [1981] 2 All E.R. 588, (C.A.).[1]

In deciding a council tenant's rights following the 1980 Act, therefore, the search for the appropriate "label" should not be as difficult a task as categorisation for Rent Act purposes (*cp.* D. Tiplady (1981) 44 M.L.R. 129, 130); in the public sector, the basic classification is simply between "secure" and "non-secure" tenancies, and tenancies granted before, as well as on and after, the commencement of the relevant provisions (October 3, 1980) can be "secure" (s. 47).

Indeed, for the public sector it will often not be necessary to make even the fundamental distinction between a lease and a licence (which still causes such difficulties in the private sector[2]), since section 48(1) of the 1980 Act provides that licences (whether or not for value) which would be secure tenancies if they were tenancies (*i.e.* the "separate dwelling" requirement in s.28(1)—discussed *infra*—must be satisfied), shall be treated as secure tenancies for the purposes of Part I of the Act; save that this is not the case where the licence is, in effect, a licensed squatting agreement, *i.e.* a licence granted temporarily to a person who entered the dwelling *or any other land*[3] as a trespasser (s. 48(2)). Thus if a licence to occupy short-life property is granted by a council to someone who was not originally a trespasser, security will *prima facie* attach, unless one of the exceptions from the definition of "secure" tenancy (shortly to be discussed) applies. Throughout this book, references to secure council "tenancies" are intended also to embrace licences, unless otherwise stated.

(b) *The basic definition in section 28*

In order to be "secure", the tenancy (whether fixed-term or periodic) must satisfy the following requirements at the time when the question falls to be decided (see the words " . . . at any time when . . . " in s. 28(1)):

(i) The property (which may be a house or part of a house, such as a flat, and may include land let together with the dwelling even though physically separated from it: s. 50(2)(*a*)) must be let *as a separate dwelling* (s. 28(1)). This expression is not defined, but it appears that in this context the relevant Rent Act cases can be applied. Thus if the tenant shares *living accommodation* (such as a kitchen or a sitting-room, but *not* merely a bathroom or a toilet) with people *other than* those who are joint tenants with him or members of his household or his lodgers or subtenants (*cf.* s. 35), then he *cannot* have a secure tenancy (*cf. Baker* v. *Turner* [1950] 1 All E.R. 834, 854, (H.L.: Lord Reid); *Goodrich* v. *Paisner* [1956] 2 All E.R. 176, (H.L.)). In effect, therefore, the sharing of living accommodation by a tenant with *other tenants* removes security, unless the sharers are joint tenants with him; so, for example, an occupier of hostel accommodation who shares essential living facilities, or a single parent or student sharing a house or flat with others though holding an individual licence, does not hold under a "secure tenancy." There is no equivalent in the 1980 Act to section 22 of the Rent Act 1977, which provides that if the tenant shares living accommodation with people other than the landlord, he can still have a protected or statutory tenancy of the separate (non-shared) accommodation.

The broad purpose behind the insertion of this "separate dwelling" requirement in the public sector was apparently to avoid security attaching to "occupiers under . . . sharing arrangements, which are basically suitable only for households or individuals at a particular stage in their life-cycle," but to allow for security "where the sharing of some facilities such as bathroom or WC is only an incidental part of the provision of otherwise permanent accommodation to one household" (D.o.E. Consultation Paper on *Housing Management, op. cit.*, at para. 16).

(ii) The interest of the landlord must belong to a prescribed public body (this is described by s. 28(1)–(2) as the "landlord condition"). The list of prescribed bodies includes: a district council, the G.L.C., and a London borough council (ss. 28(2) *(a)*, 28 (4), 50 (1)); a county council which grants the tenancy in the exercise of its reserve powers under section 194 of the Local Government Act 1972 (s. 28(2) *(d)*: these powers appear never to have been exercised by any county council); and a "housing co-operative" which holds the property on behalf of a local authority pursuant to an agreement approved by the Minister[4] (ss. 28(2) *(c)*, 50(1), and Sched. 20).

(iii) The tenant must be an *individual* (not, *e.g.* another public authority, a limited company, or a short-life housing organisation), who occupies the dwelling as his *only or principal home* (s. 28(1) and (3) describe this as the "tenant condition"). In the case of a joint tenancy, each of the joint tenants must be an individual, and at least one must fulfil this occupation requirement (s. 28(3)).

The concept of occupation as the tenant's "only or principal home" is not defined (although the Act makes clear, first, that a secure tenant need not occupy the *whole* property, since s. 35 contemplates the subletting of part and the taking in of lodgers[5]; and secondly, that a deserted spouse may by remaining in occupation keep the deserting spouse's secure tenancy alive notwithstanding his or her departure, since s. 1(5) of the Matrimonial Homes Act 1967 is amended by Sched. 25, Pt. I, para. 14 of the 1980 Act[6]). The courts may therefore be expected to take the common-sense approach of disregarding temporary absences (*e.g.* for holiday or business reasons), and to refer in cases of difficulty to relevant decisions concerning similar expressions used in other legislation. For example, with regard to the expression "occupying . . . as his only or main residence" used in section 1(2) of the Leasehold Reform Act 1967, the Court of Appeal in *Poland* v. *Earl Cadogan* [1980] 3 All E.R. 544 emphasised the following principles: first, that a tenant might satisfy the requirements of this expression even though absent for a long period, provided he was keeping the property ready for his renewed occupation; secondly, that occupation is a matter of fact and degree, indicating something more than legal possession; and thirdly, that where the absence is prolonged the onus is on the tenant to show that he has taken clear steps to maintain his occupation. On the facts, the tenant failed to discharge this burden since he had departed on a long ocean voyage without leaving a forwarding address, and after making preliminary arrangements for subletting the whole property.[7]

An instructive case on the other side of the line in *Frost* v. *Feltham* [1981] 1 W.L.R. 452. In issue here was the applicability of the expression "used as [his] only or main residence," contained in paragraph 4 (1) of Schedule 1 to the Finance Act 1974 and concerning tax relief on instalments of mortgage interest, to a publican in Essex who bought a house in Wales on mortgage: this house was the only one he had ever owned, and it was kept fully furnished, but he only spent two or three days each month there. Nevertheless, Nourse J. held that the publican was entitled to the tax relief he sought, since the property was used as his "main" residence, though not as his "only" residence: the judge made clear that where a person lives in two or more places, the question of which he uses as his principal residence cannot be decided solely by reference to the way in which he divides his time between the two.

In this context one must beware of cases decided in relation to the Rent Act expressions "statutory tenancy" and "resident landlord," since the relevant provisions of the Rent Act 1977 (ss. 2 and 12) refer to occupation "as his residence," whereas section 28(3) of the 1980 Act is much more narrowly drafted in its reference to "*only or principal* home"; further, it must be borne in mind that the mere failure to occupy by a Rent Act *protected, i.e.* contractual, tenant (as opposed to a Rent Act *statutory* tenant), is not inconsistent with the continuance of the tenancy, so that no surrender will necessarily be implied (see, *e.g. Legg* v. *Coole and Sheaff* (1978) LAG Bul. 189, (C.A.)). Thus, as mentioned earlier, any temptation to equate a Rent Act protected or statutory tenancy with a Housing Act secure tenancy must be firmly resisted.[8]

(c) *Exemptions from the definition in section 28*

Assuming that the three basic conditions for a secure tenancy set out above are satisfied, the tenancy may nevertheless fail to be secure if it falls within one of the exemptions listed in Schedule 3.[9] An outline account of the more important of these exemptions now follows, but reference should be made to the Schedule itself[10] for the details of each relevant exemption.

(i) Long tenancies

Tenancies granted for a term certain exceeding 21 years cannot be secure (Sched. 3, para. 1). Thus "equity-sharing" schemes involving long leases[11] are excluded from the provisions of the tenants' charter, and long leases of flats granted to former secure tenants pursuant to the "right to buy"[12] cannot themselves be secure tenancies.

(ii) Tenancies granted to employees

A tenancy granted to an employee of the landlord authority, *or* to an employee of certain specified public bodies other than the landlord authority, is not secure if the contract of employment requires the employee to occupy the dwelling for the better performance of his duties, as is the case for example with many resident caretakers (Sched. 3, para. 2). Relevant here will be the case-law concerning the difficult distinction often made for Rent Act purposes between service occupiers (who are unprotected, because they are licensees *required* to occupy the property in order to carry out their duties), and service tenants (who are protected as tenants because they are merely *permitted* to reside in their employer's property)[13]; we have seen that section 48 of the 1980 Act has removed, for *most* purposes relating to a secure tenancy, the distinction between a lease and a licence as such. Shelter has estimated that there are over 200,000 public sector tenants (excluding servicemen and employees of nationalised industries) living in tied accommodation.

There is also a separate exemption from the definition of secure tenancy, which applies where a tenancy is granted to an employee *of the landlord authority*, the tenancy is to terminate when the employment ends, and the dwelling forms *part* of (or is situated in the grounds of) a building held by the landlord authority for educational purposes or (in effect) for people with designated special needs: this exemption would cover, for example, certain resident employees in schools or children's homes or old people's homes (Sched. 3, para. 3); the tenant does not need to be *required* to occupy for the better performance of his duties here, in order for the tenancy to be exempt (*cp.* para. 2, *supra*).

(iii) Tenancies of land acquired for development

A tenancy is not secure if the dwelling is on land which was initially *acquired* for development within the meaning of section 22 of the Town and County Planning Act 1971 (as opposed merely to being currently *required* for such development), and the dwelling is used by the landlord authority, pending development, as temporary housing accommodation (Sched. 3, para. 4). The problem with this exemption is that it does *not* cover short-life property as such: the authority must have acquired the property for development within the technical definition in section 22(1) of the 1971 Act ("the carrying out of building, engineering, mining, or other operations . . . or the making of any material change in the use of any buildings or other land"). It is still not clear in law that the complete *demolition* of a building would of itself be "development" (see, *e.g.* J. Alder, *Development Control* (1979), p. 48); and improvement work which does not materially affect the external appearance of the building is specifically exempted from the definition of development by section 22(2) *(a)* of the 1971 Act. If, therefore, the authority acquired the land to do work which falls *outside* this technical definition of development, any short-term leases (or licences) would *prima facie* attract security unless one of the other exemptions applies, and could therefore provide long-term headaches for the authority. This problem remains notwithstanding the availability of a special mandatory ground for possession here (see the 1980 Act, Sched. 4, Pt. I, gd. 8), since before possession can be awarded on this ground the court has to be satisfied as to suitable alternative accommodation for the tenant.[14]

There is thus a distinct danger that authorities may prove reluctant to lease (or licence) their short-life properties to someone who does not fall within one of the other exempt categories. Paradoxically, in view of section 48(2) *(supra)*, there is more incentive for authorities to grant licences of short-life properties where squatters have already taken the law into their own hands by trespassing, than in a situation where potential licensees ask permission before they occupy; this is almost an incentive to squat!

One way out of this difficulty would be for the authority to grant a licence of property to a special short-life borrowing agency, which would in turn licence the property to the intended occupants. Provided this intermediate licensing agency is not a housing association registered with the Housing Corporation (and therefore is not itself a "public landlord" for secure tenancy purposes: see s. 28(2) *(b)*), all should be well. The licence granted by the authority to the agency would not require the Minister's consent within the new section 104 of the Housing Act 1957 (introduced by s. 91 of the 1980 Act),[15] since it would not be a "disposal"[16]; the agency itself could not hold a secure tenancy (or "secure licence"), since it would not satisfy the "tenant condition" in section 28(3) of the 1980 Act *(supra)*; and the licence by the agency to the individual occupiers would neither attract security under the 1980 Act (the agency not being a designated public landlord), nor under the Rent Act 1977 (which does not, broadly speaking, cover mere *licences*: since the agency itself only held under a licence it could not of course carve out a sub-*lease* therefrom); see further *The Housing Act 1980: Its implications for the short-term use of vacant property*, H.E.O. (Shelter), 1981, pp. 23–25.

(iv) Tenancies granted to homeless persons

A tenancy granted in pursuance of sections 3(4), 4(3) or 5(6) of the Housing (Homeless Persons) Act 1977 (*i.e.* the *temporary* duties[17]) will not normally be secure until the expiry of 12 months beginning with the authority's notification to the tenant pursuant to section 8 of the 1977 Act (Sched. 3, para. 5 of the 1980 Act). Although it is somewhat rare in these "temporary" cases for the accommodation to be made available for more than 12 months from the notification under section 8, authorities will have to "diary ahead" if they are to ensure that security cannot arise, so that where necessary the tenant can be switched to other accommodation before the deadline is reached. Where accommodation is granted pursuant to section 4(5) of the 1977 Act (*i.e.* where the applicant is found to be in priority need and unintentionally homeless), security will normally attach immediately if no other exemption applies.

(v) Tenancies granted to those securing employment

A tenancy granted temporarily by an authority to someone who has already secured employment in its area and was not previously resident there will not normally be secure until the expiry of 12 months from the grant (Sched. 3, para. 6).

(vi) Tenancies granted under "North Wiltshire" schemes

A subtenancy granted temporarily by an authority, pursuant to an arrangement with (normally) a private landlord under what is popularly called a "North Wiltshire" scheme,[18] will not be secure (Sched. 3, para. 7). This scheme involves a short-term arrangement under which a dwelling is leased *to* the authority *by* (normally) a *private* landlord (*i.e. not* by another body capable of granting secure tenancies, though the landlord could be, *e.g.* a government department such as the Property Services Agency), with vacant possession, and for use as temporary housing accommodation on terms allowing the head landlord to obtain vacant possession from the authority on the expiry of a specified period or when required by him. The authority will then sublet the property, with no danger of creating a secure (sub) tenancy.

Thus a private landlord can avoid the restrictions in the Rent Act 1977 by (in effect) using the council as his letting agent. Such schemes can be regarded as "shortholds without the aggro."[19] However, if the private landlord charged the authority a rent which it considered to be excessive, it would appear to be legally entitled, as head tenant, to take the unsporting step of having a "fair rent" registered by the rent officer under Part IV of the Rent Act 1977, provided that the property was let to it as "*a separate dwelling*" (see s. 1 of the Rent Act 1977, and *cp. St. Catherine's College* v. *Dorling* [1979] 3 All E.R. 250, (C.A.)).

(vii) Tenancies granted temporarily during works

A tenancy is not secure if it is granted temporarily, during the period when works are being carried out on the tenant's previous dwelling, and the tenant was *not* a secure tenant of that previous dwelling (Sched. 3, para. 8). This would cover for example a private sector tenant who has been temporarily displaced while his landlord carries out the work required by an authority's improvement notice served under Part VIII of the Housing Act 1974. If such a temporarily "decanted" tenant was in fact a *secure* tenant of the previous dwelling, then the new tenancy will normally also be secure, although the council will have a discretionary ground for possession (under Sched. 4, Pt. I, gd. 6) when the work on the previous dwelling is completed.[20]

(viii) Student tenancies

Tenancies granted to students cannot normally be secure until six months from the end of the student's course (Sched. 3, para. 11; S.I. 1980/1407 designates the relevant courses for the purposes of this exemption).

(d) *Secure tenancies and the right to buy*

Quite apart from these exemptions from the definition of a *secure tenancy*, there are several exceptions to the *right to buy*, which is normally one of the rights enjoyed by secure tenants[21]; the two lists of excluded categories (exemptions from secure tenancies on the one hand, and exceptions to the right to buy on the other), must not be confused.

2. *The Form of the Tenancy Agreement*

Most council tenancies are periodic, and on a weekly basis. Under the general law, leases the length of which will not initially exceed three years need neither be under seal nor even in writing (see the Law of Property Act 1925, s. 54 (2)). Oral council tenancies are still perfectly legal even after the Housing Act 1980, which does not insist on a written tenancy agreement as such (*cp.* the Green Paper on *Housing Policy*, Cmnd. 6851, 1977, at para. 11.07, and the Tenants' Rights, etc. (Scotland) Act 1980, s. 16). The Housing Act 1980 merely requires that where under a secure tenancy there is no formal lease or tenancy agreement in writing, the council must provide the secure tenant with a *written statement* of all the terms of the tenancy other than those implied by law (and where there is a formal lease or tenancy agreement in writing but it fails to set out all the terms agreed, *e.g.* because it refers to a list of conditions kept at the council's offices, then again a *written statement* of the omitted terms, other than those implied by law, must be given): section 41(3) *(b)*. This written statement must be supplied, in the case of post-October 3, 1980 tenancies, on the grant of the tenancy or as soon as practicable thereafter, or, if the tenancy was granted before October 3, 1980, by October 3, 1982[22]: s. 41(4). The court can pronounce by simple declaration on the *accuracy* of this written statement (s. 86(2)), but the tenant cannot obtain the court's opinion as to the *reasonableness* of the stated terms of the tenancy as such (save in eviction proceedings[23]).

Thus in practice the tenancy agreement itself will still often be made orally, but subject to certain conditions set out in some ancillary document such as the rent book. Sometimes the tenant is required to sign these tenancy conditions (see, *e.g.* Lord Wilberforce in *Liverpool C.C.* v. *Irwin* [1976] 2 All E.R. 39, 43, (H.L.), pointing out that in such a case " . . . the contract takes effect as soon as the tenants sign the form and are let into possession"); but signature is not essential, since the tenant's acceptance of the conditions can be inferred merely from his entry into possession, and the conditions sometimes expressly provide that the tenant's possession of the property is conclusive evidence of his acceptance of those conditions.

If the document takes the form of a written lease or written tenancy agreement (as opposed to a printed list of conditions forming the basis of an oral or deemed acceptance by the tenant), then this can actually prove disadvantageous to the tenant, since a written lease for a periodic tenancy is subject to stamp duty at the rate of 50p per £50 where the rent exceeds £250 per annum (see the Stamp Act 1891, Sched. 1; Finance Act 1974, s. 49(1), Sched. 11, Pt. I, para. 10); and even a written *contract* for such a tenancy must be stamped as if it were a lease (Stamp Act 1891, s. 75(1)). No doubt many council tenants (and some of their advisers) fail to consider the stamp duty implications where the lease or tenancy agreement itself is in writing; yet if a document subject to stamp duty is not properly stamped it is not admissible in court, save on a solicitor's undertaking to pay the duty and penalties for late stamping (Stamp Act 1891, s. 14(1); *Parkfield Trust Ltd.* v. *Dent* [1931] 2 K.B. 579, 582).

3. *Rent Books*

Quite apart from the formalities considered so far, under section 1 of the Landlord and Tenant Act 1962 the council must provide a "rent book" where the rent is payable weekly, even if the tenancy itself is oral. Further, the 1962 Act can cover *licences* as well as tenancies, for section 1(1) refers to a right to occupy property as a residence "granted . . . by a contract or conferred by an enactment."

Paradoxically, neither the 1962 Act nor the relevant regulations (*infra*) actually require the recording of the rent payments in the rent book. Instead, the rent book is really more of a vehicle for the provision of information to the tenant, although as regards secure tenants this role has been rather overshadowed by the provisions in the Housing Act 1980 relating to the supplying by the landlord of both a written statement of the tenancy terms (s.41(3)(*b*), *supra*), and explanatory information relating thereto (s. 41(1), (3) *(a), infra*).

The rent book must contain the landlord's name and address (1962 Act, s. 2(1) *(a)*), and a summary of the statutory provisions relating to overcrowding (Housing Act 1957, s. 81(1)). Unlike a private landlord, a council is not obliged to insert particulars of its rent rebate scheme[24] in the rent book (see the Housing Finance Act 1972, ss. 19(4), 24(11)); but since the council must furnish details of its rebate scheme to the tenant on or before the commencement of the tenancy (1972 Act, s. 24(6)), it will often prove convenient to include this information in the rent book.

If the council fails to provide a rent book when under an obligation to do so, or fails to include the relevant information therein, it is guilty of a criminal offence (Housing Act 1957, s. 81(1); 1962 Act, s. 4), but it may still claim the rent from the tenant (*Shaw* v. *Groom* [1970] 1 All E.R. 702, (C.A.)). Although the information to be included in rent books provided by council landlords is much less than that required to be provided by most private landlords (*cf.* D. C. Hoath [1978] J.S.W.L. 3, Rent Act 1977, ss. 14, 19(5) *(aa)*), nevertheless, since authorities have been urged to prosecute landlords contravening these requirements (M.H.L.G. Circular no. 59/62 on *Landlord and Tenant Act 1962*, 1962, para. 3), they should themselves set a good example!

4. *The Terms of the Tenancy*

(a) *General*

Prior to the Housing Act 1980, the terms of council tenancy agreements had frequently been criticised for their one-sidedness in setting out in detail the obligations of the tenant, without spelling out his rights as against the landlord (see, *e.g.*: *Liverpool C.C.* v. *Irwin* [1976] 2 All E.R. 39, 43, (H.L.: Lord Wilberforce); the National Consumer Council's paper on *Tenancy Agreements*, 1976, *passim*; the H.S.A.G. Report on *Tenancy Agreements*, 1977, paras. 8–9; and the Green Paper on *Housing Policy*, *op. cit.*, at para. 11.06). Even after the Housing Act 1980, the detailed tenancy terms are still broadly speaking up to the individual council to decide, in the exercise of its power of "general management, regulation and control" conferred by section 111(1) of the Housing Act 1957. The courts in England and Wales have no such discretion as that conferred by section 17 of the Tenants' Rights, etc. (Scotland) Act 1980, under which a tenant who wishes to vary any tenancy term which restricts his use or enjoyment of the property can take the matter to court, if the council refuses to agree to the variation, and the court can make such order as it thinks fit. Nevertheless, the Housing Act 1980 regulates the terms relating to secure tenancies in three principal ways.

First, breach of the terms of the tenancy agreement will not automatically entitle the council to possession, since such a breach only provides a "reasonableness" ground (under s. 34 and Sched. 4, Pt. I, gd. 1, discussed in Chapter 7). Thus if a council were to require that "the tenant shall see that the bath is used only for the purpose for which it is intended,"[25] or that "no breeding of animals may take place without consent from the Housing Officer,"[25] a tenant in breach of such conditions could now only be evicted if the court considered this course to be reasonable.

Secondly, in order partially to ensure that the tenant is made aware of his basic rights, the 1980 Act imposes on councils certain duties to provide their secure tenants with information about the terms of their tenancies. We have already noted that section 41(3) *(b)* imposes a duty to provide the secure tenant with a written statement of the terms of the tenancy (*i.e.* the actual terms, not merely a summary), insofar as these are not already set out in a formal lease or written tenancy agreement and are not implied by law. There is also a quite separate obligation imposed on councils under section 41(1)–(2) under which they must, by October 3, 1982[22] and thereafter from time to time, publish up-to-date information about their secure tenancies explaining "in simple terms"[26] the *effect* of: (i) the express terms of such tenancies; (ii) Parts I and III of the 1980 Act (*i.e.* the basic "charter" rights, including the right to improve); and (iii) sections 32 and 33 of the Housing Act 1961 (*i.e.* certain implied repairing obligations[27]). A copy of this information, when published, must be supplied to every secure tenant (s. 41(3) *(a)*). However, the information to be provided under section 41 will not necessarily be comprehensive: thus the tenant does not have to be told about any *implied* terms beyond those in the 1961 and 1980 Housing Acts, such as the landlord's implied obligations concerning quiet enjoyment, non-derogation from grant, and certain additional repairing responsibilities[28]; nor need the tenant be informed of his *remedies* for disrepair.[28] Nevertheless, it is fair to point out that some councils (*e.g.* Basildon and the London Borough of Hackney) issued very full "information packs" to their tenants even before the 1980 Act; in many respects these provided more detail than is now required by section 41, and it is to be hoped that after the 1980 Act councils will generally be prepared to provide more information than that actually required by the section.

Thirdly, certain specific provisions are implied by the 1980 Act into *every* secure tenancy, and therefore apply notwithstanding any stipulation to the contrary. These provisions will now be examined.

(b) *Specific provisions*

(i) Lodgers

At common law, if the lease is silent on the point, the tenant has complete freedom to take in lodgers. However, prior to the 1980 Act, most council tenancy agreements expressly prohibited the tenants from taking in lodgers without the council's consent (93 per cent. of the 318 tenancy agreements examined by the National Consumer Council contained such a clause[29]), and some councils would only give consent if the tenant agreed to pay an additional "lodger charge." Councils had however often been urged actively to encourage their tenants to take in lodgers, by removing prohibitions or financial disincentives, in order to help to alleviate the housing problem generally and to remedy the under-occupation of council properties in particular (see, *e.g.* the C.H.A.C. Report on *Council Housing Purposes, Procedures and Priorities*, 1969, at para. 200, and D.o.E. Circular no. 24/75 on *Housing: Needs and Action*, 1975, para. 28). In pursuance of this policy, section 35(1) of the Housing Act 1980 now provides that it is a term of *every* secure council tenancy that the tenant may allow any persons to reside as lodgers in the dwelling, even without the landlord's consent.

Section 35 does not expressly prohibit the imposition of "lodger charges" (pursuant to s. 111(1) of the Housing Act 1957). However, a D.o.E. sample of authorities in 1977 revealed that less than 3 per cent. were then still imposing lodger charges, and the D.o.E. stated that since there was no evidence that charges were being levied which were a disincentive to the taking of lodgers, there appeared to be "no case for imposing an express statutory bar" (*Housing Management: Consultation Paper on A Tenants' Charter*, D.o.E., 1977, Annex 4, paras. 4–5);

moreover, section 35(1) of the 1980 Act does not require the tenant even to inform the council that he has taken in a lodger, so that the council may well be unaware that an opportunity to claim a lodger charge has arisen (though the requirement to disclose lodgers could be imposed by the tenancy agreement).

The increases in council rents which are currently being implemented by Ministerial "persuasion"[30] could cause many tenants to exercise the statutory right to take in lodgers.

(ii) Disposals of *part* of the property: subletting part or otherwise parting with possession of part

If a lease contains no prohibition on subletting, then at common law the tenant may sublet without the landlord's consent. However, prior to the 1980 Act, local authorities were obliged by section 113(5) of the Housing Act 1957 to "make it a term of every letting that the tenant shall not assign, sublet or otherwise part with the possession of the premises, or any part thereof, except with the consent in writing of the authority"; the insertion of such a "qualified" covenant against disposal of the property attracted the implied proviso under section 19(1)(*a*) of the Landlord and Tenant Act 1927 that, notwithstanding any express provision to the contrary, the landlord's consent was not to be unreasonably withheld.

Section 113(5) of the 1957 Act has now been repealed by section 35(4) and Schedule 26 of the 1980 Act. Instead, under section 35(2) of the 1980 Act it is a term of *every* secure council tenancy that the tenant will not, without the written consent of the council, sublet *part* of the dwelling or otherwise part with the possession of *part* thereof; but such consent (which may be retrospective) must not be unreasonably withheld or given subject to conditions (*e.g.* as to rent levels for the sublease[31]): if consent is unreasonably withheld or given subject to conditions, it shall be treated as given, or given uncon-

ditionally, as the case may be (ss. 35(3), 36(2)–(3)). It
therefore remains important here to distinguish between
the taking of lodgers (*i.e.* a licence), for which no consent
is needed, and a *subletting* of part of the property (*i.e.* a
disposal conferring a proprietary interest), for which
consent is required[32]; even though, as noted earlier, for
most other purposes relating to secure tenancies the
distinction between a lease and a licence has been
removed by section 48.

Thus following a disposition of *part* of the property, the
original tenancy remains secure, but if the authority's
consent was not requested or was properly withheld, a
"reasonableness" ground for possession arises under
Schedule 4, Part I, ground 1.[33] The burden lies on the
authority to show that the consent was reasonably
withheld (s. 36(1)[34]), and the following matters (*inter alia*)
are relevant: that statutory overcrowding would result if
consent were to be given, or that the authority proposes to
carry out works which will affect the accommodation
likely to be used by the proposed subtenant (s. 36(1)).

The tenant must be given written reasons for any refusal
of consent, and if the authority fails to respond to the
tenant's request for consent within a reasonable time the
consent is taken to have been withheld (s. 36(4)). The
county court has jurisdiction to decide this consent issue
by simple declaration (s. 86(2) *(a)*).

Whether or not the subletting is with consent, the
subtenant cannot normally gain any security against the
authority after the ending of the head tenant's tenancy,
since the Act does not exclude the basic common law rule
that an interest derived out of the tenant's estate will fall
with the tenancy[35] (although the subtenant can enjoy the
appropriate protection as against the head tenant: the
subtenancy will normally be classed as a "resident
landlord" tenancy, and therefore as a restricted contract,
pursuant to ss. 12 and 20 of the Rent Act 1977, unless
substantial board is provided, *i.e.* meals, etc., of an
adequate nature). However, it appears that if the head

tenant voluntarily surrenders the tenancy to the authority, or gives notice to quit to the authority, the sublease (even if it was not granted with the consent of the authority) will be capable of binding the authority, and the portion of the property sublet will become subject to a direct secure tenancy provided that the "separate dwelling" requirement in section 28(1) (*supra*) is satisfied (*cf. Mellor* v. *Watkins* (1874) L.R. 9 Q.B. 400, *Parker* v. *Jones* [1910] 2 K.B. 32).

(iii) Disposals *inter vivos* of the *whole* of the property: assigning the tenancy, subletting the *whole* property, or otherwise parting with possession of the *whole* property

We have noted that section 35(2) of the 1980 Act only governs disposals of *part* of the property. Since section 113(5) of the 1957 Act (*supra*) has been repealed, an *absolute* covenant against assigning the tenancy, or subletting the *whole* property, or otherwise parting with possession of the *whole* property, can now be inserted as a term of the tenancy; conversely, such disposals of the whole can now be absolutely permitted (*i.e.* without the need for the council's consent) under the terms of the tenancy. However, no matter what the terms of the tenancy may provide, the 1980 Act tries to ensure that the tenant cannot transfer his "charter" rights to whoever he pleases, since the recipient may not be in housing need at all; on such a disposal of the whole, therefore, section 37 provides that the *secure* tenancy (and thus the whole package of "charter" rights) will normally cease forthwith, although the (common law) tenancy itself will continue on a purely contractual basis.

Section 37(1) provides that if a secure tenancy (whether fixed-term or periodic) is *assigned*, even through death,[36] then it *ceases* to be a secure tenancy *unless* the assignment is made pursuant to a court order under section 24 of the Matrimonial Causes Act 1973,[37] or to someone in whom the tenancy would or might[38] have vested under the statutory succession provisions in section 30[39] had the tenant died immediately before the assignment (treating, for these purposes, a fixed-term tenancy as if it were a periodic tenancy[40]). Thus if a secure tenant assigns his tenancy while alive, or dies, then if the transferee is neither his spouse nor any other "member of his family,"[41] the transferee cannot enjoy the "charter" rights even if the lease permitted such a transfer and even if the transferee occupies the property as his only or principal home (see the "tenant condition" in s. 28(3)[42]).

Further, if a secure tenant *sublets* the *whole* of the property, or otherwise *parts with the possession* of the *whole* of the property, then again the tenancy will cease to be secure, whether the lease permitted or prohibited the disposition (s. 37(2)); and here it matters not whether the subtenant or new possessor happens to be the tenant's spouse or other "member of his family" (*cp.* the exceptions to s. 37(1), *supra*): this is consistent with the "tenant condition" in section 28(3), which imposes as one condition of a secure tenancy that the *tenant himself* must normally occupy the property as his only or principal home.[42]

If a tenancy ceases to be secure under section 37 following a disposal of the whole (whether by way of assignment, subletting or otherwise parting with possession), that tenancy cannot later become secure again (even if, for example, the council takes rent from the assignee, or the subletting is ended): section 37(3).

(iv) Disposals on death

No council tenancy agreement before the 1980 Act ever went so far as to prohibit the tenant from dying, and a bequest of a tenancy in the tenant's will cannot be a breach of a covenant against assignment.[43] Prior to the 1980 Act, however, the lack of security for council tenants gave authorities considerable control in practice over the tenant's choice of successor, although the deceased tenant's spouse or adult child was often permitted to take over the tenancy.[44]

The 1980 Act now regulates succession to a *secure* council tenancy. It is necessary to consider the position regarding *fixed-term* secure tenancies separately from the position regarding *periodic* secure tenancies.

Fixed-term secure tenancies

Where the secure tenancy is for a *fixed term* and the tenant dies, the tenancy will only cease to be secure if *either* (i) the tenancy is disposed of by the tenant's personal representatives to someone who is not a "member of the tenant's family" who would or might[45] have taken under the statutory succession provisions relating to periodic secure tenancies had the tenancy been periodic (*infra*); *or* (ii) it is known that when the tenancy has been so disposed of, it will not pass to such a person: sections 28(5), 37(1). Thus, broadly speaking, if the relevant beneficiary under the will or intestacy is a "member of the tenant's family," the *secure* tenancy, and not merely the contractual tenancy, will pass following the death; while if the relevant beneficiary is *not* a "member of the tenant's family," the *secure* tenancy will end, but the *contractual* tenancy will pass, so that the council will not normally be entitled to possession until the end of the fixed term.

Periodic secure tenancies

Where the deceased tenant's secure tenancy is *periodic*, the secure tenancy can vest by virtue of the Act (regardless of the terms of the tenant's will and even though the tenancy must remain contractual[46]), in a "member of his family" who can satisfy certain stipulated residence requirements: *i.e. either* the tenant's spouse if he or she occupied the property as his or her only or principal home at the time of the tenant's death; *or* (failing such spouse) the tenant's parent, grandparent, child, grandchild, brother, sister, uncle, aunt, nephew, niece, or cohabitee[47]: but a non-spouse successor must not only have occupied the property as his or her only or principal home at the time of the tenant's death, *but must also have resided with the tenant throughout the period of twelve months before the death* (though it is not necessary for such successor to have resided, throughout this period, in the same house in which the tenant finally died): sections 30, 50(3). Relationships by marriage or the half-blood count as full relationships, as do step-relationships and illegitimate relationships (s. 50(3)); and adopted children are separately treated as the natural children of the adopters under the Children Act 1975, s. 8 and Sched. 1.

Where there are two or more claimants, the spouse has priority, and as regards other members of the family the authority can decide the matter if the relevant members cannot agree[48] which one of them is to succeed—a jurisdiction unlikely to be welcomed by many authorities[49] (s. 30(3): the additional use of the word "one" in s. 30(1) makes it quite clear that there cannot be joint statutory succession).

However, in effect only one statutory "succession stage" is possible, for section 30 does not apply if the deceased tenant was himself a "successor" (s. 30(1)); and the expression "successor" here has a very wide definition in section 31(1). The effect is that under a periodic secure tenancy the dead tenant is normally treated as himself having been a (first) "successor" (and therefore no further statutory succession is permitted on his death) if the tenancy vested in him under section 30, or he was a joint tenant and became the sole tenant (*e.g.* on the death of the other joint tenant), or he became the tenant on the tenancy being assigned to him or on its being vested in him on the death of the previous tenant; but a tenant to whom the tenancy was assigned pursuant to an order under section 24 of the Matrimonial Causes Act 1973[50] is only treated as a "successor" for these purposes if the other party to the marriage was originally a "successor".[51] Further, section 31(2) provides that where, within six months of the coming to an end of a periodic secure tenancy, the tenant becomes tenant under *another* periodic secure tenancy, and the tenant was a "successor" as regards the former tenancy, and under the new tenancy either the dwelling or the landlord (or both) is (or are) the same as under the former tenancy, then the tenant is a successor in respect of the *new* tenancy also (thus prohibiting any statutory succession on his death), unless the new tenancy agreement otherwise provides; this devious provision, whereby successorship may be carried forward from one tenancy to another, will often operate in practice where the former tenancy has been ended by a possession order obtained on the "under-occupation" ground.[52]

These complicated succession provisions differ significantly from those in Schedule 1 of the Rent Act 1977 (where "members of the family" are not expressly defined, their residence requirement is only six months, and a second statutory succession stage is permitted). It is suggested that the difficulties presented by the prohibition on a second succession to a secure periodic tenancy (and by the wide definition of "successor" in s. 31) are excessive; a second succession should be permitted, as in the private sector: authorities would then still be adequately safeguarded against under-occupation by non-spouse successors, through the availability of the "under-occupation" ground for possession.[52]

(v) Improvements

Under section 81(2) of the 1980 Act, it is a term of *every* secure council tenancy that the tenant can make improvements to the property with the landlord's written consent, which cannot be unreasonably withheld. The details of this new "charter" right are discussed in Chapter 5.[53]

5. Variation of the Terms of the Tenancy

It is clear at common law that a landlord cannot vary the terms of the tenancy without the agreement of the tenant. However, it was quite common before the 1980 Act for councils expressly to reserve the right to add to or vary the tenancy conditions (21 per cent. of the agreements examined by the National Consumer Council contained such a provision[54]), and the validity of such a "unilateral variation clause" was upheld in the rent increase case of *G.L.C.* v. *Connolly* [1970] 1 All E.R. 870 (C.A.), although the court added the proviso that reasonable notice of the variation had to be given. In the absence of such a unilateral variation clause, a council could only alter a term of the tenancy (other than the rent) by first ending the tenancy (if periodic) by notice to quit, and then offering a new tenancy incorporating the appropriate alteration (a practice disapproved of by the H.S.A.G.[55] in view of the distress it often caused to tenants); but a special procedure, prescribed by section 12 of the Prices and Incomes Act 1968,[56] allowed authorities to vary the *rent* by notice of increase without service of a notice to quit and even if the agreement contained no unilateral variation clause.

The Housing Act 1980 alters the variation rules so far as secure tenancies are concerned. As will be seen,[57] the authority will often be subject to preliminary consultation duties under sections 42 and 43 where the change relates to a matter of "housing management," but this expression does not include matters relating to rent or charges for services or facilities (s. 42(3)). Assuming that such consultation, where applicable, has taken place, then section 40 provides that (except for a term of the tenancy which is implied by any enactment, *e.g.* under the Housing Acts of 1961 or 1980), the terms of a secure tenancy can only be varied[58] by one of the three methods prescribed by the section. These methods do *not* include service by the authority of a notice to quit and the substitution of a new tenancy: indeed, as will be seen in Chapter 7, a periodic secure tenancy cannot be ended by a notice to quit served by the *landlord* at all. The three prescribed methods of variation are as follows.

First, *by ad hoc agreement* between the council and the tenant (s. 40(3) (*a*)): this will usually only be feasible where the variation affects a very small number of tenants.

Secondly, *by the council or the tenant alone* in accordance with any provision in the tenancy agreement (or any agreement varying it), but *only* to the extent that the variation relates to rent, rates or services (s. 40(3) (*b*)); thus a "unilateral variation clause" for a secure tenancy can now *only* be used in relation to these matters.[59]

Thirdly, *by the council alone* in the case of a *periodic* secure tenancy, by a notice of variation served on the tenant (s. 40 (4)). Before serving the notice of variation, the council must normally serve a preliminary notice giving the tenant information about the variation and an opportunity to comment thereon within a reasonable time (s. 40(6); and the council must then consider any comments from the tenant regarding this preliminary notice (s. 40(6)). Further, the notice of variation itself must normally be accompanied by information as to the nature and effect of the variation (s. 40(6)). But these "information" duties in section 40(6), relating to the preliminary and actual notices of variation, do *not* apply where the variation relates to the rent or to payments in respect of rates services or facilities provided by the council (s. 40(7)); one rather unconvincing reason given for these exclusions was that "such proposals will generally receive wide publicity among tenants well in advance of their operation" (D.o.E. Consultation Paper on *Rights in Respect of Tenancy Agreements*, para. 16).

The notice of variation must also specify the variation and the date on which it takes effect, and the period between the date on which it is served and the date on which it takes effect must not be shorter than the rental period of the tenancy, nor shorter than four weeks (s. 40(5)). Prior to the effective date of the variation, the tenant may serve a valid notice to quit,[60] whereupon the notice of variation will be ineffective (even for the remainder of the contractual tenancy) unless the tenant, with the council's written consent, withdraws the notice to quit before the effective date of the variation (s. 40(8)); but before using this drastic method of avoiding the effect of the variation,[61] the tenant should appreciate that on expiry of the notice to quit there will no longer be any tenancy, secure or otherwise, so that if he fails to leave, the council can issue possession proceedings without having to establish a Housing Act ground.

Notes

[1] The case was concerned with the question (answered in the negative) of whether a council tenant could rely on the new statutory protection where the authority had ended his tenancy by notice to quit and commenced proceedings before the coming into force of the security provisions of the 1980 Act on October 3, 1980, but the hearing of the action had taken place after that date. Many county court judges had been unsure of the rights of such tenants in this "transitional" situation, and it is unfortunate that the draftsmen did not cater explicitly for this problem (*cp.* the Rent Act 1965, s. 20, and s. 88(5) of the Housing Act 1980).

[2] *cp.*, *e.g.* *Heslop* v. *Burns* [1974] 3 All E.R. 406, (C.A.), *Marchant* v. *Charters* [1977] 3 All E.R. 918, (C.A.); see further, *e.g.*: M. Partington, *Landlord and Tenant* (2nd ed., 1980), Chap. 3; D. Yates and A. J. Hawkins, *Landlord and Tenant Law* (1981), pp. 8–25; however, even before the 1980 Act, the Court of Appeal had assumed that the same basic administrative law principles (see Chap. 7) would govern the decision to evict a council licensee as would govern the decision to evict a council tenant: see *Cleethorpes B.C.* v. *Clarkson* (1978) LAG Bul. 166.

[3] Despite these very wide words, presumably there must be *some* connection between the original trespass and the present licence, even if there has been a series of intervening licences: if the present licensee had happened to "gate-crash" a council committee meeting in 1947, his present security would surely not be affected!

[4] See Chap. 9.

[5] See *infra*, pp. 24–7; *cf. Harris* v. *Swick Securities Ltd.* [1969] 3 All E.R. 1131, (C.A.).

[6] See *infra*, p. 75.

[7] Although in fact the property was never sublet. Note that subletting of the whole property by a secure tenant in fact causes automatic statutory cessation of security under s. 37(2), discussed *infra*.

[8] In addition, note that in the case of a secure tenancy, unlike a Rent Act protected tenancy, there is no rateable value ceiling above which protection is removed, there is no minimum rent to be charged before protection can attach, and payments for board or attendance do not as such exclude protection (*cp.* the R.A. 1977, ss. 4, 5 and 7).

[9] In addition, a secure tenancy may cease to be secure (*i.e.* it will lose statutory protection although the contractual term will continue) following certain acts of disposal: see s. 37 of the 1980 Act, discussed *infra*.

[10] The annotated version in A. Arden, *The Housing Act 1980*, (Current Law Statutes Reprints), may be found particularly helpful.

[11] See *infra*, p. 197.

[12] See *infra*, p. 174.

[13] This distinction, which is often somewhat blurred in practice, is discussed by, *e.g.* A. Arden in (1974) LAG Bul. 108 and in *The Housing Act 1980*, *op. cit.*, notes to Sched. 3, para. 2.

[14] See *infra*, p. 158. The Minister stated (in H.C. Standing Committee F on the Housing Bill, April 24, 1980, cols. 2402–2403) that the purpose of the "acquisition for development" exclusion was to facilitate developments such as road schemes, and not the normal improvement programmes of councils, for which the special ground for possession against a secure tenant contained in Sched. 4, Pt. I, gd. 8 was designed; it is nevertheless submitted that gd. 8 will not prove enough of itself to ensure the adequate use of councils' short-life properties.

[15] See *infra*, pp. 194–5.

[16] See by analogy the Ministerial Letter dated September 2, 1980 on *Sales of Council Houses and Flats and Disposal of Housing Land*, para. 12.

[17] See further D.C. Hoath, *Homelessness* (1982).

[18] The scheme originated in North Wiltshire in 1975, but was used by several other authorities even prior to the 1980 Act, in order to achieve the occupation of private sector property which would otherwise not be let by the owner because of Rent Act restrictions. The viability of such schemes is preserved by the present exemption in the 1980 Act, and further encouragement is afforded by s. 80, through the relaxation of the private landlord's repairing obligations (see *infra*, p. 102).

[19] *cf.* the well-publicised but ill-drafted provisions in the 1980 Act, ss. 51–55, whereby private landlords can, by following a somewhat tortuous path, "get their tenants by the shortholds."

[20] *Infra*, p. 157.

[21] See *infra*, pp. 175–7.

[22] This time-scale seems excessively leisurely, in view of the fact that breach of the tenancy conditions is a (reasonableness) grounds for possession under Sched. 4. Pt. I, gd. 1 (see *infra*, pp. 155–6).

[23] See *infra*, p. 155.

[24] See *infra*, pp. 141–2.

[25] These conditions are not the product of the writer's warped imagination: they are actual tenancy conditions, recorded in the National Consumer Council's paper, *op. cit.*, at pp. 5, 13. Note also the "dog passport" condition imposed by one London council, under which each dog belonging to a council tenant had to be licensed with the council on an annual basis upon production (by the tenant) of a *photograph of the dog*: *The Guardian*, September 28, 1979.

[26] Thus merely photocopying the relevant statutory material will *not* suffice! It is interesting that, as regards, *e.g.* the right to buy, councils are expected to achieve a degree of clarity of exposition, pursuant to s. 41(1), which eluded the draftsman of the relevant provisions of the 1980 Act itself.

[27] Explained at pp. 98–102, *infra*.

[28] See *infra*, pp. 102–119.

[29] *Op. cit.*, at p. 40.

[30] *Infra*, pp. 131–2.

[31] Similarly, s. 36(3) would appear to preclude the insertion by the council of an "Adler"-type clause, whereby the tenant must first offer to surrender the tenancy to the landlord before applying for a licence to sublet: *cf. Adler* v. *Upper Grosvenor St. Investment Ltd.* [1957] 1 All E.R. 229; *Bocarda S.A.* v. *S. & M. Hotels Ltd.* [1979] 3 All E.R. 737, (C.A.); C.G. Blake [1980] Conv. 418, 426.

[32] For the distinction between a lease and a licence, see the references in note 2. In practice, the council may have difficulty in establishing that the tenant of a small house or flat has taken in a *subtenant*, rather than a lodger.

[33] See *infra*, p. 155.

[34] *cp.* s. 19(1) (*a*) of the Landlord and Tenant Act 1927, *supra*, under which it had been held that the burden lies on the *tenant* to show that the withholding of consent was unreasonable (see, *e.g. Shanly* v. *Ward* (1913) 29 T.L.R. 714). Rather anomalously, s. 36 of the 1980 Act does not expressly exclude the 1927 Act (*cp.* the exclusion of s. 19(2) of the 1927 Act in s. 81(1) of the 1980 Act, relating to improvements, which is discussed *infra*, p. 120); but clearly the "burden" rule in s. 36(1) of the 1980 Act must here prevail regarding partial disposals.

[35] If in such a case the authority's consent to the subletting had not been obtained in breach of s. 35(2), the authority could evict the subtenant by using the swift "squatters" eviction procedure in R.S.C. Ord. 113 or C.C.R. Ord. 26: *Moore Properties (Ilford) Ltd.* v. *McKeon* [1977] 1 All E.R. 262.

[36] See *infra*, pp. 28–9.

[37] See Chap 4; it was not necessary for s. 37(1) specifically to exempt transfers made by court order pursuant to Sched. 2 of the Matrimonial Homes Act 1967 (*infra*, pp. 78–80), since these do not operate by way of assignment by the tenant but purely "by virtue of the [court's] order and without further assurance" (see Sched. 2, Pt. II, para. 2(1) of the 1967 Act).

[38] The rather confusing use of the word "might" in this context appears to be intended to validate, *e.g.* an assignment by a widower of his secure tenancy to *both* of his two adult sons who live with him, even though only *one* could in fact have inherited the tenancy had he died, since (as will be seen) s. 30 does not permit joint succession.

[39] See *infra*, pp. 29–31.

[40] As will be seen, the succession provisions in s. 30 itself relate only to periodic tenancies.

[41] See *infra*, pp. 29–30.

[42] *Supra*, pp. 11–13.

[43] See, *e.g. Crusoe* d. *Blencowe* v. *Bugby* (1771) 3 Wils. K.B. 234, 237. Even a weekly tenancy can in law be disposed of by the tenant's will or under his intestacy (see, *e.g. Youngmin* v. *Heath* [1974] 1 All E.R. 461, (C.A.)); but possibly the assent by the tenant's personal representatives giving effect to the bequest, or on the intestacy, might break a covenant against assignment.

[44] See, *e.g.* the *Consultation Paper on A Tenants' Charter, op. cit.*, Annex 1, at para. 15.

[45] See note 38, *supra*.

[46] The Rent Act concept of the "statutory tenancy" is inapplicable: *supra*, pp. 8–9.

[47] The actual wording in s. 50(3) is "liv[ing] together as husband and wife," which clearly excludes "gays"; for analogous Rent Act cases concerning statutory succession by cohabitees, see, *e.g.*: *Dyson Holdings Ltd.* v. *Fox* [1975] 3 All E. R. 1030, (C.A.), *Helby* v. *Rafferty* [1978] 3 All E.R. 1016, (C.A.), *Carega Properties S.A.* v. *Sharratt* [1979] 2 All E.R. 1084, (H.L.), and *Watson* v. *Lucas* [1980] 3 All E.R. 647, (C.A.); see further B. Berkovits [1981] J.S.W.L. 83 (arguing *inter alia* that the courts have been over-much influenced here by the presence or absence of a sexual relationship); for the position of cohabitees who are no longer on speaking terms but are forced to share the same flat, *cf. Adeoso* v. *Adeoso* [1981] 1 All E.R. 107, (C.A.), *infra*, p. 77.

[48] The landlord does not have to be notified before such an agreement becomes valid: *cf. General Management Ltd.* v. *Locke* (1980) 255 E.G. 155, (C.A.).

[49] *cp.* the Rent Act 1977, Sched. 1, para. 3, which provides that in cases of disputes between potential statutory successors in the private sector, the *county court* shall decide the matter.

[50] See Chap 4; similarly, where the secure tenancy is transferred by

court order pursuant to Sched. 2 of the Matrimonial Homes Act 1967 (*infra*, pp. 78–80), and the former tenant-spouse was a "successor" for s. 31 purposes, then the transferee is also deemed to be a successor: see Sched. 2, Pt. II, para. 2(3) of the 1967 Act.

[51] Perhaps an example will help in unravelling this tortuous provision. Assume that Y, who satisfies the 12 months' residence requirement, wishes to take the secure periodic tenancy of her dead mother, Mrs. X, a widow. Y will be eligible if Mrs. X was the original tenant or gained the tenancy from her husband Mr. X under s. 24 of the M.C.A. 1973 where he was the original tenant; but Y will not be eligible if Mrs. X gained the tenancy from Mr. X on his death, or if she gained the tenancy from him under s. 24 of the 1973 Act but he was then himself a "successor," *e.g.* through having taken the secure tenancy on his mother's death. Y therefore had some interest in fomenting matrimonial discord between her parents!

[52] See *infra*, p. 160.

[53] See *infra*, pp. 120–2; in practice, the council may decide to give "blanket" consents to all its tenants relating to specified minor improvements (such as the installation of additional power points, provided the work is carried out to Electricity Board standards).

[54] *Op. cit.*, at p. 41.

[55] *Op. cit.*, at para. 19.

[56] Discussed *infra*, at p. 134.

[57] *Infra*, pp. 210–11.

[58] "Variation" for these purposes includes addition and deletion, and the conversion of a monthly tenancy into a weekly tenancy or *vice versa*, but not a change in the premises let (s. 40(9)); of course, the landlord will need a possession order to compel a change of premises, and it will be seen in Chap. 7 that the offer of suitable alternative accommodation is not of itself a ground for possession.

[59] See further p. 133, *infra*.

[60] The notice to quit must be in writing, and be given not less than four weeks before the date on which it is to take effect (see the Protection from Eviction Act 1977, s. 5(1)); the notice must further expire at the end of a completed period of the tenancy.

[61] *cp.* the more liberal provision in s. 17 of the Tenants' Rights, etc. (Scotland) Act 1980, whereby if a tenant refuses to agree to a variation, he can take the dispute to court, which can make such order as it thinks fit; see also *supra*, p. 22.

Chapter 3

THE ALLOCATION AND TRANSFER OF COUNCIL TENANCIES

1. *General*

The H.S.A.G. stated in 1978 (before the statutory "right to buy" was introduced) that the allocation and transfer aspects of council housing management "generate[d] more interest among the public at large than any other" (*Allocation of Council Housing*, Introduction, at para. 1; this Report is hereafter referred to as the "H.S.A.G. Report"). In particular, for those families who are unable or unwilling to become owner-occupiers and who find that they cannot improve their housing conditions in the shrinking privately-rented sector, the securing of a council house will often be the realisation of a long-cherished ambition; and the importance of both allocation and transfer policies has been enhanced in recent years by the high capital value of some council housing, together with the introduction by the Housing Act 1980 of the generous "right to buy" (discussed in Chapter 8), under which council tenants may be able to acquire their properties with very attractive discounts off the market price.

It has been estimated by Shelter that there were 1.2 million families registered on council house waiting lists in England and Wales in June 1980, a rise of 12 per cent. from the previous year's figure (although we shall see that these lists do not reliably indicate the *need* for council housing); and the 1969 C.H.A.C. Report on *Council Housing Purposes, Procedures and Priorities* (hereafter referred to as the "Cullingworth Report"[1]) stated (at para. 54) that each year local authorities allocated about 350,000 houses, over 200,000 to households living in the private sector or without separate accommodation, and about 145,000 to existing council tenants transferring to different houses (*i.e.* about one-quarter of the one-and-a-half million households moving each year were being housed by local authorities).

What sort of people succeed in gaining council houses? The Cullingworth Report had pointed out in 1969 (*op. cit.*, at para. 26) that in allocating council housing (*i.e.* in making the dual decision of who should get a house, and which particular house each successful applicant should receive), authorities were having to face a situation involving "[f]ewer houses to rent, an increasing dependence upon council housing, more single-person and elderly households, [and] a decreasing supply of large family type houses." Nevertheless, by the early 1970s the vast majority of council households still consisted of families with children: the 1977 Green Paper on *Housing Policy* noted that in 1971 only 4 per cent. of council tenants were men and women of working age living alone, and that many authorities were not even admitting such people to their waiting lists (Cmnd. 6851, at p. 116). The government therefore urged all authorities to reconsider their allocation policies with a view to ensuring that they were able to judge the priorities to be given to new categories of applicant, for example couples without children, single working people and students, and mobile households (*Housing Policy*, *op. cit.*, at p. 79); and the need to cater for these "non-traditional" applicants will become much more acute during the 1980s if the privately rented sector continues to shrink and private sector housebuilding rates remain low.

There is also the difficulty that (as will be seen) authorities have primary statutory responsibilities to house people displaced from their accommodation by some form of public action (*e.g.* clearance or redevelopment), and certain categories of homeless people, so that in some areas there is little council accommodation left over even for those who are at the top of the general waiting list.

Since these problems are subject to considerable regional variations, it is not possible to prescribe any single method of selection for general use. We shall see that the legal provisions purporting to govern the allocation process are vaguely worded, and do not attempt substantially to interfere with the very wide discretion enjoyed by authorities in this area. The Cullingworth Report considered that more central intervention could prove less effective than the existing system, and that the need was for a "clearer lead from central government, not greater control" (*op. cit.*, at para. 64). Although, as we shall see, the H.S.A.G. Report made several useful suggestions, it also broadly sought to preserve councils' discretion in allocation matters (see particularly at paras. 7.2–7.3); and the relevant provisions of the Housing Act 1980, which will be discussed shortly, are mainly concerned with the securing of wider publicity for allocation schemes rather than with "policing" them as such.

However, some disquiet has been felt at the extent of the discretion enjoyed by authorities in this important area, and at the possibility of abuse (see for example the 1976 Report of the Welsh Consumer Council on *Council Housing*, at p. 16; also in 1976, the vice-chairman of one authority's housing committee was found to have voted in support of his own application for a council house: *The Times*, October 5, 1976). In view of the importance of allocation and transfer policies, and the fact that as regards such policies "[t]he management powers of local authorities . . . [still] flourish luxuriantly as a jungle of discretion,"[2] it might be expected that lawyers would take an active interest in these matters. But this particular jungle appears to be more the stamping-ground of M.P.s and local councillors (who are sometimes able successfully to champion individual "hard cases") than of lawyers. We shall see that the relevant cases which have reached English courts have concerned rehousing obligations following public action, homelessness, or the assignment of council housing from one spouse to another on marriage breakdown: in these particular areas there is some reasonably specific statutory material, yet in none of them have the judges shown any general inclination to interfere with the policies of housing authorities. A broad attack on one council's selection powers was mounted in the Northern Ireland High Court case of *Campbell & Casey* v. *Dunganon R.D.C.* (1971, unreported), where Gibson J. held that although the council had not been operating its selection rules properly, the plaintiffs failed, since they could not show that the council had acted in bad faith (noted in D.W. Pollard (ed.), *Social Welfare Law*, at para. B. 459).

Complaints about allocations and transfers have however been finding their way to the Local Commissioners (or "ombudsmen") appointed under Part III of the Local Government Act 1974 to investigate "maladministration" by local authorities. General "consumer's guides" to using the local ombudsmen may be found in, for example, *Roof*, September 1980, at p. 154 (J. Bash), and *Your Local Ombudsman* (Commission for Local Administration, 1979); see also D. J. Hughes, *Public Sector Housing Law* (1981), Chapter 12.

Maladministration was established, for example, where district councillors were permitted to choose from a short list of applicants earmarked by council officers as being in special need of rehousing, and these councillors had repeatedly passed over the complainants in favour of people in less housing need, even though the complainants were living in a caravan after having been advised by the council to leave their house because of its dangerous condition (Investigation 4537, 1978, reported in [1978] J.P.L. 121); while in another case a council was found guilty of maladministration where it refused to register a young mother on the housing waiting list, despite the general recommendations in paragraphs 18 and 23 of D.o.E. Circular no. 78/77 on *Housing for One-Parent Families* (1977) that single parents should be given ready access to waiting lists and that rehousing should not necessarily depend on the obtaining of a divorce or legal separation (Investigation 52C, 1978, reported in *Roof*, March 1979, at p. 61).

These were cases where the allegations against the authority were relatively specific and could easily be proved. More generalised complaints of "discrimination" would appear to stand little chance of success: thus in Investigation 414H, 1976 (discussed in the Commission for Local Administration's Report for the year ending March 31, 1976), no maladministration was found where the' complainant alleged that homeless persons in less need than herself had been allocated houses before her, that there was no adequate "points" allocation scheme,[3] and that a person who had complained to the local press about preferential treatment had been allocated a house shortly afterwards. For a full investigation of the role of the local "ombudsmen" regarding allocation and transfer complaints, see D. J. Hughes and S. R. Jones [1979] J.S.W.L. 273.

A complaint to the Commissioners can take a long time to resolve; the reference must normally be made via a local councillor, although it need not specify an act of "maladministration" as such, provided it contains an allegation that the complainant has suffered injustice arising from a specified act or omission of the local authority (*R.* v. *Local Commissioner for Administration, ex p. Bradford M.C.C.* [1979] 2 All E.R. 881, (C.A.)). Even a finding of maladministration will not necessarily achieve the result contemplated in the Commissioner's report, since there is at present no obligation on the authority to comply with the report's recommendations, and some reports have in fact been ignored (see further the Justice Report on *The Local Ombudsman—a review of the first five years*, 1980). There is no appeal against a Commissioner's decision.

Having discussed the general difficulties involved, we can now turn to the law and practice relating to the allocation and transfer of tenancies.

2. *The Law*

The allocation and transfer policies of authorities may be affected by various statutory provisions, some being directly relevant (concerning, *e.g.* rehousing obligations following slum clearance or redevelopment), and others being indirectly relevant (concerning, *e.g.* the prohibition of discrimination on the grounds of race or sex). A few of these provisions have been the subject of litigation, but the broad discretion of authorities has remained largely intact.

(a) *The Housing Act 1957*

Allocation and transfer policies are obviously affected by the amount of housing which individual authorities have available, so that it is important initially to ask what obligations govern the provision of council housing.

By section 42(1) of the Housing Act 1957, where an authority proposes to declare an area of unfit houses to be a "clearance area" (*i.e.* in order to purchase the area and demolish the houses), it must first be satisfied that it can provide or secure the provision of "suitable accommodation" for those who will be displaced by the clearance, insofar as such accommodation does not already exist. However, the court will be slow to quash a compulsory purchase order following the declaration of a clearance area on the ground that the accommodation provided for rehousing is "not suitable": it has been held that "suitable accommodation" for these purposes does not mean ideal or identical accommodation, and that the question is one for the council and not for the court to decide, unless the council can be shown to have acted arbitrarily, or otherwise irregularly or improperly: *Savoury* v. *Secretary of State for Wales* (1976) 31 P. & C.R. 344.

Under section 76 of the 1957 Act, if it appears to a local authority that it should make a report on overcrowding in its district, or if the Minister so directs, then the authority must make an inspection and submit a report to the Minister showing the number of new houses required to abate the overcrowding, together with proposals for providing them.

A more general duty to consider housing conditions and the need for the provision of further housing is laid down by section 91 of the 1957 Act (as amended by s. 90 of the Housing Act 1980; see also s. 70 of the Housing Act 1969, and the H.S.A.G. Report on *The Assessment of Housing Requirements*, 1977); further, section 3(1) of the Chronically Sick and Disabled Persons Act 1970 (as amended by Sched. 26 of the Housing Act 1980) requires every authority, in discharging its duty under section 91 of the Housing Act 1957, to have regard to the special needs of the chronically sick and disabled. Section 92 of the 1957 Housing Act permits authorities to provide accommodation by way of erection, conversion, acquisition, alteration, enlargement, repair or improvement.

An authority cannot provide "council housing" by circumventing sections 91 and 92 of the Housing Act and deciding instead to compel a private developer to provide equivalent housing through the device of attaching conditions having this effect to his planning permission: *R.* v. *L.B. of Hillingdon, ex p. Royco Homes Ltd.* [1974] 2 All E.R. 643, (D.C.). Here the authority granted planning permission to a developer subject to conditions (*inter alia*) that the dwellings conformed to the standards required for local authority housing, and were first occupied by persons on the authority's housing waiting list. The developer obtained an order of *certiorari* to quash the planning permission, since the conditions were *ultra vires* the authority: they required the developer to assume at his own expense a significant part of the authority's housing responsibilities.

These provisions in the Housing Act 1957 in effect leave to the discretion of the individual authority the decision as to the amount and type of council housing which it will actually provide, but they do go some way towards ensuring that it will at least be aware of the *need* for council housing in its area.

Turning now to the separate question of the allocation of such council housing as has been provided by the authority, section 111(1) of the Housing Act 1957 provides that the "general management, regulation and control of houses provided by a local authority . . . shall be vested in and exercised by the authority," so that in effect authorities can "pick and choose their tenants at their will" (*per* Lord Porter in *Shelley* v. *L.C.C.* [1948] 2 All E.R. 898, 900, (H.L.)).

However, this wide discretion is qualified by section 113(2) of the 1957 Act, which provides that the authority must ensure that in selecting its tenants it gives a "reasonable preference" to persons who are "occupying insanitary or overcrowded houses, have large families or are living under unsatisfactory housing conditions," and to persons towards whom it is "subject to a duty under section 4 or 5 of the Housing (Homeless Persons) Act 1977." We shall see later that where an insanitary house is unfit, and action is taken by the authority pursuant to Part II or III of the 1957 Housing Act, special rehousing obligations are imposed by the Land Compensation Act 1973; while overcrowding, family size and unsatisfactory living conditions are all factors which in practice will normally be catered for by the authority's individual selection scheme relating to those on the general waiting list. The duty to *house* homeless persons with a "priority need"[4] under section 4 or 5 of the Housing (Homeless Persons) Act 1977 can be discharged either by providing council housing, or by securing that "some other person" provides the accommodation (s. 6(1)); it is significant, however, that section 113(2) of the 1957 Act (as amended) in effect requires authorities to give a "reasonable preference" to *all* people who are homeless or threatened with homelessness, whether or not in "priority need," so that even single homeless people must be given such "reasonable preference."

It has been pointed out that this duty imposed by section 113(2) is "[o]bviously . . . so wide as to constitute no restriction at all" (J. B. Cullingworth, *Housing and Local Government* (1966), at p. 121). Nevertheless, it might be possible to persuade a court that an authority operating, for example, a straight "date order" allocation scheme where success depends entirely on "waiting time" without any allowance being made for cases of hardship, is in breach of section 113(2), so that it should be required to review its scheme: see M. Grant, *Local Authority Housing: Law Policy and Practice in Hampshire* (1976), at p. 5.[5]

(b) *The Land Compensation Act 1973*

It is necessary to deal with the position of those eligible for rehousing by the local authority under the Land Compensation Act 1973 separately from the position of those on the general housing waiting list, since the 1973 Act imposes special duties on authorities regarding those displaced by, *e.g.* clearance or redevelopment, and in practice many authorities treat those covered by the 1973 Act as a quite distinct group from those on the waiting list (though some authorities operating "points" allocation schemes[3] still award households displaced by clearance or redevelopment a large number of "points," thus technically bringing them within such schemes: see the Cullingworth Report, *op. cit.*, at para. 135, and the H.S.A.G. Report, *op. cit.*, at para. 2.25).

Under section 39(1) of the Land Compensation Act, where a person is displaced from residential accommodation in consequence of certain types of public action, and "suitable alternative residential accommodation on reasonable terms is not otherwise available" to him, then the relevant local authority must ensure that such accommodation will be provided.

The public action covered by section 39 is: the acquisition of land by an authority possessing compulsory purchase powers (*e.g.* where a "clearance area" has been declared relating to unfit property under section 42 of the Housing Act 1957[6]); the improvement or redevelopment of land previously acquired by such an authority (*cf. R.* v. *Corby D.C., ex p. McLean* [1975] 2 All E.R. 568, (D.C.); *Armstrong* v. *G.L.C.* (1980) LAG Bul. 269 (Lambeth County Court)); the making or acceptance of a housing order or undertaking (including, by s.29(7), a demolition or closing order relating to unfit property under Part II of the Housing Act 1957, although these unfitness procedures do *not* apply to *council* houses as such: see *R.* v. *Cardiff C.C., ex p. Cross, The Times,* April 11, 1981, (D.C.)[7]); and the service of an improvement notice under Part VIII of the Housing Act 1974.

Section 39 does not define which classes of residents it intends to cover. The section would appear to extend beyond tenants and sub-tenants to any residents who are displaced, "whether families (with or without children) or lodgers or single residents" (see D.o.E. Circular no. 18/74 on *Homelessness,* 1974, App., para. 7), with the exception of trespassers and those permitted to reside in property pending its demolition or improvement (these last two categories being specifically excluded by section 39(3)). Certain caravan dwellers are included by section 40.

However, in order to qualify for rehousing, the displaced resident must have been in occupation at a particular time, which is defined in detail by section 39(6) and depends on the type of public action involved.

A major difficulty with section 39 lies in deciding whether "suitable alternative residential accommodation on reasonable terms" is "otherwise available" (for if it is so available, the duty disappears). This will be a matter of fact, but some authorities have argued that they have no duty to rehouse single residents (despite the fact that Circular 18/74, *supra,* envisaged that single residents will *prima facie* be eligible), since they should be able to find suitable accommodation in the privately rented sector. Evidence from accommodation agencies, etc., should assist in showing that in many parts of the country this assessment of opportunities in the private sector is quite unrealistic.

Assuming that an authority accepts that it has an obligation to rehouse a displaced resident, what sort of accommodation can he expect? Section 39(1) requires that the accommodation offered shall be on "reasonable" terms, so that it need not be on identical terms, or even similar terms, to the previous accommodation. It appears, indeed, that the accommodation may legally be subject to far worse terms (*e.g.* regarding security) than those governing the previous accommodation. In *R.* v. *Bristol Corp., ex. p. Hendy* [1974] 1 All E.R. 1047, (C.A.), a tenant who had been protected by the Rent Acts was displaced from his flat following the making of a closing order by the local authority. He argued that the authority had to provide him with permanent accommodation giving him equivalent security of tenure to that which he formerly enjoyed under the Rent Acts, and that the authority's offer of temporary accommodation, to be followed by the allocation when practicable of a council house on the normal terms, was insufficient; this argument would still have relevance even after the introduction of statutory security of tenure for council tenants by the Housing Act 1980, since we have seen that certain tenancies of "short-life" property and other short-term arrangements do not attract security.[8] His application for an order of mandamus to compel the authority to perform its duty under section 39 of the 1973 Act was dismissed by the Court of Appeal, which held that the authority was not required to give the applicant priority for a council house over those on the general housing waiting list. Scarman L.J. considered that even if the court's interpretation of the section was mistaken, it was not in any event a proper case for mandamus, since the authority was doing "all that it honestly and honourably [could] to meet the statutory obligation" (at p. 1051).

There is no easy answer to the question of the priority

for council housing as between "1973 Act" claimants and those on the general waiting list. However, in many areas the quality of accommodation offered pursuant to the 1973 Act is in practice markedly superior to that offered to the *homeless* under the Housing (Homeless Persons) Act 1977, so that it *may* be very important for an applicant to show that he falls within the 1973 Act. The Commission for Racial Equality has pointed out that a typical allocation scheme in order of the *quality* of the properties offered is: first, "decants" (*i.e.* Land Compensation Act cases, notwithstanding *Hendy's* case, *supra*); secondly, transfers (see *infra*); thirdly, waiting list cases (see *infra*); and finally, the homeless (*Local Authorities and the Housing Implications of Section 71 of the Race Relations Act 1976*, 1980, p. 12); see also the H.S.A.G. Report, *op. cit.*, at para. 2.26: " . . . a number of . . . authorities allocate only the least desirable vacancies to homeless households and/or permit them only a limited choice, or no choice."

(c) *The Rent (Agriculture) Act 1976*

Under section 28(7) of the Rent (Agriculture) Act 1976, an authority is under a duty to use its best endeavours to provide suitable alternative accommodation for certain agricultural employees, whose employers require their houses for other employees and cannot themselves provide the required alternative accommodation.

(d) *The Race Relations Act 1976*

It is unlawful for an authority to discriminate against a person on racial grounds (*i.e.* grounds of colour, race, nationality or ethnic or national origins), in the terms on which the premises are offered, or on which his application for the premises is refused, or in his treatment in relation to any list of applicants: see sections 1, 3 and 21(1) of the Race Relations Act 1976. Further, section 71 of the 1976 Act imposes a duty on every local authority to

endeavour to eliminate racial discrimination and promote
racial harmony in the carrying out of its various functions.
If the Act is broken, remedies are available to the person
discriminated against and to the Commission for Racial
Equality (see sections 57–62).

The practical implications of the race relations legislation for authorities and their prospective tenants are
considered later.

(e) *The Sex Discrimination Act 1975*

It is similarly unlawful for an authority to discriminate
against a woman (or man) on the ground of her (or his)
sex or marital status, in the terms on which the premises
are offered, or by refusing the application, or in its
treatment of her (or him) in relation to any list of
applicants: see sections 1, 2 and 30(1) of the Sex
Discrimination Act 1975. If the Act is broken, remedies
are available to the person discriminated against and to
the Equal Opportunities Commission (see sections
66–71). The impact of the 1975 Act on local government
services, including housing, is discussed in D.o.E. Circular no. 1/78 on *Sex Discrimination Act 1975—Provisions
Affecting Local Government* (1978).

3. *The Practice*

We have seen that the law allows authorities considerable
discretion in allocating their housing. It is now necessary
to examine in outline the practices of authorities concerning allocations (to those who are not existing council
tenants), and transfers and exchanges (which involve
existing council tenants changing their accommodation).

(a) *Allocations*

(i) The housing waiting list

All authorities keep "housing waiting lists" on which
general applicants for council housing (not being "clearance

or redevelopment" cases or homeless persons) may register, and from which the authorities will make their allocations in accordance with their individual selection schemes. Authorities usually keep not only general lists based on the characteristics of applicants, but also separate lists of applicants for different types of properties (family houses, single person's accommodation, old peoples' dwellings, etc.): this reflects the dual nature of the allocation process, *i.e.* in deciding not only who should be allocated council housing, but also which particular dwelling each successful applicant should receive. It is an offence under section 1(1) of the Accommodation Agencies Act 1953 for anyone to demand or accept payment for registering or agreeing to register details of any person seeking the tenancy of a house or flat: although this prohibition was designed to cure abuses in the private sector, authorities' housing lists would not appear to be exempt.

Registration on a housing list is not always allowed automatically: sometimes the applicant must first satisfy a condition. The most common condition is one requiring residence in the authority's area for a designated minimum period. The imposition of such minimum residential qualifications for acceptance on a housing list has been repeatedly criticised: see, *e.g.* the Cullingworth Report (which considered it to be "fundamental that no one should be precluded from applying for, or being considered for, a council tenancy on any ground whatsoever": *op. cit.*, at para. 169), the Report of the Committee on *One-Parent Families* (Cmnd. 5629, 1974, at p. 384), the Green Paper on *Housing Policy* (which stated that the case for legislation preventing this practice was being considered: *op. cit.*, at pp. 79–80), and the H.S.A.G. Report (which supported the complete abolition of residential requirements "as a long term objective": *op. cit.*, at para. 6.10).

Residential qualifications for housing lists are already illegal for the London boroughs, which must register every application which is made to them by residents in their areas, under section 22(3) of the London Government Act 1963; however, most London boroughs impose requirements of between one and five years' residence (depending on the particular borough) anywhere in the Greater London area before the applicant is eligible for *consideration* (as opposed to acceptance on the list).

Residential qualifications have still not been generally prohibited by statute for England and Wales (but *cp.* s. 26(2)–(3) of the Tenants' Rights, etc. (Scotland) Act 1980). One reason often advanced for their abolition is that it is only possible for the authority to assess housing needs if it admits all applicants to its list.[9] In fact, even the most comprehensive housing lists may be poor indicators of need, since they may well be out of date, or contain the names of people who are registered on the lists of other authorities also or who have registered merely as a cautionary measure: see further the H.S.A.G. Report on *The Assessment of Housing Requirements*, 1977, paras. 5.18–5.19, the 1978 H.S.A.G. Report, *op. cit.*, at paras. 13.11–13.12, and I. Sier, *Roof*, March 1981, at p. 3.

(ii) Who should do the selecting?

Before we examine the various types of allocation schemes, it is relevant to consider who should operate them: for even the very best of schemes depends ultimately for its effectiveness on the ability of those applying it.

Most commentators consider that the individual decisions on allocations, unless particularly difficult, should be left to the officers of the housing department rather than to the members of the housing committee, since the matter is not (or should not be) a political one, and councillors might be subject to undesirable pressures (see, *e.g.* the 1959 C.H.A.C. Report on *Councils and their Houses: Management of Estates*, at p. 13, J. B. Cullingworth, *Housing and Local Government, op. cit.,* at pp. 77–78, the Cullingworth Report, *op. cit.,* at paras. 119–123, and the H.S.A.G. Report, *op. cit.*, at para. 13.2).

Whether the final decision is to be taken by housing officials or councillors, the applicant will previously have been seen, often at home, in order to check the facts on his application form, and to make a preliminary assessment regarding his claim to council housing and the sort of property which he ought to be offered. Much disquiet has been voiced at the way in which this vitally important initial "visiting" stage is frequently conducted. The Cullingworth Report considered the selection and training of housing visitors to be "often quite inadequate for the task" (*op. cit.*, at para. 84), and an estate manager for one of the London boroughs has said that housing visitors are "notoriously self righteous, lower middle-class, ex-policewomen" (see the Shelter Report, *Homes Fit For Heroes*, 1975, at p. 19). The fault may partly lie with the system within which some housing visitors are forced to operate: for example, one authority was reported in 1973 to be grading families by a coding system using abbreviations like "DSBF" (meaning "dirty stove, bugs and fleas")[10]; compare the adverse comments on the "grading" of applicants based upon their housekeeping standards in the H.S.A.G. Report, *op. cit.*, at para. 7.17.

(iii) Types of schemes

Allocation schemes differ greatly in matters of detail, but they tend to fall into four main types: "date order" schemes (where allocation is generally on the basis of "first come, first served"), "points" schemes (where allocation is generally made to those amassing sufficient "points," *e.g.* for overcrowding), "merit" schemes (where each application is treated on its merits), and "combined " schemes (involving, *e.g.* a "points" scheme for families, a "date order" scheme for single applicants, and a "merit" scheme for "special cases").

The Cullingworth Report examined a sample of some 30 selection schemes. It considered that "date order" schemes were only acceptable in areas with no real housing problem, and then only if "individual hardship cases and key workers" were treated separately (*op. cit.*, at para. 128). The Report judged "points" schemes to be "excellent in concept but exceedingly difficult to devise in detail with fairness," and emphasised that they should be kept up to date (*op. cit.*, at para. 130); it also stressed that points merely for length of residence (rather than for length of housing need) were undesirable except for the purpose of deciding between cases of equal housing need (*op. cit.*, at para. 170). The H.S.A.G. Report approved of points schemes as being "particularly suitable where there is still considerable housing stress," but warned authorities against making such schemes too complicated (*op. cit.*, at para. 7.9).

"Merit" schemes were disapproved of by the Cullingworth Report for being "unworkable" (*op. cit.*, at para. 133), and the H.S.A.G. Report, after noting that very few merit schemes still remained, recommended their total discontinuance (*op. cit.*, at paras. 2.31, 7.5); while on "combined" schemes, the Cullingworth Report noted that every authority which it examined operated in effect a sort of "combined" scheme, since cases of "exceptional hardship" were always dealt with separately, although the definition of "exceptional" varied (*op. cit.*, at para. 135).

The Cullingworth Report was unable to recommend an ideal all-purpose selection scheme, since each scheme had to be devised in the light of local conditions (*op. cit.*, at para. 125, a conclusion endorsed by the H.S.A.G. Report, *op. cit.*, at para. 7.4). But the Cullingworth Report did make some general observations: for example, authorities were urged to stop adopting "moralistic" attitudes towards "unmarried mothers, cohabitees, 'dirty' families, and 'transients' " (*op. cit.*, at para. 96), and to give more weight to "social need" as a separate priority, *i.e.* by taking into account both the housing conditions of an individual household and its ability to cope with those conditions, with the highest priority going to those unable to cope with bad conditions (*op. cit.*, at paras. 117–118). The Report also stressed that cases of severe ill-health should similarly be dealt with as having priority outside the general selection schemes (*op. cit.*, at para. 136). The H.S.A.G. Report reemphasised that housing need should be the main criterion for deciding priorities (*op. cit.*, at para. 4.2).

The following general advice has been given to applicants for council housing seeking to "beat the system": "Letters from doctor, social worker and psychiatrist are useful, the active interest of a councillor helps, advocacy from an advice centre is an advantage. Persistence, not merit, is rewarded and by proving not only housing need but also a capacity to cause trouble, rehousing often follows" (*Limits of the Law*, Community Development Project, 1977, at p. 31). This passage may be thought over-cynical, but it is still worth heeding.

(iv) Special cases

Certain types of applicant raise particular difficulties, and some of these merit separate consideration here.

The homeless. There has long been a tendency for some authorities to regard homeless families as potential "queue jumpers" for council housing, especially if they have been evicted from their previous accommodation for rent arrears; this tendency has increased since the imposition of the duty to house certain categories of the homeless on housing authorities rather than social services authorities: see sections 4 and 5 of the Housing (Homeless Persons) Act 1977,[11] which replaced the recommendations in D.o.E. Circular no. 18/74 on *Homelessness* (1974). Nevertheless, the H.S.A.G. Report stated its conclusions on this "queue jumping" dilemma in uncompromising terms: " . . . it is essential that people should not be penalised in terms of quality by the urgency of their need: every applicant, from whatever allocation group, should be offered the best available property consistent with his degree of priority, and not the poorest that he is likely to accept because of his desperation" (*op. cit.*, at para. 4.22); in practice, however, the "queue jumping" stigma is still often attached to homeless applicants (see, *e.g.* J. Forsyth, *Roof*, March 1979, at p. 36), who can consequently get a very raw deal in terms of the accommodation offered (see S. Billcliffe, *Roof*, July 1979, at p. 118).[12]

Single applicants and one-parent families. The traditional recipients of council housing have been married couples with children, and the elderly. "Points" schemes and residential qualifications tend to place the single applicant and the one-parent family at a disadvantage, as was recognised for example in the Report of the Committee on *One-Parent Families*, which recommended that a lone parent should qualify for the same number of points as a married couple with a comparable family (*op. cit.*, at pp. 382–384). The H.S.A.G. Report urged that the needs of single people should be carefully considered, that they should be accepted on to housing lists, and that specific assessment and allocation policies should be introduced for them (*op. cit.*, at paras. 10.13–10.16).

With regard to the type of housing which should be offered to one-parent families in particular, D.o.E. Circular no. 78/77 on *Housing for One-Parent Families* (1977) advised authorities to integrate them with other families amongst the housing stock, in order to avoid any stigma which might arise from segregation (Annex B, para. 4); while the H.S.A.G. Report emphasised the need for battered women to be allocated "ordinary family accommodation," in order to ensure that "places in emergency refuges are freed to meet short term needs" (*op. cit.*, at para. 10.8).

Rent arrears.   Many authorities will not consider allocating their normal housing stock to tenants with rent arrears. Both the Cullingworth Report (*op. cit.*, at para. 350) and the H.S.A.G. Report (*op. cit.*, at para. 6.21) recommended that rent arrears should not automatically preclude a family from obtaining a council house; indeed, the Cullingworth Report emphasised that authorities should in fact take increased responsibility for families with arrears, since they are "the most vulnerable" (*loc. cit.*).

Coloured people.   The problems experienced by coloured applicants are largely the result of the adverse effects on them of general rules adopted by authorities (regarding, *e.g.* residential qualifications), rather than of any conscious discrimination (see, *e.g.* W. W. Daniel, *Racial Discrimination in England* (1968), at pp. 178–182, the Cullingworth Report, *op. cit.*, at paras. 366–376, the Green Paper on *Housing Policy*, *op. cit.*, at p. 118, and the H.S.A.G. Report, *op. cit.*, at paras. 11.2–11.3). Nevertheless, there is some evidence of racial discrimination in the allocation process, proceeding from a variety of motives (see, *e.g. Colour and the Allocation of GLC Housing*, 1976, the H.S.A.G. Report, *op. cit.*, at paras. 11.1–11.2, and *Roof*, September 1979, at p. 145). There is also evidence of racial harassment being experienced by coloured families on the estates to which they are allocated (see *Racial Harassment on Local Authority Housing Estates*, Commission for Racial Equality, 1981).

Particular concern has arisen regarding the danger of creating "ghettoes" of coloured people: the Cullingworth Report suggested that *voluntary* dispersal should be "an aim, but not the overriding preoccupation of policy" (*op. cit.*, at para. 406), and the 1975 White Paper on *Race Relations and Housing* considered that obstacles to dispersal should be removed if possible, but that people "must be free to make up their own minds whether or not to move from established communities" (Cmnd. 6232, at

p. 9). The 1976 Report from the Community Relations Commission on *Housing in Multi-Racial Areas* pointed out that there is nothing wrong with all-black estates in the abstract, but that in practice they are likely to form on poor-quality estates and to become targets for political criticism (at pp. 33–34). Under the Race Relations Act 1976[13] the *compulsory* dispersal of households on racial grounds is clearly unlawful, as is a quota system such as allocating only one house in five to a black family (*Local Authorities and the Housing Implications of Section 71 of the Race Relations Act 1976*, C.R.E., 1980, p. 13).

The keeping of specific records of coloured people was sanctioned as an aid to avoiding discrimination by for example the Cullingworth Report (*op. cit.*, at paras. 414–427), the White Paper on *Race Relations and Housing* (*op. cit.*, at pp. 6–8), the Report on *Housing in Multi-Racial Areas* (*op. cit.*, at p. 36), the H.S.A.G. Report (*op. cit.*, at para. 11.8), and the Report on *Local Authorities and the Housing Implications of Section 71 of the Race Relations Act 1976* (*op. cit.*, at pp. 10–11); see also R. Franey, *Roof*, March 1979, at p. 56.

(v) Publicity

Prior to the Housing Act 1980, there had been several calls for more publicity to be given to allocation schemes: see, *e.g.* the Cullingworth Report (*op. cit.*, at para. 75), the Green Paper on *Housing Policy* (*op. cit.*, at pp. 79–80), and the H.S.A.G. Report (*op. cit.*, at para. 4.12). Nevertheless, it was estimated in 1978 that "rather less than half of all English authorities [were] . . . satisfying Government policy on publication" (S. Winyard, *Roof*, July 1978, at p. 106).

Under section 44 of the 1980 Act, however, councils must now publish a *summary* of their rules relating to allocations, transfers and exchanges, and must have a *complete set* of these rules readily available (s. 44(1)–(2)); a copy of the summary must be supplied on request free of charge, while a copy of each set of rules must be supplied on request, on payment of a reasonable fee (s. 44(5)). It has been suggested that these publication requirements may not be very helpful in practice, since authorities can comply with the law merely by publishing their eligibility requirements and basic schemes (s. 44 refers to "rules . . . for determining priority as between applicants" and "rules . . . governing the procedure to be followed in allocating [the authority's] housing accommodation"), without revealing the crucial aspects of how long applicants have to wait and what sort of property (and area) they are likely to be offered (V. Karn, *Roof*, January 1981, at p. 15). However, some authorities (*e.g.* Manchester and Sheffield) do regularly publish in the local press comprehensive information as to how long applicants will have to wait for properties in each particular area.

There is a separate provision in section 44(6) whereby at the request of an applicant for housing, the authority must furnish him free of charge with details of the particulars given by him to the authority, and recorded by it as relevant to his application; again, however, this right may be of limited practical use to the applicant, since he has no right to see the whole file relating to his application, nor has he the right to be given the reasons behind the authority's ultimate assessment of his particulars for the purpose of its allocation scheme.

(vi) Voluntary "mobility" schemes

The need for prospective (and actual) council tenants to move across local authorities' boundaries has often been emphasised (see, *e.g.*: D. Jordan, *Roof*, January 1977, at p. 18; the H.S.A.G. Report, *op. cit.*, Chapter 9, which pointed out—at para. 9.3—"the important role that greater mobility of labour can play in assisting economic recovery"; and D.o.E. Circular no. 71/77 on *Local Government and the Industrial Strategy*, 1977, paras.

25–26). Under the London Inter-Borough Nomination Scheme (I.B.N.S.), which began on April 1, 1978, each participating London borough had to set aside 15 per cent. of its available lettings for nominees from other boroughs who were either applicants for council housing or existing council tenants.

A National Mobility Scheme was agreed between the majority of housing authorities with effect from April 1, 1981; like the I.B.N.S., it is a *voluntary* scheme, and Shelter saw this as one of its major weaknesses, given "the fiercely parochial attitude of some councils" (*Roof*, May 1981, at p. 2.); however, more than three-quarters of the housing authorities in England and Wales are now operating the scheme.

Under this national scheme, people who are high on waiting lists, and existing public sector tenants who want to move to a different region for employment or strong social reasons, can be helped by participating authorities. The scheme is in two parts: there is a "knock-for-knock" arrangement for mobility *within* county areas, whereby each participating authority offers a given number of lettings each year for people within the same county who need to change from one district to another; there is also a seperate arrangment for mobility *between* county areas, under which each particpating authority makes available at least one per cent. of its annual lettings (a rather low minimum figure, given the likely demand), for people who need to move in from outside the county boundaries.

An applicant under the scheme should initially apply to his local authority; the scheme is however co-ordinated through a National Mobility Office, the cost of which is met by the D.o.E. pursuant to special provisions in section 46 of the Housing Act 1980. It is somewhat paradoxical that this scheme was introduced at the very time when the best council housing stock was beginning to be depleted through enforced council house sales. For further information on the National Mobility Scheme, see J. Shears, *Roof*, July 1981, at p. 29.

(b) *Transfers and exchanges*

(i) General

Contrary to what might be expected, council tenants appear to move as often as the rest of the population, although they have hitherto tended to move relatively shorter distances than the other tenure groups (see D. V. Donnison, *The Government of Housing*, 1967, p. 210, J. B. Cullingworth, *Housing and Local Government, op. cit.*, at pp. 79–80, 124, and the technical volume in the Green Paper on *Housing Policy*, *op. cit.*, Pt. I, at pp. 90–96). Since the new National Mobility Scheme (*supra*) covers existing council tenants wishing to move (as well as people high on waiting lists), long-distance moves by council tenants may now be expected to increase.

Moves in the public sector may however sometimes benefit primarily the authority rather than the tenant, particularly in cases of under-occupation (which authorities have been urged by the government to minimise, *e.g.* by encouraging tenants to transfer from under-occupied family houses to smaller units: see D.o.E. Circular no. 18/74, *op. cit.*, App., para. 9(v)). The 1953 C.H.A.C. Report on *Transfers, Exchanges and Rents*, while warning against the "fallacious assumption that housing problems can be reduced to a matter of impersonal arithmetic," suggested that in cases of "indefensible under-occupation" the tenant should be forced to pay the full unsubsidised rent (at pp. 2–4); but elderly occupants who may have spent most of their lives in a council house and raised a family in it will often be understandably reluctant to leave, and should not be pressured into doing so (see, *e.g.* V. Karn, *Roof*, September 1979, at p. 139). In any event, we shall see that where the tenancy is secure, "under-occupation" is only a statutory ground for possession in extremely limited circumstances.[14]

There is a technical but significant difference between a "transfer" and an "exchange": a "transfer" takes place where an existing council tenant moves to vacant accommodation also owned by the local authority, thus leaving his previous property available for re-allocation; whereas an "exchange" involves an interchange of properties between a council tenant and another council tenant (perhaps in a different area), or a private sector tenant, and does not depend on a vacancy (see *Transfers, Exchanges and Rents, op. cit.,* at pp. 3–5, and the H.S.A.G. Report, *op. cit.,* at p. 1, note 1).

There is also the seperate concept of the "assignment" of a council tenancy, whereby the tenant himself assigns his tenancy to a third party: the usual result of this, as was noted in Chapter 2, is the automatic cessation of the *secure* tenancy.[15] The problems concerning the devolution of council tenancies on death were also discussed in Chapter 2[16]; and the special difficulties arising in relation to assignments and transfers on marriage breakdown will be separately discussed in Chapter 4.

(ii) Transfers

Where a tenant requests a transfer, the authority often has to make a difficult decision between his claim and the claims of applicants at the head of the general waiting list. The H.S.A.G. Report found that few authorities had any formal scheme for deciding priorities either as between general waiting list applicants and transfer applicants, or as between transfer applicants *inter se* (*op. cit.,* at paras. 2.46, 2.48). Yet a lack of a proper policy on transfers can cause a "bottleneck" effect in the general waiting list, since "[a] family offered a poor house in an unattractive area may . . . refuse it, no matter how desperate they are, because they will not easily be able to get a transfer" (V. Karn, *Roof*, January 1981, at p. 15). The publication requirements in section 44 of the 1980 Act (*supra*) extend to transfer schemes also, so that some authorities have had to introduce formal transfer arrangements for the first time. Sometimes the same system of "points" will be used for transfer cases as for general waiting list cases, but often authorities can adopt a lower standard of need for transfer cases, since a transferring tenant will vacate a property which the authority can use.

Some authorities insist upon strict conditions being satisfied before a transfer application will be entertained, for example, a satisfactory record of rent payments (this condition was adopted in 1976 by all the Welsh authorities who permitted transfers: see the Welsh Consumer Council's Report on *Council Housing, op. cit.,* at p. 27).

(iii) Exchanges

Authorities normally adopt a more liberal attitude towards exchanges, since unlike transfers they do not involve any vacant accommodation and will help at least two families. It is possible for exchanges to be arranged between council tenants and tenants in the private sector, but these have not proved popular, *inter alia* because of private landlords' suspicions that unsatisfactory council tenants might be "dumped" on them: see *Transfers, Exchanges and Rents, op. cit.,* at pp. 6–7.

Exchange schemes are subject to the general publication requirements imposed on councils by section 44 of the 1980 Act (*supra*). However, tenants desiring exchanges may themselves have difficulty in publishing their needs to other tenants who might be interested: some advertise in the local press, or make use of the various commercial concerns which disseminate exchange information nationally.[17] There have been several calls for a central computerised[18] exchange bureau, covering the whole country (see, *e.g. Roof,* January 1978, at p. 9). However, the Cullingworth Report found "considerable scepticism" among authorities for such a proposal, although some support was evident for regional or subregional bureaux (*op. cit.,* at paras. 183–184); and the H.S.A.G. Report concluded that although the idea of a national or regional computerised exchange bureau was "superficially attractive," the results were "unlikely to justify the cost and effort involved," since past experience indicated that only a very few of the potential exchanges identified by exchange bureaux actually came to fruition (*op. cit.*, at paras. 9.12–9.15). By section 22(5) of the London Government Act 1963, however, the G.L.C. is required to maintain exchange facilities for accommodation in the Greater London area, and may charge for this service notwithstanding the Accommodation Agencies Act 1953[19]; a computerised exchange agency was instituted by the G.L.C. in 1975.

The machinery whereby an "exchange" is to be technically effected needs careful consideration. We have seen that an *assignment* by a secure tenant of his tenancy normally results in the cessation of security under section 37(1) of the Housing Act 1980, regardless of the terms of the tenancy[15]: thus if security (and the right to buy) is to be preserved for the respective tenants in their new accommodation, the tenancies of their former dwellings should be *surrendered* to the council, and new (secure) tenancies should then be granted by the council to them as "incoming" tenants. However, legislation is to be introduced with retrospective effect in order to prevent councils from arranging exchanges by way of requiring assignments of the tenancies (a method whereby some councils had neatly side-stepped both the right to buy and statutory security of tenure): see *Hansard* (Commons) July 28, 1981, Vol. 9, cols. *442–3*.

(iv) Removal expenses

Under section 93 of the Housing Finance Act 1972 an authority may pay the removal expenses of a tenant moving from a council house, whether into another council house or into a private dwelling. The provision in section 46 of the Housing Act 1980 for central government funding of mobility schemes[20] only covers general administrative costs, and not the removal costs incurred by individual tenants.

4. *Reform*

Valerie Karn wrote recently that "housing management . . . has arrived in 1981 trailing clouds of the Poor
Law and 'less eligibility,' parish relief and residential
qualifications, charity and moral judgments" (*Roof*, January 1981, at p. 23). The Housing Act 1980 has done little
to remove such attitudes where they still exist, though the
new publication requirements should ensure the demise of
excessively discretionary "merit" allocation schemes.

There would seem to be no reason in principle why the
courts should not be prepared to interfere with an unfair
allocation scheme or procedure, in an appropriate case,
by the use of the prerogative orders (mandamus, prohibition and *certiorari*). The granting of these orders is of
course a matter of discretion, but the courts have granted
orders of *certiorari* quashing the grant of planning
permission by an authority (*R.* v. *L.B. of Hillingdon, ex p.
Royco Homes Ltd.* [1974] 2 All E.R. 643, (D.C.)[21]), and
quashing an authority's decision that it owed no duty to
the applicant under the Housing (Homeless Persons) Act
1977 (*R.* v. *Hillingdon L.B.C., ex p. Streeting* [1980] 3 All
E.R. 413, (C.A.)); and an order of prohibition has been
granted for the purpose of controlling the procedure for
the issue by an authority of hackney carriage licences (*Re
Liverpool Taxi Owners' Association* [1972] 2 All E.R. 589,
(C.A.)). The function of allocating council housing may
be said to be primarily administrative rather than judicial
or quasi-judicial, but this will not prevent the issue of the
prerogative orders if the authority fails to act fairly (see,
e.g. the *Liverpool Taxi Owners* case, *supra*, at pp. 594,
596, and the *Royco Homes* case, *supra*, at p. 648), or if it
fails to publish its allocation scheme in accordance with
section 44, *supra* (see, *e.g.* D. Yates [1981] J.S.W.L. 129,
132). Further, an applicant who is denied housing in clear
contravention of the authority's rules as published pursuant to section 44 may well have a claim by way of
declaration or injunction, since "there would seem to be

little other purpose in permitting people to find out that they have been *wrongfully* denied housing" (A. Arden (1981) LAG Bul. 38, 39).

However, certain additional reforms are needed even if the judges prove willing to involve themselves in this area, and some specific proposals have been mentioned where appropriate in the foregoing discussion. More generally, dissatisfaction regarding allocation processes could be reduced by the introduction of a statutory requirement for authorities to produce published "grievance procedures," giving rights of appeal within the particular authority, in the light of circulars from the D.o.E.[22] The H.S.A.G. Report noted that few authorities had any formal appeal procedures for applicants to contest decisions, and recommended their general introduction, which would provide "an important role for councillors" (*op. cit.*, at paras. 2.59, 13.9).

Statutory "grievance procedures" are already established in some other areas of local authority housing activities: for example, a tenant applying for a rent rebate under the Housing Finance Act 1972[23] has a right to be given the authority's decision in writing, following which he may make a complaint to the authority within one month, which it must consider, and it must then inform him in writing of its reasons for confirming or altering its original decision (see Sched. 4, Pt. I, para. 15 of the 1972 Act).

It is difficult to see why an applicant for permanent council housing (who under the 1980 Housing Act can be regarded as applying also for a full "package" of rights, including in particular the right to buy), should not at least have the basic right to be given the reasons for the authority's refusal to grant his application the priority which he anticipated, or to be informed of the way in which his individual "points" score has been assessed (rather than being left to guess at these matters from a perusal of the authority's published scheme). Homeless applicants have the right under section 8 of the Housing (Homeless

Persons) Act 1977 to be notified of the authority's reasons if their claims are rejected (and those seeking house renovation grants have a similar right, under s. 80 of the Housing Act 1974); "normal" applicants for council housing should be in no worse a position.

Notes

[1] The chairman of the sub-committee responsible for this report was Professor J. B. Cullingworth.

[2] A. W. Bradley (1974) XIII Jo. S.P.T.L. 35, 41.

[3] "Points" schemes are discussed *infra*, pp. 54–5.

[4] "Priority needs" are listed in s. 2 of the 1977 Act, and the Minister may by order specify further categories; for a detailed assessment of the 1977 Act and the difficult case law thereon, see, *e.g.* D. C. Hoath, *Homelessness* (1982).

[5] Published by the Hampshire Legal Action Group.

[6] See *supra*, p. 44.

[7] See further *infra*, p. 114.

[8] See *supra*, pp. 15–18.

[9] See, *e.g.* the Cullingworth Report, *op. cit.*, at para. 169.

[10] Manchester Free Press, Issue 21, November 1973, quoted in C. Ward, *Tenants Take Over*, 1974, at p. 17.

[11] *Supra*, p. 46.

[12] See also *supra*, p. 50.

[13] See *supra*, pp. 50–51.

[14] *Infra*, p. 160.

[15] *Supra*, pp. 27–8.

[16] *Supra*, pp. 28–31.

[17] There appear to be about 10 commercial exchange bureaux, together with one non-profit making bureau (Locatex): see *Roof*, September 1979, at p. 141.

[18] Computerisation can prove a mixed blessing: see the case reported in *The Times*, June 16, 1977: "Computer error turned squatter into a tenant."

[19] This Act makes illegal the keeping of accommodation lists for gain (see *supra*, p. 52), but it has been restrictively interpreted: see *Saunders* v. *Soper* [1974] 3 All E.R. 1025, (H.L.).

[20] See *supra*, p. 61.

[21] For the facts see *supra*, p. 45.

[22] See further: the Report of the Committee on *Conduct in Local Government*, Cmnd. 5636, 1974, Vol. 1, pp. 34–35; N. Lewis (1976) 54 *Public Administration* 147, 154–7; N. Lewis and R. Livock (1979) 2 U.L. 133; N. Lewis and P. Birkinshaw, *Welfare Law and Policy* (ed. M. Partington and J. Jowell, 1979), p. 130; and the Code of Practice on *Complaints Procedures*, issued under the auspices of the Commission for Local Administration in 1978.

[23] See *infra*, pp. 141–2.

Chapter 4

THE COUNCIL HOUSE AS A FAMILY HOME

1. *General*

In the last chapter we examined in general terms the system of allocation and transfer of council tenancies. However, where a council house is occupied by spouses or cohabitees and the relationship breaks down, the resultant difficulties merit special treatment: the 1977 H.S.A.G. Report on *Tenancy Agreements* recognized that such a breakdown "brings with it a whole series of problems about the tenancy and who remains in the dwelling . . . until any legal processes take effect" (at p. 4); and in some respects the security provisions of the Housing Act 1980 have caused further complications. Yet the 1980 Act also contains several important provisions which cater for the special interests of the tenant's "family" even where there has been no discord between the spouses or cohabitees, particularly as regards assignments[1], succession rights[2], and the "right to buy."[3]

There is no reason to think that the incidence of "marriage" breakdown is any less in the publicly-rented sector than in the privately-rented and owner-occupied sectors; indeed, since it is still true that "[c]ouncil tenants include relatively few of the youngest and oldest and very few single householders" (D.V. Donnison, *The Government of Housing*, 1967, at pp. 210–11), the problem of deciding what is to be done with a council house when the occupying spouses (or cohabitees) fall out is a common one, concerning which there is a growing body of case law. The solution of this problem demands just as much care on the part of those advising the parties as if the house were owner-occupied, since the result can be of equally crucial importance: Ormrod L.J. recognized in 1975 that "[w]here . . . the wife has a secure home in a council flat, then she has what in these days is a very valuable asset" (*Browne* v. *Pritchard* [1975] 3 All E.R. 721, 725, (C.A.)), and the "value" of a council tenancy has since been enhanced by the very generous "right to buy" provisions in the 1980 Act, discussed in Chapter 8. Further, the availability of council housing to one of the spouses may prove relevant to settling a dispute involving a former matrimonial home which was either owner-occupied or privately rented (see, *e.g. Browne* v. *Pritchard* [1975] 3 All E.R. 721, (C.A.), *Martin* v. *Martin* [1977] 3 All E.R. 762, (C.A.)).

Quite apart from the strict legal position, however, there was some evidence prior to the 1980 Act indicating that a wife involved in a marital dispute where the matrimonial home was a council house had in practice less chance of remaining in the home than if it were owner-occupied or privately rented, at least until a divorce or separation order was obtained (see the Shelter Housing Action Centre's 1977 Report on *Violence in Marriage*, suggesting *inter alia* that the greater financial commitment or "sense of permanence" involved in owner-occupation might partly account for this discrepancy[4]). It may well be that the 1980 Act has caused a greater awareness among council tenants and their partners that council tenancies attract "rights," so that legal advice may now be sought more swiftly following the breakdown of the relationship.

In viewing a council house as a family home or matrimonial asset, there has long been the fundamental problem that the interests of at least one of the parties to the dispute may well differ from the interests of the local authority, which may for example be particularly concerned to avoid "under-occupation" following the departure of one or more of the family members from the dwelling. It will be seen that the discretion of authorities in situations of family breakdown has been substantially curtailed by the introduction of statutory security of tenure by the 1980 Act. We shall therefore consider separately the position of the spouses or cohabitees *inter se*, before turning to the position of the authority itself (although in practice, of course, these two issues cannot be viewed entirely separately, since for example the authority's views will be considered by the court in deciding the destination of the tenancy following divorce).

As a preliminary issue, however, the matter of joint tenancy agreements will be discussed.

2. *Joint Tenancy Agreements*

The traditional practice of putting council tenancy agreements in the husband's name alone has been largely displaced by the increasing use of joint tenancies. Indeed, the National Consumer Council's 1976 paper on *Tenancy Agreements*, having "taken note of the Sex Discrimination Act 1975,"[5] proposed (at pp. 22–23) a model agreement which stated: "Normally the council will not consider granting anything other than a joint tenancy to a husband and wife." In the case of cohabitees, however, many authorities still appear to be reluctant to grant joint tenancies.

Where the spouses or cohabitees do hold under a joint tenancy, the tenancy will be "secure" if at least one of them occupies the dwelling as his or her "only or principal home," providing the normal conditions are satisfied (see s. 28(3) of the Housing Act 1980 and Chapter 2, *supra*); the "right to buy" can be exercised either jointly by both of the tenants, or by one of them following an agreement to that effect (see ss. 1(4), 4(1) of the 1980 Act, discussed in Chapter 8, *infra*); and on the death of one joint tenant the other will take the secure tenancy automatically under the common law right of survivorship rather than under section 30 of the 1980 Act,[6] although in such a case the survivor is treated as a statutory "successor" under section 31(1), so that there can be no transmission of the *secure* tenancy to a "member of his [or her] family" under section 30 on his or her own death.[6]

If the relationship breaks down while both joint tenants are still alive, the existence of a joint tenancy can sometimes have an important psychological effect on the "weaker" party, in that he or she may be more reluctant to leave merely at the "stronger" party's bidding. However, it will be seen that as far as short-term legal remedies on the breakdown of the relationship are concerned, it may make little difference in practice whether the spouses or cohabitees hold as joint tenants or whether the tenancy is solely in one partner's name. It will also be seen that in the case of spouses the court is given a wide discretion to decide the long-term destination of the tenancy pursuant to a decree of divorce, nullity or judicial separation, whether or not the tenancy is currently in joint names. Indeed, the 1977 H.S.A.G. Report considered that there were "as many arguments in favour of, as there [were] against, tenancies in joint names," and suggested that prospective tenants should be given the chance to choose between a joint tenancy and a sole tenancy in the light of appropriate guidance furnished by the authority (*op. cit.*, at p. 5; but *cf.* the 1978 H.S.A.G. Report on *The Housing of One Parent Families*, para. 3.29, which saw "strong advantages to joint tenancies"); while the 1977 S.H.A.C. Report argued that "in the Public Sector the availability of joint tenancies is not the issue most crucial to a wife's rights" (*op. cit.*),[7] and that the real problem is that of responsibility for rent arrears. The general significance of rent arrears in cases of matrimonial breakdown will be discussed later,[8] but it may be mentioned here that where there is a joint tenancy each partner is equally liable for the rent even if the arrears were due purely to the "fault" of one of them, whereas where the tenancy is in the name of one partner alone, the non-tenant partner is under no legal liability for rent arrears.

We shall see that the broad matrimonial jurisdiction under which the court can "switch" the tenancy from one spouse to another does *not* apply to cohabitees; thus the 1978 H.S.A.G. Report considered that joint tenancies were "a great advantage" for "common-law wives" (*op. cit.*, at para. 3.30).

3. *The Position of the Parties to the Marriage or Cohabitation Inter se*

It will be seen that the security provisions of the Housing Act 1980 have in effect removed the power which authorities previously enjoyed to intervene at an early stage after the breakdown of the relationship by "switching" the tenancy from one spouse or cohabitee to the other (by way of determination and re-grant). Thus a spouse or cohabitee must rely on the normal legal remedies available in respect of the "family" home: in the case of a spouse, these remedies may be either short-term or long-term, whether or not he or she currently has an interest in the tenancy; but in the case of a cohabitee, only short-term remedies are normally available unless he or she already has an interest in the tenancy. These remedies will now be discussed, with particular emphasis on those aspects most relevant to council housing.

(a) *Short-term remedies*

(i) Spouses

Whether the tenancy is in joint names, or in the sole name of one spouse, each has the right to remain in occupation until a court orders otherwise. This right exists at common law, either by virtue of any proprietary interest the spouse may have (see, *e.g. Bull* v. *Bull* [1955] 1 All E.R. 253, (C.A.)), or by virtue of the husband's duty to provide a roof over his wife's head regardless of whose name the house is in (see, *e.g. National Provincial Bank*

Ltd. v. *Ainsworth* [1965] 2 All E.R. 472, (H.L.), *Gurasz* v. *Gurasz* [1969] 3 All E.R. 822, 823, (C.A.)). The court also has *inherent* jurisdiction to *exclude* one spouse from the home while matrimonial proceedings are pending, even if he or she is the sole tenant (*Jones* v. *Jones* [1971] 2 All E.R. 737, (C.A.), a council housing case); in exceptional circumstances, this inherent jurisdiction to exclude can even be exercised after the parties have been divorced (see, *e.g. Phillips* v. *Phillips* [1973] 2 All E.R. 423, (C.A.), *Beard* v. *Beard* [1981] 1 All E.R. 783, (C.A.): both these cases also concerned council housing).

The right to remain in occupation has been separately conferred by statute, under section 1 of the Matrimonial Homes Act 1967 (unless, by s. 1(9), the spouse is entitled to a legal estate in the property either solely or as joint tenant,[9] in which case he or she will of course have an equivalent right to occupy at common law). In particular, an occupying spouse may keep the *secure* council tenancy of the other spouse "alive" even though the latter spouse has deserted the occupying spouse, since by section 1(5) of the 1967 Act (as amended by Sched. 25, Pt. I, para. 14 of the Housing Act 1980) a spouse's occupation under section 1 of the 1967 Act is to be treated as occupation by the tenant-spouse for the purposes of section 28(3) of the 1980 Act (which requires a secure tenant to *occupy* the dwelling[10]): thus a secure tenant who has deserted his wife cannot affect her occupation rights by purporting to surrender the tenancy to the authority (*cf. Middleton* v. *Baldock* [1950] 1 All E.R. 708, (C.A.), *Hoggett* v. *Hoggett* [1979] J.S.W.L. 365, (C.A.)); further, section 1(5) of the 1967 Act entitles the occupying non-tenant spouse to pay the rent due from the other spouse, so that rent arrears and the consequent threat of possession proceedings[11] may be avoided.

Where one spouse is exercising these statutory "rights of occupation" under section 1 of the 1967 Act, either spouse may apply to the court for an order "declaring, enforcing, restricting or terminating those rights or

prohibiting, suspending or restricting the exercise by
either spouse of the right to occupy . . . or requiring
either spouse to permit the exercise by the other of that
right" (s. 1(2); see, *e.g.* the council housing case of *Glover*
v. *Glover* (1974) 124 N.L.J. 810 (Birmingham County
Court)). The reference in section 1(2) to "prohibiting"
occupation shows that, at least in theory, the court now
has power to grant a *permanent* exclusion order (*cp.* the
council housing case of *Tarr* v. *Tarr* [1972] 2 All E.R. 295,
(H.L.), the effect of which was reversed by the amend-
ments to s. 1(2) of the 1967 Act introduced by s. 3 of the
Domestic Violence and Matrimonial Proceedings Act
1976). Similar powers to those conferred by section 1 of
the 1967 Act are available to the court where the spouses
jointly hold the *legal estate*, under section 4 of the
Domestic Violence and Matrimonial Proceedings Act
1976. However, the statutory rights of occupation under
the 1967 Act normally cease on the death of the tenant or
on the termination of the marriage *inter vivos* (s. 2(2)).

Quite apart from the 1967 Act, under sections 1 and 2 of
the Domestic Violence and Matrimonial Proceedings Act
1976 one spouse can seek a *county court* injunction against
the other, without the need to claim any further relief in
the proceedings, which can have the effect of (*inter alia*)
excluding him or her from the matrimonial home, and to
which in certain circumstances a power of arrest may be
attached. Despite the title of this Act, no violence needs
to be shown before an exclusion order (as opposed to a
power of arrest) can be granted: *Spindlow* v. *Spindlow*
[1979] 1 All E.R. 169, (C.A.), a council housing case; and
it is immaterial which spouse has the legal interest in the
property: *cf. Davis* v. *Johnson* [1978] 1 All E.R. 1132,
(H.L.), another council housing case. The 1976 Act can
usually provide speedier relief than that obtainable under
section 1 of the Matrimonial Homes Act (*supra*), but it is
designed to provide essentially short-term remedies: for
the duration of exclusion orders and powers of arrest, see
Hopper v. *Hopper* [1979] 1 All E.R. 181, (C.A.), and

Practice Notes at [1978] 2 All E.R. 1056, [1981] 1 All E.R. 224.

There is a completely separate jurisdiction relating to short-term remedies conferred on *magistrates' courts* under section 16 of the Domestic Proceedings and Magistrates' Courts Act 1978, whereby orders may be made excluding one spouse from the matrimonial home, even though no other matrimonial proceedings have been begun: but here the applicant must normally be able to show that the respondent has committed an act of violence and that the applicant or a child of the family is in danger of being physically injured by the respondent (s. 16(3); *cf. McCartney* v. *McCartney* [1981] 1 All E.R. 597, (D.C.)). As with the 1976 Act, a power of arrest may be attached under the 1978 Act in certain circumstances (s. 18), and the procedure is designed to secure speedier relief than that normally obtainable under section 1 of the Matrimonial Homes Act (see ss. 16(5), 17(2) of the 1978 Act).

(ii) Cohabitees

Of the short-term remedies available to spouses which have just been discussed, the provisions in sections 1 and 2 of the Domestic Violence and Matrimonial Proceedings Act 1976 (but not s. 4 thereof) apply equally to those "living with each other in the same household as husband and wife" although they are unmarried (see ss. 1(2), 2(2), and *Davis* v. *Johnson* [1978] 1 All E.R. 1132, (H.L.)); even if the relationship has broken down, the parties may still be "living with each other . . . " for these purposes if their accommodation is so small that they cannot live separate lives: *Adeoso* v. *Adeoso* [1981] 1 All E.R. 107, (C.A.), a case concerning cohabitees who were joint tenants of a one-bedroom council flat.[12] However, neither sections 1 and 2 of the Matrimonial Homes Act 1967 nor sections 16 to 18 of the Domestic Proceedings and Magistrates' Courts Act 1978 (*supra*) offer any protection to cohabitees.

(b) *Long-term remedies*

(i) Spouses

If a long-term solution is sought regarding the destination of the council tenancy following marriage breakdown, then the parties may be able to agree between themselves as to which of them should retain or gain the tenancy: if so, then section 37(1) of the Housing Act 1980 provides, broadly speaking, than an assignment from one spouse to the other shall not cause any cessation of the secure tenancy.[13] Failing any such agreement, however, then (as will be seen) the introduction of statutory security of tenure has meant that the authority cannot now itself terminate a secure council tenancy and "switch" it to the "deserving" spouse; nevertheless, the *court* can decide the ultimate destination of the tenancy under Schedule 2 of the Matrimonial Homes Act 1967 or section 24 of the Matrimonial Causes Act 1973, but (in either case) only where a decree of divorce, nullity or judicial separation is granted.

Schedule 2 of the Matrimonial Homes Act 1967

Prior to the Housing Act 1980, the jurisdiction in section 7 of the Matrimonial Homes Act 1967 for the court to order the transfer of a tenancy from one spouse to another was limited to protected or statutory tenancies under the Rent Act 1977 (and even in the case of such tenancies, the order could only be made between decree nisi and decree absolute of divorce or nullity). The exclusion of council tenancies from this jurisdiction was justified in the 1956 Report of the Royal Commission on *Marriage and Divorce* (which made the proposal eventually enacted in s. 7 of the 1967 Act) on the grounds that "it would be undesirable to interfere with the rights of the landlord to this extent in respect of [non-Rent Act] tenancies," and that in any event in the case of periodic tenancies outside the Rent Act "it is not possible to afford the wife effective protection, since the landlord would always be free to give her notice to quit" (Cmd. 9678, p. 186). Nevertheless, there had been several suggestions that section 7 should be extended to council tenancies even if their tenants were not given security of tenure (see, *e.g.* the Report of the Committee on *One-Parent Families*, Cmnd. 5629 (1974), at p. 388), and in D.o.E. Circular no. 78/77 on *Housing for One-Parent Families* (1977) it was pointed out that the extension of section 7 to council tenancies would be expected to "follow from the grant of security . . . [to] public sector tenants" (Annex A, para. 24).

The extension of section 7 to council tenancies duly followed the introduction of statutory security in 1980: the relevant change was initially made by paragraphs 15–17 of Part I of Schedule 25 of the Housing Act 1980, but these provisions were themselves repealed, and replaced with significant modifications, by the Matrimonial Homes and Property Act 1981. Section 7 of the 1967 Act (as amended by s. 6 of the 1981 Act) now merely refers to Schedule 2, in which the relevant provisions are contained.

By paragraphs 1 and 2 of Schedule 2 of the 1967 Act, the court, on granting a decree of divorce, nullity *or judicial separation*, or (with leave of the court[14]) *at any time thereafter*, may order the transfer of the interest of one spouse under a *secure* council tenancy (whether as sole or joint tenant) to the other spouse. In such a case the transfer of the secure tenancy operates "by virtue of the order and without further assurance" (para. 2(1)): the tenancy is *not assigned* by the existing tenant-spouse, so that the court's power to order the transfer will not be ousted by the presence in the tenancy agreement of a prohibition against assignments, whether drafted in absolute or qualified form.[15] Nevertheless, although the council's *consent* is not required, it has the right to be heard by the court before any such order is made (see para.8(1) of Sched. 2 and r.107(4) of the Matrimonial Causes Rules 1977, S.I. 1977/344).

Any demand made by the council in such proceedings that the transferee-spouse (not being an existing joint tenant) should discharge rent arrears due from the other spouse should be firmly resisted, especially since paragraph 2(2) of Schedule 2 expressly provides that the other spouse is only exempt from liability under the terms of the lease in respect of obligations *falling due on or after* the date of transfer. Prior to the Housing Act 1980 it was quite common for authorities to refuse a transfer of a tenancy to a wife unless she paid off her husband's rent arrears, despite the fact that she was under no legal liability to do so and such a requirement would normally have been an illegal "premium" if demanded by a *private* landlord (*cp.* the Rent Act 1977, ss. 119, 128; *Hampstead Way Investments* v. *Mawdsley* (1980) 9 C.L. 115: Barnet County Court); but now that the transfer of council tenancies is largely removed from the scope of an individual council's discretion, such demands for the discharge of the previous tenant-spouse's arrears should be rare, save for example where a new tenancy of a separate property is offered to a displaced spouse, and even in these cases the making of such demands were disapproved of in the 1978 H.S.A.G. Report (*op. cit.*, at para. 4.24). Requirements that a wife should discharge her estranged husband's rent arrears in order to retain or obtain council accommodation have been held by the Local Commissioners to amount to "maladministration"[16] (see *e.g.* Investigation 1854 (C) H, 1976, and Investigation 4692 H, 1977, referred to by D. J. Hughes and S. R. Jones [1979] J.S.W.L. 273, 286–7). The Tenants' Rights, etc. (Scotland) Act 1980 actually makes it illegal for a council to refuse to house a person until he or she has repaid rent arrears attributable to any tenancy of which he or she was not a tenant (s. 26(6)), and thought should be given to importing this provision south of the Border.

Section 24 of the Matrimonial Causes Act 1973

Under section 24(1) (*a*) of the Matrimonial Causes Act, the court has a general power to order that one spouse shall transfer to the other (or to or for the benefit of a child of the family) "such property as may be so specified." In making such an order, the court must take into account under section 25 "all the circumstances of the case" including certain specified matters, for example the "income, earning capacity, property and other financial resources" of the parties. The order can be made on granting the decree or (with leave of the court) at any time thereafter (ss. 24(1), 26(2); Matrimonial Causes Rules 1977, S.I. 1977/344, r. 68(2)).

Even prior to the Housing Act 1980, the courts had (eventually) accepted that transfer of property orders under section 24 of the 1973 Act could be made relating to council housing (see, *e.g. Thompson* v. *Thompson* [1975] 2 All E.R. 208, (C.A.), *Hale* v. *Hale* [1975] 2 All E.R. 1090, (C.A.), *Hutchings* v. *Hutchings* (1976) 237 E.G. 571, (C.A.), and *Rodewald* v. *Rodewald* [1977] 2 All E.R. 609, (C.A.); *cp.* the earlier doubts relating to a "mere tenancy from a council" expressed by Dunn J. in *Brent* v. *Brent* [1974] 2 All E.R. 1211, 1215). However, the courts tended to consider very carefully the council's views before making the order, despite the fact that the council had (and has) no statutory right to be heard in section 24 proceedings (*cp.* Sched. 2, para. 8(1) of the 1967 Act, *supra*). The need for the court to consult the council was important not only because the lack of security of tenure would enable a council speedily to end a tenancy transferred to an "unwelcome" spouse, but also because (as noted in Chapter 2[17]) under the (now-repealed[17]) section 113(5) of the Housing Act 1957 councils had to make it a term of every letting that the tenant could not assign (or sublet) without the council's written consent (see, *e.g. Regan* v. *Regan* [1977] 1 All E.R. 428), and under section 24 of the 1973 Act the court's order can only be effected by the assignment of the tenancy by the tenant (*cp*. Sched. 2 para. 2(1) of the 1967 Act, *supra*). For a discussion of the general problems which section 113(5) presented in this context, and of the relevance of section 19(1) (*a*) of the Landlord and Tenant Act 1927 (which provides that the landlord's consent to an assignment, where required, cannot be unreasonably withheld[18]), see the first edition of this book, at pp. 57–59, and D. Yates, (1977) 41 Conv. (N.S.) 309, 313–317.

After the Housing Act 1980, a tenancy agreement may now unreservedly permit, or indeed absolutely prohibit, assignments of the tenancy[19]; but there are many tenancy agreements entered into prior to October 3, 1980 which (until variation under s.40[20]) are still expressly subject to the qualified prohibition on assignments formerly required to be inserted by the (now-repealed) section 113(5) of the 1957 Act (*supra*). In such cases the old problems concerning the courts' powers to order the transfer of the tenancy under section 24 of the 1973 Act will, at least in theory, remain relevant[21] (for it is clear that the specific jurisdiction in the 1967 Act in relation to secure tenancies, *supra*, does not have the effect of excluding the use of the general jurisdiction in section 24 of the 1973 Act in relation to such tenancies: *cf*. Megaw L.J. in *Hale* v. *Hale* [1975] 2 All E.R. 1090, 1094, (C.A.)).

In practice, however, the use of the court's enlarged jurisdiction under Schedule 2 of the 1967 Act, which relates specifically to secure tenancies, will surely be regarded in most cases as much more appropriate than the general 1973 Act jurisdiction. In particular, use of the 1967 Act powers does not depend on the assignment of the tenancy by the tenant, so that any covenant against assignment need not as such be an insuperable hurdle, despite the landlord's right to be heard in the transfer proceedings. Since the courts bear in mind broadly the same criteria in deciding on transfers under the 1967 Act as those specifically listed in section 25 of the 1973 Act, *supra*,[22] it is difficult to see what advantage an applicant would normally gain by seeking a transfer under the 1973 Act rather than under the "purpose-built" procedure in the 1967 Act (as amended by the 1981 Act, *supra*). Obviously, if the tenancy is not "secure,"[23] the 1967 Act's jurisdiction will not be available; and if a transfer of the tenancy is sought to a "child of the family," only the 1973 Act can be used, and not the 1967 Act; but apart from such cases, section 24 of the 1973 Act has now been rather eclipsed, as far as council housing is concerned, by the jurisdiction in Schedule 2 of the 1967 Act.

Where a transfer is nevertheless ordered under section 24 of the 1973 Act, then the tenancy will remain secure following the assignment (assuming it was secure prior to the assignment) in view of the specific "saving" reference to the 1973 Act jurisdiction in section 37 of the Housing Act 1980 (a provision whereby a secure tenancy generally loses its security following assignment[24]). Whether the insertion by a council in its tenancy agreement of an *absolute prohibition* against assignment (which is now permitted) will prevent the court from accepting jurisdiction over the tenancy under section 24 of the 1973 Act, despite the clear recognition of this particular jurisdiction over council tenancies in section 37 of the 1980 Act, remains to be seen. The cases concerning the old "qualified" covenant prescribed by section 113(5) of the 1957 Act would indicate an affirmative answer (see, *e.g.* Sir George Baker P. in *Regan* v. *Regan* [1977] 1 All E.R. 428, 429); and these cases might be thought to apply *a fortiori* where there is an *absolute* prohibition. But arguably there are special issues of public policy arising under the Housing Act 1980[25] which require the court to reach a just decision untrammelled by the terms of the tenancy agreement: the specific recognition in section 37 of the 1980 Act of the role of the courts here surely indicates that the matrimonial jurisdiction under the 1973 Act cannot be evaded by councils in such a facile manner; and it would be somewhat unfortunate if an authority were able *absolutely* to prohibit an *assignment* of a secure tenancy, when by section 35 of the 1980 Act only a *qualified* covenant can be inserted against *sub-letting part* of a property held on a secure tenancy (*i.e.* a covenant calling for the landlord's consent, which however cannot be unreasonably withheld).[26] Any attempt by a council to impose liability on an assignee-spouse for the previous tenant-spouse's rent arrears would also be open to challenge.[27]

(ii) Cohabitees

Neither Schedule 2 of the Matrimonial Homes Act nor section 24 of the Matrimonial Causes Act extend to cohabitees. Thus the court cannot order the transfer of the tenancy from one cohabitee to the other; and the long-term rights of a party in respect of the tenancy on the breakdown of the relationship depend, not on any "matrimonial" jurisdiction as such, but primarily on whether he or she already has a proprietary interest in that tenancy, failing which he or she can only try and persuade the other partner to assign the secure tenancy to him or her (*cf.* s. 37(1) of the 1980 Act[28]) or to surrender it to the authority with a view to a re-grant to him or her (*infra*).

4. *The Position of the Local Authority*

(a) *Where no order is made pursuant to Schedule 2 of the Matrimonial Homes Act or section 24 of the Matrimonial Causes Act*

Prior to the Housing Act 1980, the council itself could intervene in an appropriate case to "switch" the tenancy from one spouse or cohabitee to the other even in advance of any court order being obtained (under, *e.g.* the Domestic Violence and Matrimonial Proceedings Act 1976, *supra*). This could be achieved by way of determination by the council of the existing tenancy by notice to quit and re-grant to the appropriate party, there being no statutory security of tenure for council tenants before the

1980 Act. The beneficiary under such an arrangement would normally be the spouse or cohabitee who was taking care of the children (if any), as Lord Gifford pointed out during the Lords' debate on the Committee stage of the Housing Bill: "Local authorities . . . make a number of very sound compassionate decisions, about which I have heard very little dispute or quarrel, when, in the early days of a separation, they have to try to help to restore a family and children to the matrimonial home by the use of the power they . . . have to transfer the tenancy" (*Hansard* (Lords) June 30, 1980, Vol. 411, col 178).

This power was particularly useful when exercised in favour of an ousted cohabitee, who was (and is) unable to apply under the "transfer" jurisdiction in the Matrimonial Homes Act or the Matrimonial Causes Act described earlier: and since no statutory "rights of occupation" can arise as between cohabitees under section 1 of the Matrimonial Homes Act (*supra*), the cohabitee to whom the tenancy was re-granted would not be subjected to any automatic statutory occupation rights in the other party.

Such transfers were often also beneficial from the council's viewpoint, since it could thereby try to ensure, for example, that a council tenant whose wife and children had left him did not continue to underoccupy a large council house, either right up until divorce proceedings or indeed indefinitely where no divorce proceedings were to be instituted: thus in *Sales* v. *Sales* (1980) 10 Fam. Law 115, (C.A.), Donaldson L.J. recognized that " . . . the council will not indefinitely tolerate the husband as a single man living in the matrimonial home"; and in the "cohabitation" case of *Spindlow* v. *Spindlow* [1979] 1 All E.R. 169, 173, (C.A.), Ormrod L.J. referred to " . . . the absurd situation [which] would arise [if] the local authority [were to] have a single man living in a three-bedroom house on his own, with a woman and two children to house in other accomodation, all at public expense."

The advantages of this power for the council to

intervene at an early stage after the break-up of a family were recognized by the Committee on *One-Parent Families* (*op. cit.*, at pp. 386–7), the D.o.E. Circular on *Housing for One-Parent Families* (*op. cit.*, Annex A, at para. 23), and the House of Commons Select Committee on *Violence in Marriage* (1975 H.C. 553–i, para. 50). Moreover, the courts had often emphasized the particular relevance of this power when considering the grant of exclusion orders under the Domestic Violence and Matrimonial Proceedings Act 1976 (*supra*) against council tenants, for they were prepared in appropriate cases to exclude the tenant (whether spouse or cohabitee) for a sufficient period to allow for the "switching" of the tenancy by the council: see for example *Davis* v. *Johnson* [1978] 1 All E.R. 1132, 1152, (H.L.: Lord Salmon), *Spindlow* v. *Spindlow* [1979] 1 All E.R. 169, 173, (C.A.: Ormrod L.J.), *Sales* v. *Sales* (1980) 10 Fam. Law 115, (C.A.: Donaldson L.J.), and *Harding* v. *Harding* (1980) 10 Fam. Law 146, 147, (C.A.: Cumming-Bruce L.J.).

After the 1980 Act, this power of early intervention which councils had possessed, whereby the tenancy could be "switched" in cases of family disputes, is generally no longer exercisable in the case of *secure* tenancies. Statutory security is conferred on secure tenants under section 34, and as will be seen in Chapter 7 there is no obviously relevant ground for possession in Schedule 4. It has been suggested (see, *e.g.* J. Luba (1981) LAG Bul. 82, 85) that councils should insert a "Thou shalt not beat thy wife"—type condition in their tenancy agreements, breach of which would afford a "reasonableness" ground for possession (under Sched.4, Pt.I, gd.1), but it is unlikely that the courts will be persuaded to treat family breakdown purely as a breach of the tenancy conditions in this way. Unlike the Rent Act regime (*cf.* the Rent Act 1977, s. 98(1)), the offer of suitable alternative accommodation is *not of itself* a "reasonableness" ground for possession, and the "under-occupation" ground (in Sched. 4, Pt. I, gd. 13 of the 1980 Act[29]) is of no avail even

against a tenant who is grossly underoccupying following
the departure of his wife or cohabitee and children,
because this ground only applies where the secure tenancy
vested in the current tenant on the *death* of the previous
tenant under section 30,[30] as being a member of the
previous tenant's family other than the spouse.[30] Indeed,
the council may be under a separate duty in such a case to
find accommodation for the displaced spouse or cohabitee
and the children under the Housing (Homeless Persons)
Act 1977.[31]. By contrast, the Tenants' Rights, etc.
(Scotland) Act 1980 includes the following among the
"reasonableness" grounds for possession:

> "The landlord wishes to transfer the secure tenancy
> of the dwelling-house to the spouse or former spouse
> of the tenant, or to a person with whom the tenant
> has been living as man and wife, where either the
> tenant or the spouse, former spouse or person
> aforesaid no longer wishes to live together with the
> other in the dwelling-house, and the spouse, former
> spouse or person aforesaid has applied to the
> landlord for the transfer of the tenancy" (s. 15 and
> Sched. 2, Pt. I, gd. 6).

A similar amendment to the English Housing Bill was
proposed by the National Women's Aid Federation, the
Women and Housing Organisation, and the Rights of
Women Organisation, but was not accepted by the
government: see *Hansard* (Lords) June 30, 1980, Vol.
411, cols. 174–179.

The old power for an English authority to "switch" the
tenancy on its own initiative can thus normally only now
be used in the case of *non*-secure tenancies. However,
even if the tenancy is secure, the authority can still
"switch" the tenancy where the tenant-spouse or cohabitee is prepared voluntarily to surrender it to the
authority, which can then re-grant the tenancy to the
other partner. Alternatively, an authority may perhaps be
able indirectly to put pressure on a grossly under-

occupying tenant in this situation, by way of legitimately increasing the rent.[32]

Further, it is arguable that where the parties to the marriage or cohabitation are *joint* secure tenants under a periodic council tenancy, the "deserving" party and the council may have a particularly devious solution whereby the council's pre-1980 Act freedom to intervene can be restored: for the "deserving" party *may* be able to determine the secure joint tenancy by giving a notice to quit[33] to the council, even without the concurrence of the other spouse or cohabitee, relying on the fact that statutory security is conferred by sections 29 and 32 of the 1980 Act through the medium of the *contract* (there being no independent "statutory tenancy" such as is conferred by the Rent Act 1977). This argument depends for its success on the proposition that at common law one of two or more joint tenants can probably serve a notice to quit terminating the tenancy, since unanimity is necessary for the continuation of a periodic joint tenancy; if all this is correct, then on expiry of the notice to quit security will cease, and the council can re-grant the tenancy in the old way, save that the new tenancy can be secure: see further *Doe d. Aslin* v. *Summersett* (1830) 1 B. & Ad. 135, *Leek & Moorlands B.S.* v. *Clark* [1952] 2 All E.R. 492, 495, (C.A.), A. Arden (1981) 131 N.L.J. 165, and J. Walton, *Law Society's Gazette*, 8.7.81, at p. 772. However, the higher courts have recently refused to apply the ordinary common law relating to joint tenancy "in all its strictness" where this would cause difficulties in the context of the Rent Act 1977 (see *Lloyd* v. *Sadler* [1978] 2 All E.R. 529, (C.A.), *Tilling* v. *Whiteman* [1979] 1 All E.R. 737, (H.L.)); and even if the technicalities of the common law rules were to be rigorously applied here, it would then be only logical to apply a relevant *statutory* technicality also, *i.e.* "for one co-owner to give such a notice [to quit] without the consent of all persons beneficially entitled will, after 1925, usually be a breach of the trusts now existing in cases of co-ownership" (see R. E. Megarry and

H. W. R. Wade, *The Law of Real Property* (4th ed.), 1975, at p. 395; *cf.* the Law of Property Act 1925, s. 26(3)); thus the giver of the notice may be liable to pay heavy damages to his or her former joint tenant for the loss of the former secure tenancy.

(b) *Where a court order is made pursuant to Schedule 2 of the Matrimonial Homes Act or section 24 of the Matrimonial Causes Act*

We have seen that *spouses* (but not cohabitees) can obtain transfers of the secure tenancy by virtue of a court order under Schedule 2 of the Matrimonial Homes Act 1967 or section 24 of the Matrimonial Causes Act 1973, where a decree of divorce, nullity or judicial separation is obtained. Whichever jurisdiction is exercised, it was suggested earlier that there is little scope for objections on the part of councils: an authority has no right to prevent an order made under the 1967 Act from taking effect (although it has the right to be heard by the court); and while the power of the court to order an assignment of the secure tenancy under the 1973 Act is technically liable to be affected by the presence of a covenant against assignment in the lease, it was suggested that the clear recognition by section 37 of the Housing Act 1980 of the 1973 Act's jurisdiction in this context should enable the courts to overcome any such prohibitive covenants. It was further argued that in either case any attempt by the council to require the discharge by the transferee of the transferor's rent arrears should be firmly resisted.

5. *Conclusions*

It has been shown that the trend of recent legislation has been to cut down the discretion of councils to interfere with the destination of a council house in cases of family disputes. The combination of statutory security of tenure and recent "family" legislation has placed the main emphasis on the views of the court rather than the views of the council, so that the "housing management" aspects of the problem have been largely subordinated to the "family welfare" aspects[34]; this may be viewed as a sensible development.

Thought should be given, however, to the introduction of a new statutory "reasonableness" ground for possession along the lines of that inserted in the Scottish Act, *supra*, allowing the authority to recover possession in order (in effect) to "switch" the secure tenancy from one spouse or cohabitee to another: this additional flexibility would of course be subject to the overview of the court (unlike the previous "free-range" council transfers), and would be particularly useful in the case of cohabitees, where a long-term solution to the family's housing problem cannot at present usually be achieved (in view of the fact that neither Sched. 2 of the Matrimonial Homes Act nor s. 24 of the Matrimonial Causes Act can be used).

Notes

[1] See *supra*, pp. 27–8.

[2] See *supra*, pp. 28–31.

[3] See *infra*, pp. 175, 178,181.

[4] The pages in this report are not numbered.

[5] Section 30 of this Act makes it unlawful to discriminate in the disposal or management of premises against a man or woman on the ground of his or her sex.

[6] See *supra*, pp. 29–31.

[7] The pages in this report are not numbered.

[8] See *infra*, pp. 80, 84.

[9] In the case of joint tenants, the court has special powers under s. 4 of the Domestic Violence and Matrimonial Proceedings Act 1976, *infra*.

[10] See *supra*, pp. 11–12.

[11] See Chap. 7, *infra*; note also that where possession is sought on one of the "reasonableness" grounds and the tenancy is terminated as a result of those proceedings as against the tenant, then the tenant's spouse, if exercising rights of occupation under the 1967 Act, has the same rights to ask the court to adjourn the proceedings, postpone the date of possession or stay or suspend execution of the possession order as

he or she would have if those rights of occupation were not affected by the termination of the tenancy: see s. 87(5)–(6) of the 1980 Act, discussed *infra*, pp. 161–2.

[12] *cp.* Ormrod L.J. at p. 110: "Of course, if this were a large household *and they were middle-class persons*, no doubt one could live upstairs and the other could live downstairs . . . " (italics supplied); the implication that "middle-class persons" do not become council tenants was not supported by any empirical data: perhaps council tenants automatically "up-class" themselves by exercising the right to buy?

[13] See *supra*, pp. 27–8.

[14] See para. 8(2) of Sched. 2 of the 1967 Act.

[15] See *supra*, pp. 25–7.

[16] See *supra*, pp. 42–3.

[17] See *supra*, p. 25.

[18] See *supra*, p. 25.

[19] See *supra*, p. 27.

[20] See *supra*, pp. 32–4.

[21] Note also the Sex Discrimination Act 1975, s. 31, which makes it unlawful for a landlord to discriminate on the ground of sex against a woman (or man) by withholding consent to (*inter alia*) the assignment of the lease to her (or him).

[22] *cf.* the Law Commission's *Third Report on Family Property*, Law Com. No. 86, 1978, pp. 251–2.

[23] See *supra*, pp. 10–18.

[24] See *supra*, p. 27.

[25] There is also the quite separate argument that a transfer by a tenant pursuant to a court order under s. 24 of the 1973 Act cannot involve the tenant in a breach even of an absolute covenant against assignment, since in reality the transfer takes effect by operation of law, and there is authority for the proposition that there will only be a breach of such a covenant if there is some *voluntary* dealing with the property *inter vivos* (see, *e.g. Slipper* v. *Tottenham & Hampstead Junction Ry. Co.* (1867) L.R. 4 Eq. 112, where a compulsory sale of a lease pursuant to a statute was held to be outside the scope of the covenant); see also a note in (1977) 96 *Law Notes* 86, 87.

[26] See *supra*, p. 25.

[27] See *supra*, p. 80.

[28] See *supra*, pp. 27–8.

[29] See *infra*, p. 160.

[30] See *supra*, pp. 29–30.

[31] See *supra*, p. 46.

[32] See the 1953 C.H.A.C. Report on *Transfers, Exchanges and Rents*, pp. 3–4. The machinery for rent-fixing is discussed in Chap. 6, *infra*.

[33] See *infra*, pp. 163–4.

[34] *cp.* the narrow approach of Dunn J. in *Brent* v. *Brent* [1974] 2 All E.R. 1211, 1216 (who saw the matrimonial dispute before him as "a

housing problem which is for the local authority to solve and not for this court") with the wider approach of Ormrod L.J. in *Hutchings* v. *Hutchings* (1976) 237 E.G. 571, 573, (C.A.), (who considered that although the courts and local authorities had to work together in these cases, the question of justice as between the former spouses was "peculiarly the sphere of the court").

Chapter 5

THE CONDITION OF THE PROPERTY: REPAIRS AND IMPROVEMENTS

1. *General*

There is considerable evidence relating to the bad condition of many council estates,[1] including those erected comparatively recently. The problems presented by novel construction methods (especially in "tower" blocks[2]) have proved particularly acute, often presenting an unhappy combination of vandalism,[3] high heating charges,[4] condensation,[5] noise,[6] and psychological problems.[7] The conditions in one notorious tower block in Liverpool (nicknamed "The Piggeries") were enshrined in the reports of *Liverpool C.C.* v. *Irwin*[8], where Lord Denning M.R. prophetically suggested that "these tower blocks ought to be demolished, just as some have been in the United States" ([1975] 3 All E.R. 658, 661, (C.A.)); Liverpool City Council has indeed since demolished several of its "tower" blocks,[9] while others have been sold off at low figures for renovation by private developers.[10] The general enthusiasm for building high-rise flats ended with the collapse of a tower block in London called Ronan Point in 1968,[11] when four people died.

In some cases a council may have "inherited" defective housing by acquiring it from the private sector. Where a council has acquired a building which may be made suitable for housing, it must make it so suitable "forthwith," and any house or building suitable for housing which is acquired by the council must be used as housing accommodation "as soon as practicable after the acquisition or . . . after the completion of the necessary work" (Housing Act 1957, s. 105(4), (4A)). These provisions are intended as "one statutory reflection of the need for unoccupied property in areas of housing shortage to be brought into use as soon as practicable" (D.o.E. Circular no. 160/74 on *Housing Act 1974: Improvement of Older Housing*, 1974, para. 14). It is quite understandable that a council will not want such properties to be reoccupied until they are at least basically sound, since otherwise it would run the risk of a private prosecution for "statutory nuisance."[12] However, if such "municipalized" properties are allowed subsequently to deteriorate to the extent that they become statutorily unfit (*i.e.* within the terms of s. 4 of the 1957 Act), then the council may decide to include them in a clearance area (*i.e.* within ss. 42–43 of the 1957 Act) with a view to their ultimate demolition; and in making such a decision the council is not obliged to take account of the fact that the properties may have become unfit through its own neglect, so that the inclusion of such properties in the clearance area cannot be challenged on this ground: see *A–G ex rel. Rivers-Moore and Others* v. *Portsmouth C.C.* (1978) 36 P. & C.R. 416.

Although there was a considerable reduction in the overall extent of defective council housing during the 1970s (see the 1977 Green Paper on *Housing Policy*, Cmnd. 6851, p. 92, Table 4), it is unlikely that this reduction will continue during the 1980s, in view of current government policies and economic factors; indeed, the incidence of defective council housing may well now begin to increase again. In particular, many people fear that the enforced sale of council housing under the statutory "right to buy"[13] will denude urban authorities of their better stock and leave them mainly with their "sink" estates; if a further moratorium on capital expenditure for new housing projects should be imposed such as that in 1980, and if repair and maintenance costs continue to escalate,[14] then a major crisis could result concerning the condition of the remaining public housing stock. Moreover, the abolition in April 1981 of the minimum space and amenity standards for the erection of council housing (the old "Parker Morris Standards"[15]) could lead to the erection of cut-price dwellings which may later prove to be very expensive to maintain; already the erection of "prefabs" has been proposed by one council.[16] It has also been suggested[17] that the changes made by sections 16–17 of the Local Government, Planning and Land Act 1980 concerning councils' direct labour departments (requiring them to cover costs and achieve a prescribed profit on the capital employed) could result in the serious deterioration of council housing due to the disbandment of such departments.

Faced with such problems, councils may be tempted to encourage "do-it-yourself" work on the part of their tenants, especially since "some two-thirds of the skilled artisan class live in council houses" (D. Fox, *Conditions of Tenancy—a possible alternative approach*, reprinted in the National Consumer Council's Report on *Tenancy Agreements*, 1976, p. 35). In the case of *minor* repairs[18] or redecoration this trend may be thought unobjectionable, provided that where the work is the council's reponsibility by statute[19] or under the tenancy agreement (or the property is in such a poor state of decoration that it would be unreasonable to expect the incoming tenant to take it in that condition without compensation), some system of financial allowances or "rent-free weeks" is implemented to compensate the tenants for the labour and cost of materials involved: this was recommended by, for example, the 1974 D.o.E. Circular on *Homelessness* (no. 18/74, App., para. 9 (iii)), the 1975 Report of the Shelter Housing Aid Centre on *Decoration Allowances*, and the 1979 National Consumer Council Report *Soonest mended* (*op. cit.*, Chapter 7).

The encouragement of tenants to undertake *major* repairing or maintenance responsibilities does however cause several difficulties.[20] First, it will be seen that secure council tenants must now be provided with written information concerning the authority's repairing obligations[21]: such tenants will probably be suspicious of attempts to encourage them to do the necessary work, even with financial incentives. Secondly, the "right to buy" conferred by the Housing Act 1980[22] must make freedom from the need to carry out major repairs and maintenance one of the few remaining reasons for continuing to hold an existing council tenancy. Thirdly, the large rent increases currently envisaged for council tenants[23] will no doubt mean that they will become more concerned to insist upon their "pound of flesh" in terms of the council's own repairing obligations. Fourthly, the scope for "do-it-yourself" activities is in any event considerably less in the case of flats, which comprise approximately one-third of council dwellings.

There are thus currently many problems involved in ensuring that the council housing stock is maintained in a proper state of repair. Yet it remains true that "[l]ocal authorities are by far the largest landlords in the country and must, by the excellence of their management, prove themselves amongst the most enlightened" (*Councils and their Houses: Management of Estates*, C.H.A.C. Report, 1959, pp. 3–4); and councils certainly do not lack well-intentioned advice (see, *e.g.* the 1978 H.S.A.G. Reports on *The Client Role in Public Sector Housebuilding* and *Organising a Comprehensive Housing Service*).

Bearing these considerations in mind, we can now examine the express and implied obligations relating to the repair and maintenance of council housing, and the legal remedies available to the tenant where they are not complied with.

2. *The Respective Liabilities of Council and Tenant*

(a) *The tenancy agreement*

Prior to the Housing Act 1980, there had been considerable criticism of the failure of many council tenancy agreements adequately to reflect the landlord's repairing obligations (see, *e.g.*: *Sleafer* v. *Lambeth B.C.* [1959] 3 All E.R. 378, 380–381, (C.A.): Morris L.J.;

Liverpool C.C. v. *Irwin* [1975] 3 All E.R. 658, 663, (C.A.): Lord Denning M.R.; *Tenancy Agreements, op. cit.*, at pp. 6, 12 and 15).

The 1980 Act tackles this problem in section 41, under which the council is required, by October 3, 1982 and thereafter from time to time, to publish up-to-date information explaining in simple terms the *effect* of (*inter alia*) its statutory repairing obligations in sections 32 and 33 of the Housing Act 1961[24] and the express terms of its secure tenancies (which may include further repairing covenants); this information must be supplied to every secure tenant (s. 41(3)).[25] Thus the tenant should eventually be aware of the landlord's basic repairing obligations even if these are not expressed in the written tenancy agreement itself (if any). It may be noted that the section requires a *simple* explanation of the relevant provisions: the handing over of photocopies of sections 32 and 33 of the 1961 Act will not suffice. However, the information to be provided relating to the council's repairing obligations is not comprehensive, since the implied terms relating to repairs other than those in the 1961 Act (such as those concerning fitness for habitation or liability for the common parts[26]) do not have to be brought to the tenant's attention, nor need he be informed of the important common-law right to use the rent-money to pay for repairs.[27]

As regards the tenant's responsibilities concerning the condition of the property,[28] it is common for the tenancy agreement expressly to require him to carry out internal decorations.[29]

An example of a model tenancy agreement stating clearly both parties' obligations relating to repairs and maintenance, and the remedies available to the tenant if the council defaults, is contained in *Tenancy Agreements, op. cit.*, at pp. 23–31: *inter alia*, this expressly permits the tenant to do the necessary work and withhold the from the rent if the council, after due notification, f carry out its repairing obligations.[30] But since tenancy agreements still fall rather short of this ideal, it remains important (despite the "disclosure" provisions in section 41 of the 1980 Act) carefully to consider the liabilities imposed by the general law concerning the repair and maintenance of council housing.

(b) *The council's implied obligations*

The following general obligations are relevant to council tenancies.

(i) Sections 32 and 33 of the Housing Act 1961: contractual liability

Repairing and maintenance obligations are implied by sections 32 and 33 of the Housing Act 1961 where three basic conditions are satisfied. First, there must be a lease or agreement for a tenancy of a dwelling, which may be a house or part of a building, such as a flat (s. 32(1), (5); see also *Brikom Investments Ltd.* v. *Seaford* [1981] 2 All E.R. 783, (C.A.)). Thus these provisions only cover leases and tenancy agreements, not licences (*cp.* s. 48 of the Housing Act 1980, which makes many of the provisions of the 1980 Act applicable to licences[31]). Secondly, the letting must be for a term of less than seven years (s. 33(1); see also *Brikom Investments Ltd.* v. *Seaford, supra*): since most council tenancies are weekly, this requirement will normally be satisfied. Thirdly, the letting must commence after October 24, 1961 (s. 33(1)): where the letting precedes this date, then in the case of weekly tenancies, including council tenancies, there appears to be an implied term that the property will be kept in "reasonable and habitable condition," if at all, by the landlord rather than by the tenant, which absolves the tenant from doing the repairs but does not actually make the landlord responsible for them: *Mint* v. *Good* [1950] 2 All E.R. 1159, 1162, (C.A.), *per* Somervell L.J.; *Sleafer* v. *Lambeth B.C.* [1959] 3 All E.R. 378, (C.A.).

The covenants are to keep in repair the structure and

exterior of the dwelling (including drains, gutters and external pipes), and to keep in repair and proper working order the installations in the dwelling for the supply of water, gas and electricity, for sanitation (including basins, sinks, baths and sanitary conveniences), and for space heating or water heating (s. 32(1)). Any tenant's repairing covenant is ineffective insofar as it relates to these items (s. 32(1)), and any attempt to exclude the statutory provisions is void (s. 33(7)), save that the county court may with the consent of the parties allow the exclusion or modification of the statutory provisions if it considers it reasonable to do so (s. 33(6): such applications seem to be very rare).

Difficult questions of fact may need to be resolved regarding whether an item falls within section 32. Windows appear to be part of the "structure" of the house (*Boswell* v. *Crucible Steel Co.* [1925] 1 K.B. 119, (C.A.); but *cf. Holiday Fellowship Ltd.* v. *Hereford* [1959] 1 W.L.R. 211, (C.A.); A. Samuels (1975) 39 Conv. (N.S.) 91). Steps and flagstones used for the purpose of access to the house are part of the "exterior" of that house (*Brown* v. *Liverpool Corp.* [1969] 3 All E.R. 1345, (C.A.)); but paving slabs which are not a necessary means of access to the house have been held, on the facts, not to be part of the "exterior" of that house (*Hopwood* v. *Cannock Chase D.C.* [1975] 1 All E.R. 796, (C.A.)). Section 32 imposes an obligation to decorate the exterior, so far as is necessary to prevent deterioration of the fabric of the property (*cf. Monk* v. *Noyes* (1824) 1 C. & P. 265).

In the case of a block of flats, there are particular problems in deciding the scope of section 32 in respect of an individual flat within that block. These problems were considered by the Court of Appeal in *Campden Hill Towers Ltd.* v. *Gardner* [1977] 1 All E.R. 739, which held: first, that the "exterior" extends to the outside walls of the individual flat (even though those walls are not included in the letting), the outside of the inner party walls of that flat, and the outer sides of the horizontal divisions between that flat and the flats above and below it; secondly, that the "structure" extends to the structural framework and beams directly supporting the floors, ceilings and walls of the individual flat; thirdly, that the "installations" cover only those installations in the "physical confines" of the individual flat; and fourthly, that repairs to other parts of the block or to installations outside the individual flat (such as a central heating boiler in the basement) are not covered by the section.

The obligation to "keep" in repair imposes a liability to put the house into repair if it is in disrepair at the commencement of the tenancy: *Proudfoot* v. *Hart* (1890) 25 Q.B.D. 42, (C.A.); *Liverpool C.C.* v. *Irwin* [1976] 2 All E.R. 39, 57, (H.L.) (*per* Lord Edmund-Davies).

However, there are several restrictions on the landlord's liability.

First, by section 32(2), the section does not require the landlord to do repairs for which the tenant is liable under his obligation to use the premises in a "tenant-like manner,"[32] nor to rebuild or reinstate the premises in cases of destruction or damage by fire, or by tempest, flood, or other inevitable accident, nor to repair or maintain anything which the tenant is entitled to remove from the property.

Secondly, by section 32(3) regard must be had, in determining the standard of repair required, to the age, character, locality and prospective life of the house. This can be applied to the considerable advantage of the landlord, as in *L.B. of Newham* v. *Patel* [1979] J.P.L. 303, (C.A.): in this (council housing) case it was held that where the property is very old and with a short life, the landlord could not be compelled to carry out substantial repairs; and it was also suggested that if demolition is imminent, the standard of repair required should be nil: the effect would be to make section 32 completely useless in such a case, and whether the legislature intended such a result must be seriously doubted.

Thirdly, certain cases on express covenants established

that a covenant to "repair" did not extend to requiring the covenantor to rebuild the property or to remedy "serious inherent defects" (see, *e.g. Torrens* v. *Walker* [1906] 2 Ch. 166; *Brew Brothers Ltd.* v. *Snax (Ross) Ltd.* [1970] 1 Q.B. 612, (C.A.)); this qualification seemed to apply to section 32 also. It has recently been decided, however, that there is *no* rule that inherent defects *automatically* fall outside a repairing covenant: it is a matter of degree whether the work in question "can properly be described as repair," or whether it involves the production of "a wholly different thing from that . . . demised" (in which case the work falls outside the repairing obligation), and in deciding this question "the proportion which the cost of the disputed work bears to the value or cost of the whole premises, may sometimes be helpful as a guide" (*Ravenseft Properties Ltd.* v. *Davstone (Holdings) Ltd.* [1979] 1 All E.R. 929, *per* Forbes J.; see further P. F. Smith [1979] Conv. 429). This "inherent defect" problem does not appear to arise if the action is for failure to keep an installation in "proper working order" within section 32(1) (*b*) (rather than for failure to repair the structure and exterior within section 32(1) (*a*)): see Lord Edmund-Davies in *Liverpool C.C.* v. *Irwin* [1976] 2 All E.R. 39, 57, (H.L.).

Fourthly, unless the landlord knows of the defect, he will not be liable to the tenant for resulting injury or damage: and this limitation applies even where the tenant was unable to tell the landlord of the defect because it was hidden: *O'Brien* v. *Robinson* [1973] 1 All E.R. 583, (H.L.). The imposition of this "knowledge" requirement was criticized by J. I. Reynolds in (1974) 37 M.L.R. 377, and defended by M. J. Robinson in (1976) 39 M.L.R. 43 and by the Law Commision in its Report on *Obligations of Landlords and Tenants*, Law Com. No. 67 (1975) at pp. 33–36. However, the requirement is well established, and the tenant will be wise to have some written evidence (*e.g.* a copy letter) showing that the landlord was aware of those defects known to the tenant; knowledge of the defect on the part of the landlord's employee will be imputed to the landlord himself (*Sheldon* v. *West Brom-wich Corp.* (1973) 25 P. & C.R. 360, (C.A.)). If there has been no consequential injury or damage caused by the disrepair, then the requirement of the landlord's know-ledge of the defect naturally causes no difficulty, since when the tenant seeks his remedy for the disrepair, such knowledge must necessarily ensue. Also, it may be possible to circumvent the "knowledge" rule by bringing an action under section 4 of the Defective Premises Act 1972.[33]

Fifthly, under section 80 of the Housing Act 1980, section 32 of the 1961 Act does not apply to leases granted after October 3, 1980, *to* certain public bodies, including local authorities: this amendment only affects short leases *to* these public bodies, not leases *by* them, and it is designed to encourage private owners to release their properties to public bodies for short-term lettings falling outside the definition of a "secure tenancy" (see Sched. 3, para. 7 of the 1980 Act[34]).

On breach of the covenants in section 32, the tenant may sue for damages or specific performance. He may also repudiate the tenancy, but a council tenant would be unlikely to want to lose his home.

(ii) Section 6 of the Housing Act 1957: contractual liability

This provision is of rather less use to council tenants. Section 6 of the 1957 Act states that where there is a letting (as opposed to a licence) of a house (or part of a house) at a rent which at the start of the tenancy did not exceed, broadly, £80 per annum in inner London or £52 per annum elsewhere (or half these figures where the tenancy commenced before July 6, 1957), then, notwith-standing any contrary stipulation, a condition is implied that the house is fit for human habitation at the start of the tenancy, coupled with an undertaking that it will be kept fit by the landlord during the tenancy. If the rent was originally within the relevant statutory limit, it is probably immaterial that it later exceeds that limit (*cf. Gable Construction Co. Ltd.* v. *I.R.C.* [1968] 2 All E.R. 968; *Jenkin R. Lewis & Son Ltd.* v. *Kerman* [1970] 3 All E.R. 414, (C.A.)).

The matter of fitness is dealt with by section 4 of the 1957 Act, which states that a house is unfit for human habitation if and only if it is defective in respect of one or more of certain prescribed matters (repair, stability, freedom from damp, etc.) to such an extent that it is not reasonably suitable for occupation in that condition. This definition has been amplified by government Circulars (M.H.L.G. nos. 55/1954, 69/1967, 68/1969), but the standard remains a low one and is arguably inadequate for modern housing needs: see D. Ormandy (1977) LAG Bul. 206. The fact that the disrepair may be quickly and cheaply remedied is irrelevant to the question of unfitness: *Summers* v. *Salford Corp.* [1943] 1 All E.R. 68, (H.L.) (where a defective sash cord rendered the house unfit).

Again, knowledge of the defect is a precondition of the landlord's liability: *McCarrick* v. *Liverpool Corp.* [1946] 2 All E.R. 646, (H.L.). A useful way for the tenant to ensure that the question of unfitness is properly investigated by the local authority is to set in motion the procedure in section 157(2) of the Housing Act 1957, by which he may complain of the unfitness of the house to a local justice of the peace or parish or community council, and these bodies will then have power to complain to the authority's medical officer of health[35] in writing that the house is unfit, whereupon the medical officer must inspect the house forthwith and report on it to the local authority giving his opinion as to unfitness (for examples, see (1973) LAG Bul. 117 and *Roof*, March 1977, at p. 60; and for a specimen letter to a justice of the peace together with a model form of complaint from the justice of the peace to the local authority, see T. Hadden, *Housing: Repairs and Improvements*, 1979, Appendix F, pp. 194–5). This procedure in section 157(2) can of course be used effectively to draw the council's attention to the state of the property even where the tenancy is outside section 6 of the 1957 Act.

Liability under section 6 will only arise, however, if the house is capable of being made fit at reasonable expense: *Buswell* v. *Goodwin* [1971] 1 All E.R. 418, (C.A.); moreover, the section will not apply where a council is retaining, pursuant to powers in the Housing Act 1957, unfit houses which are capable of providing accommodation which is adequate for the time being (see the 1957 Act, ss. 29(4), 48(4)).

Breach of the condition or undertaking allows the tenant to sue for damages or specific performance. He may also repudiate the tenancy for breach of the condition, but is unlikely to wish to take this course.

There is also a quite separate condition implied at common law that on the letting of a *furnished* dwelling the property will be reasonably fit for human habitation at the start of the tenancy (see, *e.g. Smith* v. *Marrable* (1843) 11 M. & W. 5); however, since furnished lettings of council properties are very rare, this common law fitness condition will not be further dealt with here.

(iii) Common parts: contractual liability at common law

At common law, if a landlord retains in his occupation or control such common parts of the building as are essential to the enjoyment of the property let, then he owes to the tenant an implied contractual obligation to use reasonable care to maintain those common parts in a reasonably safe condition, and so that they do not cause injury to the tenant or damage to the premises let to him: *Dunster* v. *Hollis* [1918] 2 K.B. 795. This implied contractual obligation was reaffirmed by the House of Lords in *Liverpool C.C.* v. *Irwin* [1976] 2 All E.R. 39. *Irwin's* case also significantly extended the obligation, holding that it may be broken if the common parts have not been kept reasonably fit for the tenant's use, even though neither injury nor damage results, so that the tenant could in appropriate circumstances recover damages merely for inconvenience or discomfort.

In *Irwin's* case the tenants occupied a maisonette on the ninth floor of a "tower" block, and complained (*inter alia*) that the lifts constantly failed, the stairs were improperly lit, and the rubbish chutes were often blocked. The House of Lords first implied easements for the tenants and their licensees to use the stairs and rubbish chutes, and a "right in the nature of an easement" to use the lifts (the "conditions of tenancy" gave no such rights expressly); it was then decided that the council was under an implied obligation, imposed by the general law as a legal incident of the subject-matter of this kind of agreement (*i.e.* the letting of a high-rise block in multiple occupation), to take reasonable care to maintain the common parts (the lifts, the stairs, the lighting on the stairs, and the chutes) in a state of reasonable repair and efficiency. The judgments showed a healthy disinclination to leave such problems to be resolved only by political or administrative pressures.

Yet this implied obligation is not absolute: it is a duty merely to take reasonable care, and in *Irwin's* case the tenants did not in fact succeed in showing that the council was in breach of this duty. Further, it is clear that authorities wishing to avoid any contractual liability to their tenants with regard to the repair and lighting of the common parts and the maintenance of lifts, rubbish chutes etc. may expressly exclude it in their tenancy agreements, to the extent permitted by the Unfair Contract Terms Act 1977.

Apart from contractual liability, a council might be liable in *tort* in respect of the *safety* of the common parts under the Occupiers' Liability Act 1957. As "occupier" of the common parts a landlord owes, by section 2 of this Act, 'a "common duty of care": this is a duty to take reasonable care to ensure that people lawfully on the premises (and their belongings: see s. 1(3)) will be "reasonably safe." This provision is concerned only with safety, not with convenience or comfort. Although the landlord can exclude liability as against the tenant in the lease (to the extent permitted by the Unfair Contract Terms Act 1977), such exclusion would be ineffective as against the tenant's visitors (s. 3 of the 1957 Act).

(iv) The Defective Premises Act 1972: tortious liability

By section 4(1) of the Defective Premises Act 1972, where premises are let either under a tenancy which puts on the landlord an obligation to the tenant for the maintenance or repair of the premises (including, by section 4(5), statutory obligations imposed, *e.g.* by section 6 of the Housing Act 1957 or section 32 of the Housing Act 1961), or under a tenancy which gives the landlord an express or implied right to enter to maintain or repair (s. 4(4)), then the landlord owes, to all persons (including the tenant) who might reasonably be expected to be affected by defects in the premises, a duty to take reasonable care to see that they and their possessions are reasonably safe from injury or damage caused by such defects. Further, this duty is owed not merely where the landlord knows of the defect (through notification by the tenant or otherwise), but also where he ought to have known of it (s.4(2)), which is considerably wider than the "knowledge" element required for a contractual claim for breach of a repairing covenant.[36] The landlord cannot exclude this liability in the tenancy agreement (s. 6(3)). A similar duty may be owed by licensors (s.4(6)).

Another section of the Defective Premises Act caters for the situation (more common in the public sector than the private sector) where the landlord himself has been responsible for the building of the dwelling: by section 1(1), such a landlord owes a duty to every person acquiring an interest in the dwelling to see that the work is properly done, with proper materials, and that the dwelling will as regards that work be fit for human habitation. Councils are clearly within this section, since section 1(4) extends the duty to those who "in the course of a business which consists of or includes providing or arranging for the provision of dwellings," or "in the exercise of a power of making such provision or arrangements conferred by or by virtue of any enactment," arrange for another to do the relevant work. This liability also cannot be excluded by the tenancy agreement (s.6(3)).

Section 1 only applies where the work was begun after January 1, 1974 (*Alexander* v. *Mercouris* [1979] 3 All E.R. 305, (C.A.)). But similar obligations arise at common law, and also cover work carried out on the property after erection; see, *e.g. Dutton* v. *Bognor Regis United Building Co. Ltd.* [1972] 1 All E.R. 462, (C.A.), *Batty* v. *Metropolitan Property Realizations Ltd.* [1978] 2 All E.R. 445, (C.A.), and section 3 of the 1972 Act (though this common law liability can be excluded by the agreement, to the extent permitted by the Unfair Contract Terms Act 1977). Further, councils have been held liable in tort at common law to occupiers of houses for breach of the duty to take reasonable care to see that the building regulations are obeyed (see *Dutton's* case, *supra*; *Anns* v. *L.B. of Merton* [1977] 2 All E.R. 492, (H.L.)); and one council has been held liable in negligence for failing to take all reasonable steps to exterminate cockroaches from a tenant's flat (*Sharpe* v. *Manchester M.D.C.*, 1977, (C.A.): *Roof*, May 1977, at p. 92).

(c) *The tenant's implied obligations*

The tenant's implied obligations are comparatively simple and can be dealt with briefly. Assuming that he is a weekly tenant, he is normally under no implied repairing or maintenance obligations. But he is liable for "voluntary waste" (*i.e.* positive acts of injury to the property: "doing that which ought not to be done"), though not for permissive waste (*i.e.* neglect or omission: "failure to do that which ought to be done"): see R. E. Megarry and

H. W. R. Wade, *The Law of Real Property* (4th ed.), 1975, at p. 104. The tenant's liability for "voluntary waste" extends to the acts of himself, his family and his guests: *Warren* v. *Keen* [1954] 1 Q.B. 15, 20, (C.A.). Further, the tenant must use the property in a "tenant-like manner," *i.e.* he must take proper care of it: he must, *e.g.* turn off the water if going away during the winter, clean the chimney and windows when necessary, mend fuses, unstop sinks, etc.: *Warren* v. *Keen* [1954] 1 Q.B. 15, 20, (C.A.) (*per* Denning L.J.). Subject to these obligations, and subject to any permissible express liabilities imposed on him by the tenancy agreement, the tenant will not be liable to carry out repairs, maintenance or decorations.

3. *Legal Remedies Open to the Tenant*

It may happen that a council house is in disrepair, and the tenant has satisfied himself that the authority is liable to put the property right in view of its implied obligations (*supra*), but due to management problems or less identifiable reasons the tenant's requests for the work to be done have not been heeded. What is his next step? The Shelter Report *Homes Fit For Heroes* (1975) commented: "When tenants form themselves into strong groups and get publicity the lack of repairs on Council estates comes to the public notice, but usually the tenants come to believe that nothing can be done and that it is not worth the trouble of getting organized" (at p. 7). In fact, however, there is considerable scope for initiative on the part of the individual tenant, without the need for the formation of an "action group." The tenant may feel that he is "always under a distant threat of eviction if he is too vociferous about repairs" (*Homes Fit For Heroes*, at p. 3), but we shall see that the Housing Act 1980 now provides considerable safeguards against the possibility of arbitrary eviction.[37]

There are five principal[38] ways in which a tenant may take action regarding disrepair: he may deduct the appropriate sums from the rent, complain to the Local Commissioners, complain to a local councillor, complain to a justice of the peace, or take court proceedings.

(a) *Deductions from the rent*

This needs handling with care. It is clear that a tenant cannot simply cease paying rent where the landlord has failed to repair, since the covenant to pay rent is independent of the covenant to repair: see *Taylor* v. *Webb* [1937] 2 K.B. 283, 290 (du Parcq J.), and *Camden Nominees* v. *Forcey* [1940] Ch. 352. Indeed, a tenant who induces other tenants to join a "rent strike" over the state of their properties may be liable, not just to pay his own arrears of rent and (subject to the discretion of the court) to be evicted, but also to be sued in tort for inducing the other tenants to break their tenancy agreements (as in *Forcey's* case); and where two or more tenants join together to try to prevent other tenants from paying their rent, they may thereby commit the tort of conspiracy (see the "rent strike" case of *R.* v. *Parnell* (1881) 14 Cox C.C. 508). Thus the tenant should not simply cease paying rent on account of the disrepair.

However, a tenant has an "ancient common law right" first to pay for the necessary repairs himself, and thereafter to deduct the "proper cost" from future rent: he will then not be liable to be sued for such rent: *Lee-Parker* v. *Izzet* [1971] 3 All E.R. 1099. Nevertheless, the law's traditional dislike of self-help as a remedy means that even a tenant who can afford to pay for the repairs outright should tread very warily: he should inform the council in writing of his intentions, enclosing estimates for the job and giving it a final chance to do the necessary work before he puts it in hand; for the possible use of the remedy by several tenants in combination, where the landlord is in breach of the same repairing obligation owed to all of them in respect of a single expensive item (*e.g.* a lift[39]), see J. Burdett, *Roof*, July 1981, at p. 31.

It was originally thought that the *Izzet* remedy was confined to deductions by the tenant from *future* rent to pay for repairs *previously executed* at his expense, but it now appears that rent already accrued in arrears can be used in discharge of the landlord's obligations, so that the tenant can in effect "save up" the rent to pay for the repairs where he cannot otherwise afford to do them: *Asco Developments Ltd. & Newman* v. *Lower, Lewis and Gordon* (1978) 248 E.G. 683 (Megarry V.-C.). One important aspect of this common law remedy is that it operates by way of set-off against the rent rather than as a counterclaim (*cf. Cophil Properties* v. *Richard Blair* (1978) LAG Bul. 14: Lambeth County Court); thus it is a *defence* to the landlord's claim for rent, and the landlord cannot seek possession on the ground of non-payment thereof (see further Chapter 7, *infra*).

The *Izzet* remedy can only be used, however, in respect of quantified sums needed for repairs, and not for general unliquidated damages arising out of the landlord's default, such as damages for inconvenience, personal injury, etc. Nevertheless, it has subsequently been decided that there is an *equitable* right to set-off *unliquidated* damages where it would be inequitable to allow the landlord to recover the full rent: thus if the tenant claims unliquidated damages and claims *bona fide* that they would exceed the amount of the landlord's claim, he may have a complete defence: *British Anzani (Felixstowe) Ltd.* v. *International Marine Management (U.K.) Ltd.* [1979] 2 All E.R. 1063.

It must be emphasised that the precise scope of the common law and equitable remedies of set-off in this context is still far from clear, and to be absolutely safe the tenant could seek a declaration from the court before withholding his rent (as was done in *Lee-Parker* v. *Izzet* itself), although this rather defeats the object of the "self-help" procedures. For further material on these "rent-deduction" remedies, see, *e.g.*: A. Arden (1979) LAG Bul. 210; A. Waite [1981] Conv. 199; R. C. A. White (1981) LAG Bul. 182.

(b) *Complaint to the Local Commissioners*

Local Commissioners (popularly called "ombudsmen") were appointed under Part III of the Local Government Act 1974 to investigate "maladministration" by local authorities, and unjustifiable delay in carrying out repairs can amount to "maladministration" (see the Report of the Commission for Local Administration in England for the year ending March 31, 1980, at p. 11, and *Roof*, January 1976, at p. 32, November 1977, at p. 188). However, reference to the Commissioners (which must initially proceed via a local councillor) is a lengthy process, and since at present the Commissioners lack really effective "teeth" the tenant may end up frustrated and disappointed.[40]

(c) *Complaint to a local councillor*

The tenant may ask a local councillor to put pressure on the housing department in order to get repairs done (quite apart from the councillor's role as intermediary for a complaint to the Local Commissioners). Councillors who get repairs done for council tenants may receive their votes!

(d) *Complaint to a justice of the peace*

We have already noted[41] that if the disrepair results in the property being unfit for habitation, the tenant can complain to a J.P. under section 157(2) of the Housing Act 1957, which can result in an inspection and report by the medical officer of health.

(e) *Taking court proceedings*

If the tenant decides to go to court, he has a choice between two broad categories of action. He could proceed against the council in a civil court to enforce its express, or more usually implied, repairing and maintenance obligations. Alternatively, he may be able to proceed against the council in a criminal court for "statutory nuisance" under the Public Health Act 1936 or the Control of Pollution Act 1974.

(i) Civil proceedings.

The tenant can claim damages for breach of the landlord's repairing obligations. Damages for breach of contract will basically represent the difference between the value *to the tenant* of the house as unrepaired and the value to him if the landlord had duly repaired it, for the period from the date when the landlord first knew of the disrepair down to the date of the assessment of damages (*Hewitt* v. *Rowlands* (1924) 131 L.T. 757, (C.A.); but *cf.* Roskill L.J. in *Liverpool C.C.* v. *Irwin* [1975] 3 All E.R. 658, 673, (C.A.)). In considering the value of the house to the tenant, the "market value" of the tenancy is irrelevant, so that in principle the fact that a council rent may be sudsidised should not mean that the damages will only be nominal: if the house is not in the state in which the landlord has covenanted to maintain it, the tenant has suffered a loss, whatever the market value of the tenancy may be: *Devereux* v. *Liverpool C.C.* (1978) LAG Bul. 266: Liverpool County Court; in this case the judge also held that it was no defence that the council had a large housing stock and many calls on its resources. It was however suggested in *L.B. of Newham* v. *Patel* [1979] J.P.L. 303, (C.A.) that in deciding whether a council tenant had suffered any damage from a breach of the landlord's repairing obligations, it was relevant that the condition of the property had been taken into account in fixing a low rent; nevertheless, it is submitted that however low the rent may be, breach of the repairing covenant can still cause damage to the tenant: it is significant that *Hewitt* v. *Rowlands* (*supra*) does not appear to have been cited in *Patel*, and in any event no breach of covenant was found in *Patel*, so that the discussion regarding the measure of damages would appear to have been *obiter dicta*; see also *Seal* v. *L.B. of Greenwich* (1981) LAG Bul. 237 (Woolwich County Court).

The tenant may also recover any sums necessary to compensate him for injury or damage to himself or his property caused by the disrepair (see, *e.g. Walker* v. *Hobbs & Co.* (1889) 23 Q.B.D. 458, (D.C.); *Hewitt* v. *Rowlands, supra*; *Summers* v. *Salford Corp.* [1943] 1 All E.R. 68, (H.L.)); and, in appropriate cases, damages for inconvenience or discomfort (*Liverpool C.C.* v. *Irwin* [1976] 2 All E.R. 39, (H.L.); *Horrex* v. *Pidwell* [1958] C.L.Y. 1461: county court; *Seal* v. *L.B. of Greenwich, supra*).

In addition to damages, the tenant can ask for specific performance of a repairing covenant under section 125(1) of the Housing Act 1974, whether the breach relates to the property let or to the common parts of the building. The remedy of specific performance is of course discretionary (see, *e.g. Jeune* v. *Queens Cross Properties Ltd.* [1973] 3 All E.R. 97), and will not be granted where it would inflict great hardship on the landlord; however, the fact that the landlord cannot afford to pay for the work will not necessarily stop the court granting the order: *Francis* v. *Cowcliff Ltd.* (1976) 239 E.G. 977 (another case concerning defective lifts!).

A useful precedent of a plaintiff's county court particulars of claim, alleging breach by the landlord of the implied covenants in section 32 of the Housing Act 1961, is contained in (1976) LAG Bul. 16.

Insofar as a cause of action may lie in tort for the disrepair (*supra*), damages will be recoverable for injury to the person or damage to property, but not for mere disrepair and consequent inconvenience or discomfort.

(ii) Criminal proceedings

Local authorities are given extensive powers to deal with defective housing under the Housing Acts and the

Public Health Acts (for general surveys of the legislation, see, *e.g.* T. Hadden, *op. cit.*, and D. Ormandy, *Guide to Public Health and Housing Law,* P.H.A.S., 1977). However, since the initiation of any of these procedures normally depends on the local authority's environmental health department serving the relevant notice, there is an obvious problem in the case of defective council housing, and the Community Development Project's 1977 paper *Limits of the Law* commented (at p. 46) that "[i]ntervention is limited to informal internal memos which housing departments generally ignore"[42] (though we have seen that the state of the house can at least be brought formally to the authority's attention under the procedure in section 157(2) of the Housing Act 1957). As regards the general "unfitness" provisions in Part II of the Housing Act 1957, it is now clear that an authority cannot be forced to take action against itself: *R.* v. *Cardiff C.C., ex p. Cross, The Times*, April 11, 1981, (D.C.). Nevertheless, council tenants can use a special procedure relating to "statutory nuisances" contained in section 99 of the Public Health Act 1936, which allows a private individual to instigate proceedings in the magistrates' court on his own initiative. Lord Goddard C.J. pointed out in *R.* v. *Epping (Waltham Abbey) Justices, ex p. Burlinson* [1948] 1 K.B. 79, (D.C.), that the object of the Act was to "provide a cheap and speedy remedy," which is available not only to local authorities but also to "an inhabitant of the district who is seeking to use it against the local authority" (at pp. 85–6); and this procedure has been used successfully against local authorities in the case of defective council housing: see, *e.g. Salford C.C.* v. *McNally* [1975] 2 All E.R. 860, (H.L.) (discussed *infra*), and *Lambeth L.B.C.* v. *Stubbs* (1980) LAG Bul. 190, (D.C.). In practice, however, the procedure may turn out to be lengthy and complicated: see C. Blood, *Roof*, September 1979, at p. 162.

A "statutory nuisance" is defined as including "any premises in such a state as to be prejudicial to health or a nuisance" (s.92(1)(*a*)), and "prejudicial to health" means "injurious, or likely to cause injury, to health" (s.343(1)). The word "nuisance" is not defined by the Act, but has been held to mean, in this context, a public or private nuisance at common law, *i.e.* an act or omission materially affecting the comfort and quality of life of a class of the public, or a substantial interference with the use or enjoyment of property belonging to another, so that no nuisance arises where the condition of the property only affects the personal comfort of its occupiers: *National Coal Board* v. *Neath B.C.* [1976] 2 All E.R. 478, (D.C.). So in the case of a house the defects in which only affect the occupiers, it is necessary to establish that it is "prejudicial to health," as defined above. This can be shown, for example, by the presence of that recurrent condition in "high-rise" blocks, severe condensation: see *Fitzpatrick* v. *Dawnray Ltd.*, reported in *Roof*, May 1976, at p. 92; see also: D. Ormandy (1979) LAG Bul. 190; J. McQuillan and N. Finnis, *Roof*, May 1979, at p. 85; *cf.* R. Gibbs (1981) 145 L.G. Rev. 282. In the much-publicised case of *Salford C.C.*. v. *McNally* [1975] 2 All E.R. 860, (H.L.), a house was held to be "prejudicial to health" where it was found to be suffering from rising damp, perished plaster, a rotten door, and an insanitary water closet pipe; the House of Lords emphasised that the question of whether the house constituted a statutory nuisance had to be decided irrespective of the question of unfitness for human habitation, so that a house may be "unfit" without being either "prejudicial to health" or a "nuisance."

In *McNally's* case the house was a "short-life" property which the authority was using for housing under the "deferred demolition" provision in section 48(1) of the Housing Act 1957: this states that nowithstanding the general unfitness provisions of the Housing Act, a local authority which has declared a clearance area may postpone the demolition of any houses within that area which the authority considers "are or can be rendered capable of providing accommodation of a standard which is adequate for the time being," and may carry out work required for "rendering or keeping such houses capable of providing such accommodation . . . pending their demolition." The House of Lords decided that section 48(1) did not authorise the use of a house that was prejudicial to health,[43] and answered in the negative the question "whether the law is any different if the defaulting landlord happens to be, instead of a private person, none other than the local authority itself" (*per* Lord Edmund-Davies at p. 865). Yet, although we shall see that magistrates are bound to make a "nuisance order" where a statutory nuisance exists, they do have a "considerable tolerance as regards the precise terms which the nuisance order shall take," and have a "discretion in regard to the time within which the work has to be done" so as to avoid "the danger of money being spent on the house abortively in view of the subsequent demolition": *per* Lord Widgery C.J. in *Nottingham Corp.* v. *Newton* [1974] 2 All E.R. 760, 765–6, (D.C.); see also *Lambeth L.B.C.* v. *Stubbs* (1980) LAG Bul. 190, (D.C.).

Assuming that a council tenant is satisfied that his house constitutes a "statutory nuisance,"[44] he may apply to the magistrates' court under section 99 of the Public Health Act 1936 by way of information and summons (rather than by complaint): see section 42 of the Magistrates' Courts Act 1952, and *R.* v. *Newham Justices, ex p. Hunt* [1976] 1 All E.R. 839, (D.C.). The procedure for laying an information under section 99 is set out in (1975) LAG Bul. 296–7, and a model "information" and "statement of information" are contained in Hadden, *op. cit.*, Appendix E. If the local authority itself is acting under the Public Health Act 1936, it must serve an "abatement notice" on the owner of the property under section 93 of the Act, requiring him to abate the nuisance and do the necessary work; but no such notice is necessary where a private individual is proceeding by way of information under section 99: *R.* v. *Oxted Justices, ex p. Franklin* [1976] 1 All E.R. 839, (D.C.). It is essential, however, that the statutory nuisance exists (or is likely to recur) at the date of the *hearing*, and not merely at the date when the information is laid: *Coventry C.C.* v. *Doyle* [1981] 2 All E.R. 184, (D.C.).

Where the tenant proceeds under section 99, "the like proceedings shall be had, with the like incidents and consequences as to the making of orders, penalties for disobedience of orders and otherwise, as in the case of a complaint by the local authority." Thus if the tenant proves his case (bearing in mind that these are criminal proceedings involving the higher criminal burden of proof), the court *must* make a "nuisance order" requiring the authority to abate the nuisance within a time specified in the order, and/or prohibiting a recurrence of the nuisance (s.94(2)), though there is a discretion as to the exact terms of the order (*Nottingham Corp.* v. *Newton, supra*). Further, the court may impose a fine of up to £200 (s.94(2), as amended by the Control of Pollution Act 1974, s.99 and Sched. 2, para. 11), and may order the closure of the building if the nuisance renders it unfit for habitation (s.94(2)): thus the tenant runs the risk of eviction in the case of serious defects (see ss. 287–9), and the authority would not be under a duty to rehouse him under the Land Compensation Act 1973 (as opposed to the Housing (Homeless Persons) Act 1977) as he would not fall within section 39(1)(*b*) of that Act (see the definition of "housing orders" in ss. 29(7) and 39(9) of the 1973 Act).[45]

Provided he is prepared to take the risk of losing his home where its defects are serious, the tenant need not be deterred by the cost of taking section 99 proceedings. He may be eligible to obtain legal advice and assistance for the proceedings under section 2(4) of the Legal Aid Act 1974 (as amended by the Legal Aid Act 1979), and in appropriate circumstances tenants have been awarded costs under either the Costs in Criminal Cases Act 1973 or section 94(3) of the Public Health Act 1936, and also compensation under section 35 of the Powers of Criminal

Courts Act 1973 (see cases reported in *Roof*, October 1975, at p. 30, January 1976, at p. 31, March 1976, at p. 63; *Coventry C.C.* v. *Doyle* [1981] 2 All E.R. 184, (D.C.)).

It is not unknown for an authority to fail to comply with a nuisance order (see, *e.g. Roof*, March 1977, at p. 60). In such cases, provided there is no "reasonable excuse" for the failure to comply, a further fine of up to £400 may be imposed, with an additional £50 for each day during which the nuisance continues thereafter (section 95(1) of the Public Health Act 1936, as amended by the Control of Pollution Act 1974, s.99 and Sched. 2, para. 11); and the mere fact that compliance with the order will be costly, or the defendant has difficulty in raising the necessary money, will not be a "reasonable excuse" for failing to comply: *Saddleworth U.D.C.* v. *Aggregate and Sand Ltd.* (1971) 69 L.G.R. 103, (D.C.). An authority does not comply with a nuisance order merely by obtaining *vacant possession*, since it remains possible for the house to be reoccupied unless an order under secton 94(2) (*supra*) has been made: *Lambeth L.B.C.* v. *Stubbs* (1980) LAG Bul. 190, (D.C.), *Coventry C.C.* v. *Doyle* [1981] 2 All E.R. 184, (D.C.); however, where the authority *demolishes* the house, or demolition is imminent, then this may constitute a "reasonable excuse" for failing to comply with the nuisance order: *Lambeth L.B.C.* v. *Stubbs, supra*.

Apart from an action for statutory nuisance under the Public Health Act 1936, it is possible for a tenant to bring criminal proceedings against the council under section 59 of the Control of Pollution Act 1974 for nuisance caused by noise. Thus in *Joyce* v. *L.B. of Hackney* (reported in (1976) LAG Bul. 211) a council tenant took out a summons in the magistrates' court under this section alleging that noise from a boiler and ancillary equipment sited in a block of council flats was a nuisance: the council pleaded guilty, and was ordered to do specified work to abate the nuisance, while the tenant was awarded £500 costs; see also: *Piper* v. *G.L.C., Roof*, July 1977, at p. 122 (magistrates' court: nuisance caused by noisy central heating system); *A. Lambert Flat Management Ltd.* v. *Lomas* [1981] 2 All E.R. 280, (D.C.: nuisance caused by noisy lift). For further information on nuisance caused by noise, see D. Oliver (1974) LAG Bul. 130, a note in (1976) LAG Bul. 111, and G. M. Pettigrew (1977) 127 N.L.J. 130.

4. *The Tenant's Right to Improve the Property*

(a) *The general law*

The (sometimes difficult) distinction between a repair and an improvement has been explained thus: "If the work which is done is the provision of something new for the benefit of the occupier, that is . . . an improvement; but if it is only the replacement of something already there, which has become dilapidated or worn out, then, albeit that it is a replacement by its modern equivalent, it comes within the category of repairs and not improvements" (*per* Denning L.J. in *Morcom* v. *Campbell-Johnson* [1955] 3 All E.R. 265, 266, (C.A.)).

At common law, the doing of improvements was normally regarded as an act of "ameliorating waste," so that if the tenant was not expressly permitted to do the work, the landlord could in theory seek damages or an injunction; in practice, however, damages would not be recoverable where the landlord had suffered no loss, while the discretionary remedy of an injunction would usually be refused where the value of the property had been enhanced, *unless* the tenant had broken an express covenant against improving or otherwise altering the property: *Doherty* v. *Allman* (1878) 3 App. Cas. 709, (H.L.).

Prior to the Housing Act 1980, council tenancy agreements would in fact often expressly prohibit the tenant from improving or otherwise altering the property, and such express prohibitions could either be "absolute" (*i.e.* making no provision for the landlord's consent), or "qualified" (*i.e.* only prohibiting improvements, etc., done without the landlord's consent). Of the 318 council tenancy agreements examined by the National Consumer Council, 86 per cent. contained such a "qualifed" prohibition (*Tenancy Agreements, op. cit.,* at p. 40). These "qualified" prohibitions were governed by section 19(2) of the Landlord and Tenant Act 1927, which states that notwithstanding any express provision to the contrary, the prohibition is deemed to be subject to a proviso that the consent will not be unreasonably withheld; if consent was unreasonably withheld, the tenant could improve without it.

(b) *Secure tenancies: a limited right to improve*

In the case of secure tenancies under the 1980 Act (whether granted before or after October 3, 1980), section 19(2) of the 1927 Act does not apply (ss.81(1), 85(2) of the 1980 Act). Instead, by section 81(2) of the 1980 Act it is an implied term of *every* secure council tenancy[46] that the tenant will not make an "improvement" (as defined, *infra*) without the authority's written consent; thus the prohibition against improvements must now always be "qualified" rather than "absolute."

Such consent (which may be retrospective) must not be unreasonably withheld: if it is, it shall be treated as given (ss.81(3), 82(2)). The burden lies with the authority to show that the consent was reasonably withheld (s.82(1)), and the county court can decide this issue by bare declaration (s.86(2)(*a*)). The court must have regard (*inter alia*) to the extent to which the improvement would be likely to affect the safety of the property, or reduce its "saleability" or "lettability," or cause expense to the authority which it would otherwise be unlikely to incur (s.82(1)); as regards this "expense" factor, it must be borne in mind that the subject-matter of a tenant's improvement may often become the landlord's repairing or maintenance responsibility under sections 32 and 33 of the Housing Act 1961 (*supra*), and presumably it is not intended that an authority could give a "blanket" refusal merely on this ground: possible expense in the long term would surely not be a factor, although if the proposed work would be likely to cause expense to the authority in the short term, this may be a ground for refusing consent.

The consent may be given subject to a condition (s.82(2)), so that the authority could monitor the quality of the workmanship and materials, but the burden of showing the reasonableness of such a condition lies on the authority (s.82(4)).

The tenant must be given written reasons for any refusal of consent, and if the authority fails to respond to the tenant's request for consent within a reasonable time, the consent is taken to have been withheld (s.82(3)).

An "improvement" is specially and widely defined for this purpose by section 81(5) to cover: (i) any alteration in or addition to the property, the landlord's fixtures and fittings therein, or the provision of services: thus inserting a picture hook in the living-room wall falls within the definition! (see also J. E. Adams [1981] Conv. 95); (ii) the erection of wireless or television aerials: thus "piped" television schemes on council estates are to some extent safeguarded against the ravages of private enterprise, and councils can also seek to prohibit their tenants from erecting Citizens' Band radio aerials (see *The Times*, May 25, 1981); and (iii) the carrying out of external decoration (although it must be remembered that such decoration can be the landlord's legal responsibility under ss.32 and 33 of the 1961 Act, *supra*). In order to amount to an improvement, the work need not necessarily enhance the market value of the property (*cp.* s.38, *infra*): the test is not an objective one, and must be regarded purely from the tenant's point of view rather than the landlord's (see *Woolworth & Co. Ltd.* v. *Lambert* [1936] 2 All E.R. 1523, (C.A.), *Lambert* v. *Woolworth & Co. Ltd. (No. 2)* [1938] 2 All E.R. 664, (C.A.)).

Under section 81, therefore, the tenant may improve

without any legal liability and notwithstanding the authority's opposition, *if* such opposition is unreasonable; he naturally remains subject to the usual planning and building regulation requirements. If the tenant improves without first asking permission, or if he improves notwithstanding a reasonable refusal, or if he fails to satisfy any reasonable condition attached to a consent (s.83), then this will give the authority a "reasonableness" ground for possession (see Sched. 4, Pt. I, gd. 1, and Chapter 7 *infra*).

Concern has been expressed that section 81 might actually operate to the general detriment of tenants, since landlords might try to exploit this "tenant's right" by way of evading their own repairing and decorating responsibilities (see *The Tory Housing Bill*, Labour Research Dept., 1980, p. 13); this would not however appear to be a real danger in the public sector, especially since, as noted earlier, the landlord's basic repairing obligations have to be brought to the tenant's attention in writing under section 41.

(c) *Secure tenancies: reimbursement by the landlord of the cost of the tenant's improvements*

Where: (i) the authority has given its written consent to the improvement (or is treated as having done so under s.81(3), *supra*), (ii) work on the improvement was begun not earlier than October 3, 1980, and (iii) the improvement has materially added to the property's "saleability" or "lettability," then under section 38 the authority *may*, at or after the end of the tenancy, make such payment to the tenant (or his personal representatives) as it considers appropriate in respect of the improvement, but not exceeding the (historic) cost thereof after deducting the amount of any house renovation grant (as to which see *infra*). The tenant has no right to insist on such reimbursement, and even if payment is to be made he cannot receive any percentage of the increase in the property's *value* due to the improvement; what will the money paid in 1982 for the installation of central heating be worth in 2001?

In practice, however, a tenant may not need to rely on the authority's exercise of its section 38 power here, since under the general law of fixtures he may be entitled as of right to remove (during or within a reasonable time after the termination of the tenancy) those articles which he fixed to the property as domestic or ornamental fixtures, and which are capable of severance without unduly damaging the rest of the property (see further, *e.g.* R. E. Megarry and H. W. R. Wade, *op. cit.*, at pp. 715–717).

(d) *Secure tenancies: rent not to be increased on account of tenant's improvements*

Where a secure tenant has lawfully made an improvement and has borne the whole or part of the cost (or would have done so but for a house renovation grant), then under section 39 the authority cannot normally increase the rent on account of the improvement[47] to the extent that the tenant has so borne (or might without a grant have so borne) the whole or part of the cost (and where the tenant exercises the "right to buy," certain tenant's improvements must similarly be disregarded in fixing the price: see s.6(2), (5), and Chapter 8, *infra*).

However, section 39 permits increases in rent attributable to *rates* (*i.e.* where the tenant is paying an inclusive rent). Moreover, the prohibition in section 39 only applies while the person who did the improvement, or his spouse as statutory successor under section 30,[48] is the secure tenant: thus authorities can charge the "improving" tenant's non-spouse successors a higher rent, and can even increase the rent of the "improving" tenant himself while he remains as tenant if the tenancy ceases to be secure (*e.g.* because he has sub-let, or parted with possession of, the whole property: s.37(2)[49]), so that eventually authorities should be able to recoup any section 38 payment (*supra*) by way of future rent increases.

(e) *Secure tenancies: right to apply for house renovation grants*

Before the 1980 Act, council tenants were generally unable to apply for house renovation grants, because they did not satisfy the condition of having an unexpired tenancy term of at least five years (see s.57(3) of the Housing Act 1974). However, secure tenants now have the right to apply for such grants under section 106(1) of the Housing Act 1980, and do not have to supply any certificate as to their future occupation (see the new s.60(1A) of the Housing Act 1974, introduced by Sched. 12, para. 29 of the 1980 Act).

Notes

[1] See, *e.g. Soonest mended*, National Consumer Council, 1979, *Houses to Mend*, Scottish Consumer Council, 1979; see also the analysis of the English Housing Investment Programmes for 1980 by R. Matthews and E. Shaw in "HIPs Analysis — England," *Roof*, July 1981, at p. 13, which indicated *inter alia* that 52,000 council dwellings were unfit, a further 150,000 were fit but lacked basic amenities, 670,000 (*i.e.* over 14 per cent. of the council housing stock) were non-substandard but in need of major repairs, nearly 99,500 were standing empty, and over 260,000 were officially classed as "difficult to let."

[2] See the D.o.E. Survey *Families in Flats*, 1981.

[3] One council suffering expenses of up to £200,000 per year on account of vandalism even proposed that £50 rewards should be paid from its Housing Revenue Account for information leading to the conviction of vandals on its estates: *The Times*, December 12, 1979.

[4] The *minimum* acceptable level of heating for a house on one London council estate during the winter of 1977 would have cost £16.92 per week: see a letter from Lady Simpson to *The Times*, February 15, 1978.

[5] See, *e.g.* D. Ormandy (1979) LAG Bul. 190; R. Bryant, *The Dampness Monster: A Report of the Gorbals Anti-Dampness Campaign*, Scottish Council of Social Service, 1979. There was a parliamentary debate on condensation in council properties in 1978: see *Hansard* (Commons) February 28, 1978, Vol. 945, cols. 290–322.

[6] For one example of the noise problem caused by a cheap property "conversion" by a London council, see J. Burdett, *Roof*, September 1980, at p. 137.

[7] For instances of suicide, see, *e.g. Inner City Crisis: Manchester's Hulme*, Hulme People's Rights Centre, 1977, and *The Times*, May 29, 1981; for an assessment of the effects of bad housing conditions on children, see *The kids don't notice*, Shelter (undated); see further H.D.D. Occasional Paper 1/75 on *The Social Effects of Living off the Ground* (1975), and R. Franey, *Roof*, November 1977, at p. 163.

[8] The case is discussed in detail *infra*, pp. 104–5.

[9] See *The Guardian*, October 1, 1979 ("Explosive end for 'Faulty Towers' "), *The Times*, April 28, 1981, May 6, 1981.

[10] See *The Times*, November 7, 1978, February 12, 1981.

[11] In "one of the most expensive pieces of High Court litigation ever," the building contractors were held liable to the council for breach of the building contract: *The Guardian*, December 22, 1979; other councils have since considered the possibility of taking legal action against the builders of defective tower blocks.

[12] See *infra*, pp. 114–18; while it is not necessary for a house to be occupied before a prosecution for "statutory nuisance" can be brought, the chances of prosecution are obviously greater where it is occupied.

[13] See *infra*, Chap. 8.

[14] In 1979, the housing committee chairman of one London authority estimated that the repairs facing housing authorities throughout the country could cost a total of £250 million, and Leeds City Council was having to spend £4 million for remedial work on 1,500 houses built by an industrialised system: *The Guardian*, August 29, 1979.

[15] The relevance of these standards to modern conditions was debated by D. Alton and B. Crofton in *Roof*, November 1979, at p. 182.

[16] See C. Wolmar, *Roof*, May 1981, at p. 14.

[17] By I. Spence, a regional officer for the General and Municipal Workers Union: see *The Times*, May 20, 1981.

[18] The London Borough of Hackney has indicated that in order to replace a tap washer, the cost to the tenant would be 10p, compared with £3 if the council did the job: *The Times*, June 18, 1981.

[19] See *infra*, pp. 98–104.

[20] See further *Soonest mended, op. cit.*, Chaps. 2 and 7.

[21] See *infra*, p. 97.

[22] See *infra*, Chap. 8.

[23] See *infra*, pp. 131–2.

[24] See *infra*, pp. 98–102.

[25] The obligations in s.41 are discussed in more general terms *supra*, at p. 23.

[26] See *infra*, pp. 102–5.

[27] See *infra*, pp. 109–110.

[28] See *infra*, pp. 107–8.

[29] See *Tenancy Agreements, op. cit.*, at p. 15.

[30] See also *How to Gain a Better Tenancy Agreement*, Brent Federation of Tenants' and Residents' Associations, 1978.

[31] See *supra*, pp. 9–10.

[32] See *infra*, p. 108.

[33] See *infra*, p. 106.

[34] Discussed *supra*, pp. 17–18.

[35] Or equivalent officer: see the Local Government Act 1972, s.112.

[36] See *supra*, pp. 101–2.

[37] See Chap. 7, *infra*.

[38] An appeal for a reduction in rateable value is another possibility: see, *e.g. The Times*, September 6, 1977, and (1980) LAG Bul. 204.

[39] See *supra*, p. 105.

[40] See *supra*, pp. 42–3.

[41] See *supra*, pp. 103–4.

[42] Indeed, it is becoming quite common for authorities to establish *combined* housing and environmental health departments. For an account of how the conflicting loyalties to which environmental health officers are exposed can result in their neglect of the interests of council tenants, see J. Burdett, *Roof*, September 1981, at p. 12.

[43] It is clear however that no action lies in a "deferred demolition" case under the "fitness" condition in s.6 of the Housing Act 1957, *supra*: see s.48(4) of the 1957 Act; and although s.32 of the Housing Act 1961 (*supra*) could still in theory apply in such cases, the "age character and prospective life" qualification in s.32(3) of the 1961 Act (as interpreted in *L.B. of Newham* v. *Patel, supra*) would much limit its potential here.

[44] The services of an independent environmental health officer may be obtainable, *e.g.* by contacting The Register of Independent Advisers Ltd. (tel. 01–622–0556).

[45] See *supra*, pp. 47–8.

[46] In this particular context, "tenancy" does *not* include licence, since s.48 (which broadly treats council licensees as secure tenants) only extends to Pt. I of the Act, and not to Pt. III (in which the rights relating to improvements are set out).

[47] For the position in the privately rented sector, see the Rent Act 1977, s.70(3)(*b*); *cp.* also the Landlord and Tenant Act 1954, s.34, and *Ponsford* v. *H.M.S. Aerosols Ltd.* [1978] 2 All E.R. 837, (H.L.): business tenancies.

[48] See *supra*, pp. 29–30.

[49] See *supra*, p. 28.

Chapter 6

RENTS

1. *General*

(a) *The legal framework*

The legal framework within which local authorities can fix the rents of their properties is very flexible. Authorities are now clearly exempt from all of the detailed provisions for rent-fixing which govern the private sector (see the Rent Act 1977, ss. 14, 19(5) (*aa*); *cp.* the short-lived decision of the Court of Appeal in *Lambeth L.B.C.* v. *Udechuka, The Times,* April 30, 1980). Instead, they have a very wide power under section 111(1) of the Housing Act 1957 to "make such reasonable charges . . . as they may determine," and we shall see that the courts have proved most reluctant to interfere with the exercise of this power. However, an authority is normally precluded by section 39 of the Housing Act 1980 from increasing the rent on account of a tenant's improvements.[1] Further, under section 11 of the Housing Rents and Subsidies Act 1975 the Minister can make an order restricting the amount of rent which would otherwise be payable on new lettings of dwellings, or restricting or preventing rent increases; but such an order can only cover a "specified description of local authorities" or a "specified description of dwellings," and thus cannot be aimed at an individual council or council house (see s. 15(5) of the 1975 Act; *cp.* s. 15(6) which is inapplicable to orders). No section 11 orders are currently in force, which in the present political climate is hardly surprising.

The general freedom regarding the initial fixing of council rents also extends in law to the fixing of rent increases (although as will be seen the Minister now has in practice the power to "recommend" increases): section 113 (1A) of the Housing Act 1957 (introduced by the Housing Rents and Subsidies Act 1975) merely requires authorities to review rents "from time to time" and make such changes "as circumstances may require."[2]

Authorities have to maintain a "Housing Revenue Account" under section 12 of the Housing Finance Act 1972, into which is paid the rent income, together with subsidies from the central government and contributions from the general rates; and out of which must be taken the sums necessary for the capital repayments and interest on loans raised, together with the cost of management, repairs and maintenance. Any deficits in the Housing Revenue Account have to be met from the rates; but there is no longer any restriction to a working balance in the account, so that it can be allowed to show a profit which can be credited to the general rate fund, *i.e.* to non-housing expenditure (s. 134 of the Housing Act 1980).

(b) *Practical problems*

The fixing of council rents has always been an intensely political matter, which "perhaps attract[s] more discussion—and dissension—than any other aspect of local authority housing policy" (J. B. Cullingworth, *Housing and Local Government* (1960), at p. 172; the "right to buy," discussed in Chapter 8, is currently vying with rent fixing for the dubious privilege of being the most polemical aspect of council housing policies). The structure of public housing finance largely depends on Exchequer subsidies (unlike the private rented sector, where the effect of successive Rent Acts has arguably been to force the individual landlord to subsidise his tenants); but councils are often also forced to borrow heavily in order to "balance the books," an aspect which has frequently come under bitter attack (see, *e.g.* the Community Development Project's 1976 paper *Profits Against Houses*, p. 32).

Council rent-fixing has never been an exact science:

considerable regional variations have long been apparent, and R. A. Parker wrote in his 1967 paper on *The Rents of Council Houses* that "[t]he field of council rents is frankly chaotic. They are surrounded by untested assumptions, expediency, convention and lack of basic data" (p.72). The inter-relation of council rents with the authorities' (now mandatory) rent rebate schemes, and with the supplementary benefits system, is examined below, but it may be noted here that councils share with the D.H.S.S. a basic dilemma: "principles must be reconciled with some degree of administrative convenience and simplicity . . . . A highly complex scheme may be very fair, but also virtually incomprehensible" (J.B. Cullingworth, *loc. cit.*).

Some authorities with substantial numbers of council houses have long managed to keep rents down by "pooling" them, so that the rents of the newer properties are subsidised by the older properties. Although it has been suggested that this concept should be extended to nationwide rent-pooling (see, *e.g.* B. Kilroy, *Roof*, March 1977, at p. 39), this idea was rejected in the 1977 Green Paper on *Housing Policy* (Cmnd. 6851, at p. 87) on the grounds that the expense of subsidising high housing costs should fall on the community as a whole, and not solely on council tenants elsewhere who happen to enjoy low housing costs.

To these recurrent problems have been added the relatively recent difficulties caused by escalating Housing Revenue Account costs (which increased at an average rate of 116 per cent. per dwelling between 1971–72 and 1975–76: see the Green Paper on *Housing Policy, op. cit.*, at p. 27); interest repayments on loans account for the lion's share of this expenditure. The Chartered Institute of Public Finance and Accountancy has recently compared the level of council house rents as a proportion of the total cost of providing council housing in the financial year 1979–80, and concluded that the average proportion in inner London was 23 per cent., in outer London 40 per cent., in the metropolitan districts 52 per cent., and in non-metropolitan districts 55 per cent. (*Local Government Comparative Statistics,* C.I.P.F.A., 1981).

(c) *Recent changes in policy*

Against this background, it may be useful briefly to review the quite dramatic changes in policy regarding council rents which occurred during the 1970s, and then to discuss the particularly significant shift in emphasis achieved by the Housing Act 1980.

By 1972, there were still considerable variations between the rent-fixing and rebate schemes adopted by the various housing authorities, although 75 per cent. of them were operating some sort of rebate scheme.[3] The then Conservative government was concerned that the housing subsidies system appeared to be reducing council rents without paying due regard to the tenants' incomes; so the government proposed a uniform nationwide council rent-fixing scheme, geared to private sector "fair rent" principles, together with *mandatory* national rent rebate and allowance schemes for both public and private sector tenants, and a revamping of the subsidies system (see the 1971 White Paper, *Fair Deal for Housing,* Cmnd. 4728: the "central policy" of the proposals was described as one of "subsidising people, not bricks and mortar": p. 11).

These proposals were eventually enacted in the Housing Finance Act 1972. The provisions relating to mandatory rent rebates and allowances (in Pt. II) are still in force (as amended by Sched. 15 of the Housing Act 1980), but the mandatory "fair rents" scheme for council tenants (in Pts. V and VI[4]) generated intense opposition on the part of many Labour-controlled councils, and was repealed, following a change of government, by the Housing Rents and Subsidies Act 1975.

The 1975 Act broadly restored to authorities their pre-1972 freedom to fix rents as they wished,[5] although it did not affect their duty to operate a rent rebate scheme under the 1972 Act (see the 1975 Act, s. 1(1)). The 1975

Act also severely limited the extent to which authorities could make a profit from council housing, by limiting the surplus in Housing Revenue Accounts to a "working balance" (s. 1(3), a restriction since removed by s. 134 of the 1980 Act, *supra*).

In 1976 the government emphasised that since it had restored to local authorities the right to fix their own rents, it would be very reluctant to interfere with that right (*Hansard* (Commons) June 23, 1976, Vol. 913, col. 1581). By 1980, after another change of government, this reluctance was overcome, but the methods adopted in order to regain some central control over council rents were much more subtle than those adopted by the Housing Finance Act of 1972 (*supra*).

As noted earlier, the discretion in law for councils to fix their own rents remains even after the Housing Act 1980. However, the 1980 Act provides the means for rents to be raised indirectly, in such a way that central government can call the tune but councils have to field the brickbats. The method adopted is the introduction in Part VI of the 1980 Act of yet another new system of housing subsidies, with effect from the financial year 1981–82. In essence, this system is based on "deficit financing." The new central government subsidy to housing authorities is paid on the basis of costs incurred in the previous financial year, with certain additions and deductions: the starting point is the amount of subsidy which each authority had in the previous year, adjusted if necessary by the Minister (the "base amount"); to this is *added* the increased costs, as compared with the previous year, again to the extent allowed by the Minister (the "housing costs differential"); but from the resulting figure is *subtracted* the amount by which the Minister *expects* rents and rates to have increased over the same period, even if those expected increases have not been realised (the "local contribution differential"): see sections 97–100. Before deciding on this key "local contribution differential," the Minister has to consult the local authority associations (s. 100(5)): the result of this process in December 1980 was a recommendation by the Minister of rent increases averaging £3.25 per week for the following year, a very substantial rise[6] which was received with less than universal acclaim: see *Hansard* (Commons) December 15, 1980, Vol. 995, cols. 34–35.[7]

Thus authorities are being indirectly pressured to increase rents, failing which they will lose some central government subsidy and will have to make good any shortfall from the general rates; yet even this option may be more apparent than real, since under the new "block grant" system of rate support introduced by Part VI of the Local Government, Planning and Land Act 1980 (as interpreted by the D.o.E.) a council will in effect be penalised by the central government in terms of rate support grant if the average levels of its rents are lower than the regional average. For the details of the new system of council housing finance under the 1980 Acts, see, *e.g.*: H. Aughton, *Housing Finance—a basic guide,* Shelter, 1981, Chapter 1; H. Aughton, *Roof*, May 1981, at p. 6; J. Gibson, *Roof*, July 1981, at p. 19.

Councils are therefore currently placed in an unenviable position concerning rent increases: in law, the decision is theirs alone, but in practice it will very often be forced upon them if valuable subsidies are not to be lost. There has been a marked change of emphasis from the general subsidising of the "bricks and mortar" of council houses to the subsidising of individual council tenants through means-tested rent rebates and supplementary benefits.

2. *The Machinery for Implementing Rent Increases*

If a council has decided in its "discretion" to increase its rents (albeit after Ministerial prompting), what legal formalities must be observed before the increase can take effect?

At common law, it is clear that "a landlord cannot, *in*

the absence of agreement, increase the rent, against the will of the tenant, unless he gives notice to quit and determines the tenancy" (*per* Lord Denning M.R. in *G.L.C.* v. *Connolly* [1970] 1 All E.R. 870, 873, (C.A.): italics supplied). However, it will be seen that following the Housing Act 1980 councils can no longer use a notice to quit as a method of determining *secure* periodic tenancies,[8] and we have already noted the provisions of section 40 of the 1980 Act, whereby the express terms of a secure tenancy can only be varied by one of three methods, *i.e.*: (i) by ad hoc agreement; (ii) by virtue of a provision in the lease or agreement permitting unilateral variation; or (iii) by statutory notice of variation.[9]

With regard to the second method, this in effect gives statutory validity to *Connolly's* case (*supra*), where the court approved a "unilateral variation clause" under which the rent was liable to be increased "on notice being given": the court decided that it was possible to imply a term that *reasonable* notice of the increase should be given, and this qualification would surely be implicit in section 40(3)(*b*) of the 1980 Act; we have seen[9] that section 40 in fact now restricts these unilateral variation clauses, as regards secure tenancies, to matters concerning rent, rates or services. As regards the third method of variation laid down by section 40, that of notice of variation (of at least four weeks) where the tenancy is periodic, we have noted[9] that in the case of a variation relating to the rent or to payments in respect of services or facilities provided by the landlord, no preliminary notice need be served on the tenant (giving him information about the nature and effect of the variation and an opportunity to comment), nor need the notice of variation itself be accompanied by information about its nature and effect: see section 40(7). This is consistent with the general exemption of rent-fixing from the consultation process (*cf.* s. 42(3)[10]), but, as noted earlier,[9] the tenant can prevent the notice of variation from taking effect by giving a notice to quit before the effective date of the notice of variation (whereupon the notice of variation can only be effective if the tenant, with the authority's written agreement, withdraws the notice to quit): section 40(8); the tenant does not have to be told in the notice of variation of his right to end the tenancy by notice to quit (*cp.* s. 12(3) of the Prices and Incomes Act 1968, discussed *infra*).

Where the tenancy is not secure, section 40 cannot apply: thus here the authority can increase the rent by one of the pre-1980 Act methods, *i.e.* (i) by ad hoc agreement; (ii) by common law unilateral variation clause (*cf. Connolly's* case, *supra*); (iii) by notice to quit and substitution of a fresh tenancy agreement providing for the increased rent; or (iv) by the special procedure in section 12 of the Prices and Incomes Act 1968, which enables authorities to serve on the tenant a notice of increase, at least four weeks in advance, without serving a notice to quit, although the tenant must be told of his right to end the tenancy by notice to quit if he wishes (s. 12(3): this last requirement was not satisfied in *Connolly's* case, *supra*); section 12 of the 1968 Act does not apply to secure tenancies (see Sched. 25, Pt. I, para. 20 of the Housing Act 1980).

Whether or not the tenancy is secure, there is no system of "phasing" rent increases in order to ease the burden for the tenant (*cp.* s. 55 and Sched. 8 of the Rent Act 1977 which, as amended by the Housing Act 1980, broadly provide that for one year from the date of an increase in the registered rent, a private landlord can only raise the rent by *half of the excess* of the new rent over the previous rent).

3. *The Ways in which the Rent may be Challenged*

Since the rent-fixing process for council housing is much less regulated and standardised than the schemes designed for the private sector (where tenants may have their rents considered, where appropriate, by rent officers, rent assessment committees or rent tribunals), it may be asked what protection the council tenant (or other ratepayer) has against the imposition of unreasonable rents. Even a secure tenant has no right to be consulted or to be heard in relation to rent fixing (see the 1980 Act, ss. 40(7), 42(3)). The objector could, of course, try informal pressure on local councillors, coupled with an appropriate use of his vote in local elections, but what if these simple methods prove unsuccessful?

There is far less scope for individual initiative in the rent-fixing process than in the private sector. Under the Housing Act 1957, sections 171–6, the Minister could intervene where an authority had failed to exercise its powers properly, but these sections were repealed by the Local Government Act 1972, so that the Minister no longer has the corresponding power to hold a local enquiry into the council's rents (either following a complaint to him or on his own initiative) under the Housing Act 1957, s. 181, and the Local Government Act 1972, s. 250. No local enquiries into council rents were ever held under these powers in England, but three such inquiries were held in Scotland in 1958, 1961 and 1962: see R. A. Parker, *op. cit.*, at pp. 11–12.

Nevertheless, those who wish to object to the rents fixed for council housing may have three principal remedies.

(a) *District auditor*

Official intervention may be secured through the medium of the ordinary district audit under what is now Part VIII of the Local Government Act 1972: the district auditor might decide that a particular rent scheme is unreasonable and *ultra vires* because for example it unreasonably increases the deficit on the Housing Revenue Account,[11] in which case he may apply to the court for a declaration that the scheme is "contrary to law" under the Local Government Act 1972, s. 161 (excessive expenditure or the improper exercise of discretion can be "contrary to law": *Roberts* v. *Hopwood* [1925] A.C. 578, (H.L.), *Taylor* v. *Munrow* [1960] 1 All E.R. 455, (D.C.); see also *The Times,* May 20, 1980, reporting the complaints made by residents to the district auditor that a London council had acted unlawfully in making large rate increases while freezing council house rents). Any local government elector for the relevant area can make objections to the district auditor regarding the authority's accounts (s. 159(3)), and if he remains dissatisfied by the auditor's decision, the elector may appeal to the High Court or a county court (s. 161(6), (13)), which can then make the necessary declaration. Further, the Minister has power, on the application of a local government elector, to order the district auditor to hold an extraordinary audit of the authority's accounts under section 165 of the Local Government Act 1972.

(b) *Local ombudsman*

Failure by a council to deal properly with a tenant's rent problems can amount to "maladministration," allowing a complaint to be made to a Local Commissioner under Part III of the Local Government Act 1974[12]: see for example the investigation into a complaint against the Greater London Council (Investigation 1094 S, 1977) reported in *Roof*, November 1978, at p. 187.

(c) *Court action*

The cases decided on public sector rent-fixing are few compared with the decisions on private sector rents, and do not hold many prizes in store for the disgruntled council tenant or other ratepayer who wishes to challenge the rent in the courts merely on the ground of *unreasonableness* (as opposed to the presence of some defect in the council's own internal decision-making procedure[13]).

(i) Getting the case to court

The question of whether the authority's rents are "reasonable" will normally be brought before the court by a disgruntled tenant on the ground that they are too high, although the rents may also be challenged by a ratepayer (other than a tenant) on the ground that they are too low: see *Evans* v. *Collins* [1964] 1 All E.R. 808, (D.C.); such a ratepayer will normally only have *locus standi* to bring the action if he obtains the consent of the Attorney General to relator proceedings: *Barrs* v. *Bethell* [1982] 1 All E.R. 106.[14] The usual remedy sought is a declaration that the rent scheme is unreasonable, so that it is *ultra vires* the authority and so void: *Smith* v. *Cardiff Corp.* [1955] 1 All E.R. 113. An injunction may also be claimed, where appropriate, to restrain the authority from carrying out the scheme: see, *e.g. Belcher* v. *Reading Corp.* [1949] 2 All E.R. 969.

It appeared from *Smith* v. *Cardiff Corp.* [1953] 2 All E.R. 1373, (C.A.), that tenants had to proceed as individuals against the authority, since they did not have a sufficient "common interest" or "common grievance" as a class to allow one or more of them to bring a representative action on behalf of the others (claiming relief beneficial to them all) under the Rules of the Supreme Court, Ord. 15, r. 12 or the County Court Rules, Ord. 5, r. 8. But the tenants in *Smith's* case were complaining about a differential rent scheme[15] which would have benefited some 5,000 of them and adversely affected the other 8,000, so that the position may have been otherwise if all the tenants would have benefited from the declaration claimed. In such a "unanimity of interest" case the plaintiff (or plaintiffs) in a representative action may be granted a declaration or an injunction (see *John* v. *Rees* [1969] 2 All E.R. 274); indeed, it now appears that in an appropriate case *damages* may also be recovered by a plaintiff in a representative capacity, where the same damage has been suffered by all members of the particular class and those members have consented to all pecuniary remedies being granted to the plaintiff in respect of the action brought on their behalf: in such a case the plaintiff will then hold the appropriate sums on trust for the other members of the class (see *E.M.I. Records Ltd.* v. *Riley* [1981] 2 All E.R. 838; but *cf. Prudential Assurance Co. Ltd.* v. *Newman Industries Ltd. (No.1)* [1979] 3 All E.R. 507).

(ii) The difficulty of proving unreasonableness

It is clear that the burden of proving that the rent scheme is unreasonable lies firmly with the tenant (see, *e.g. Smith's* case, 1955, *supra*, at p. 121), and the conclusion was judicially drawn in 1964 that the cases " . . . cumulatively do emphasise . . . that very wide discretion which local authorities have under section 111 of the Housing Act 1957, and also the reluctance which courts have shown to interfere in matters which are very often matters of social policy and not really matters of law at all" (*per* Widgery J. in *Evans's* case, *supra*, at p. 812). Most of the decisions tend to regard council rent-fixing merely as an administrative process.

Indeed, it appears that the only case in which a court has struck down an authority's rent as being unreasonable is *Backhouse* v. *Lambeth B.C., The Times,* October 14, 1972. Here an authority resolved to increase to £18,000 a week the rent of an ordinary council house,[16] the last weekly rent of which had been £7.71 (this bizarre arrangement was designed to bring the authority's rent total above the figure which would exempt it from making the general increases in rent otherwise required by the Housing Finance Act 1972, ss. 62(1) and 63(1)). Melford Stevenson J. held that the resolution was one at which no reasonable authority could have arrived, and was not a valid exercise of the authority's powers under section 111 of the 1957 Act. A recent "substantial increase" case which fell on the other side of the "reasonableness" line, though in a different context, is *Ricketts* v. *Havering L.B.C., The Times,* July 17, 1980, in which Whitford J. upheld as reasonable a 128 per cent. increase in stallage charges at Romford Market imposed by the council as the market authority under section 52(1) of the Food and Drugs Act 1955, which (as amended) gives authorities a broad discretion in fixing stallage charges. The judge emphasised that section 52(1) "did not mean that the . . . authority had the right to impose any sort of charge it thought reasonable," but here the council had "rightly taken the view that the time was ripe to increase charges," and had "taken a reasonable view that the market was a potentially profitable operation." Of course, it is not suggested that the decision in *Ricketts* could be used to justify 128 per cent. increases in ordinary council house rents, even in the present financial and political climate!

(iii) Specific principles

Apart from indicating the heavy burden involved in proving the "unreasonableness" of an authority's rents, the cases have also laid down various specific principles.

There is a duty on the authority to maintain a balance between the interests of its tenants and those of the "general body of ratepayers" (*Belcher's* case, *supra*, at p. 983); and the rents must be objectively reasonable, not merely reasonable in the authority's opinion (*Smith's* case, 1955, *supra*, at p. 121). However, there is no duty to fix "economic" rents[17] (*Summerfield* v. *Hampstead B.C.* [1957] 1 All E.R. 221, 225–6), nor to make a profit out of the tenants by charging market rents (*Evans's* case, *supra*, at pp. 811–12); conversely, there is "no justification in the Housing Acts" for "the notion that a council house . . . must necessarily be run at a loss" (*per* Harman J. in *Summerfield's* case, *supra*, at p. 226), and the idea that tenants who have occupied council houses for a long time should be immune from rent increases "has no justification at all" (*per* Romer J. in *Belcher's* case, *supra,* at p. 981).

The authority may fix rents by reference to the needs and capacities of tenants in broad groups, rather than by reference to the needs of individual tenants, provided a balance is kept between the tenants and the ratepayers (*Evans's* case, *supra*, at p. 814). A "pooling" system may be operated whereby the rents of older housing subsidise those of the newer properties (*Summerfield's* case, *supra*, at pp. 225–6); moreover, rents may be geared to the gross rateable values of the houses (*Luby* v. *Newcastle-under-Lyme Corp.* [1964] 3 All E.R. 169, 173, (C.A.)), and many authorities use rateable values in order to adjust rent levels as between properties of various types.

There is no obligation to operate a differential rent scheme[15] (*Evans's* case at p. 812, and *Luby's* case, *supra*). But such schemes have long been judicially sanctioned (see, *e.g. Leeds Corp.* v. *Jenkinson* [1935] 1 K.B. 181, (C.A.) and *Summerfield's* case, *supra*), and the discretion to provide them survives the repeal by the Housing Finance Act 1972 of the *power* to grant rebates formerly contained in section 113(3) of the Housing Act 1957 (the contrary view expressed in *Evans's* case, *supra*, at p. 810, that the discretion to provide differential rent schemes came from the former power to grant rebates, appears to be incorrect: see *Luby's* case, *supra,* at p. 172). Nevertheless, the mandatory rent rebate scheme introduced by the Housing Finance Act 1972[18] has diminished the importance of differential rent schemes generally.

Finally, it appears that the small number of council tenants who do not hold under secure tenancies[19] cannot claim that their lack of statutory security of tenure[20] should be reflected in the fixing of lower rents for their dwellings than those fixed for their "secure" neighbours. This proposition emerges as a matter of inference from the housing trust case of *Palmer* v. *Peabody Trust* [1974] 3 All E.R. 355, (D.C.), where the landlord in question was exempt from the security provisions in the Rent Acts (see the Rent Act 1977, s.15), but the court refused to regard this as relevant to the fixing of the rent.

4. *Assistance with the Rent: Rent Rebates and Supplementary Benefit*

(a) *Rent rebates*

Public funds were used to help the poor with their rents at least as far back as the "Speenhamland settlement" of 1795, under which the measurement of need was geared to the cost of the "gallon loaf." Housing authorities were first given the power to operate rent rebate schemes by section 27(1) of the Housing Act 1930; and we have seen that they are now under a *duty* to operate uniform rebate schemes under the Housing Finance Act 1972. Not only tenants of local authorities, but also their *licensees,* may now be eligible for rent rebates, provided the licence has not been granted to a former squatter (see the new s. 18(3)(*a*), 18(4) of the Housing Finance Act 1972, introduced by Sched. 15, para. 2 of the Housing Act 1980).

For those eligible for rebate, the amount is (broadly) the difference between the tenant's actual weekly rent and a special "minimum weekly rent" (depending on the relationship between his income and his needs: S.I. 1980/1555), which he must meet himself. The maximum weekly rebate is currently £35 in the area of the Greater London Council and £30 elsewhere (S.I. 1981/332). The details of the scheme can be found in (*e.g.*) the *National Welfare Benefits Handbook*, C.P.A.G., or *Roof*, May 1981, at p. 29. The rebates are not automatically given where appropriate: they must be applied for, and will then be deducted from the tenant's rent. It has been estimated that during a sample week in May 1980, about one million council households out of a total of 5,243,000 council dwellings were receiving rent rebates, the average rebate being £4.40 per week (*The Times*, February 2, 1981).

There is also a statutory *rate* rebate scheme, which though separate from the rent rebate system uses similar calculations (see: the Local Government Act 1974, ss. 11–14; S.I. 1978/1504, S.I. 1980/1625; L. Elks (1976) LAG Bul. 82).

(b) *Supplementary benefit*

Apart from possible entitlement to rent and rate rebates, council tenants may be eligible for supplementary benefit from the Department of Health and Social Security (D.H.S.S.) under the Supplementary Benefits Act 1976, if their "requirements" exceed their "resources"; and for these purposes a sum to take account of rent (and rates) forms part of the claimant's requirements (Supplementary Benefits Act 1976, Sched. 2, para. 2; S.I. 1980/1299, Pt. IV). The rents of council tenants in Housing Revenue Account dwellings "will be met in full" (*Supplementary Benefits Handbook*, 1980, para. 6.15), and of the 2.9 million claimants receiving benefit in November 1979, approximately half were council tenants (*Supplementary Benefits Commission Annual Report, 1979*, para. 4.2). The D.H.S.S. has power to pay a tenant's rent direct to his landlord if the tenant is in arrears and the D.H.S.S. considers both that he has failed to budget for the arrears and that direct payment is in his interests (S.I. 1980/983, rr. 3, 7).

If a tenant already in receipt of a rent rebate claims supplementary benefit, then such part of the rent as is covered by the rebate will be excluded from his housing requirements for supplementary benefit purposes, and will therefore not be met by the D.H.S.S. (see S.I. 1980/1299, r. 15(6)). Conversely, if a tenant already receiving supplementary benefit becomes *prima facie* eligible for a rent rebate, then unless the Minister otherwise directs, no rebate is to be paid (s. 119(1) of the Housing Act 1980), and the tenant's supplementary benefit will continue to be calculated with regard to his full rent (*cf.* the 1977 Green Paper on *Housing Policy, op. cit.*, at pp. 109–110).

(c) *A "unified housing benefit"?*

Calls for a more comprehensive housing "benefit," which would (*inter alia*) break down the present difficult distinctions between rent rebates and supplementary benefit, were rejected by the Green Paper on *Housing Policy* (*op. cit.*, Chap. 5). Nevertheless, the D.o.E.'s 1981 consultation paper on *Assistance with Housing Costs* proposed a "unified housing benefit" which would be administered by local authorities, and would combine into a single payment rent rebates (and rent allowances in the private rented sector), rate rebates, and certain supplementary benefit housing payments. This new benefit was designed particularly to remove the hardship often unwittingly experienced at present by claimants who lose out by applying for rent rebates when they would be better off on supplementary benefit, or *vice versa*. The additional workload which the implementation of this proposal would impose on local authorities is likely to prove very unwelcome to them, given the current manpower constraints. This proposed scheme has now been embodied in Part II of the Social Security and Housing Benefits Bill 1981.

5. *Rent Arrears and their Collection*

(a) *The extent of arrears*

Despite the help available to tenants in the form of rebates and supplementary benefit, many councils have problems over rent arrears. Where substantial arrears occur, these are often due to the low incomes of the tenants rather than any irresponsibility (see, *e.g.*: L. Alpren, *The Causes of Serious Rent Arrears*, 1977, pp. 46–47; A. Harvey, *Remedies for Rent Arrears,* Shelter, 1979, p. 48; G. Porter, *Roof*, September 1978, at p. 141;

R. Franey, *Roof,* May 1980, at p. 80). In fact, however, most council tenants in arrears only owe small amounts, and the largest slice of the arrears debt is attributable to the very few tenants who are in serious arrears (see the D.o.E. discussion paper on *Rent arrears in local authority housing*, H.D.D. Occasional Paper 1/78, 1978, by P. Downey). Figures published by the Chartered Institute of Public Finance and Accountancy showed that for the financial year 1978–79 rent arrears amounted to only four per cent. of the collectable rents (*Housing Statistics, C.I.P.F.A.*, 1980).

(b) *Remedies for arrears*

Housing departments have been given detailed advice in government circulars and reports regarding alternatives to eviction in the case of rent arrears, and this guidance remains relevant even though, in the case of secure tenants, the council is prevented by the Housing Act 1980 from actually recovering possession on the ground of rent arrears unless the court considers this to be reasonable.[20]

Some of the advice has merely been platitudinous (see, *e.g.*: the 1955 C.H.A.C. Report on *Unsatisfactory Tenants*, pp. 3–4, 9, and 16; M.H.L.G. Circular no. 58/66 on *Homeless Families—Temporary Accommodation,* 1966, para. 6; and M.H.L.G. Circular no. 62/67 on *Homeless Families—Temporary Accommodation,* 1967, para. 7). But other advice has been more specifically helpful (see, *e.g.*: D.o.E. Circular no. 74/72 on *Housing Finance Act 1972: Rent Rebate and Rent Allowance Schemes*, 1972, para. 81, concerning advice to tenants as to their eligibility for rent rebates; D.o.E. Circular no. 83/72 on *Repeal of the Small Tenements Recovery Act 1838,* 1972, concerning the remedy of attachment of earnings under the Attachment of Earnings Act 1971 and the special procedure for a rent action in the county court introduced by r. 17 of the County Court (New Procedure) Rules 1971, S.I. 1971/2152, whereby rent can be recovered from a tenant still in occupation; and D.o.E. Circular no. 18/74 on *Homelessness*, 1974, App., paras. 3–4, detailing a series of eight possible measures).

The most comprehensive guidance yet was contained in the Annex to the D.o.E.'s *Code of Guidance* to the Housing (Homeless Persons) Act 1977: this Annex emphasised that rent arrears "call for a variety of approaches" (para. A1.13), and it then detailed 12 possible measures which can be used to control arrears, including the checking of the tenant's entitlement to rent and rate rebates, financial support by social services authorities by way of rent guarantees or payments of the arrears, the direct payment of the rent element in supplementary benefit from the social security office to the housing department,[21] and setting the debt aside for a period in order to give the tenant a chance to put his finances in order (para. A1.15). The Code regarded eviction as a final step, only to be taken when "unavoidable" after all the other preventive measures have failed (para. A1.16), and the subsequent introduction of statutory security of tenure by the Housing Act 1980[20] should now ensure that the commencement of possession proceedings is not treated by the authority as an automatic process even in the case of persistent defaulters.

(c) *"Distress"*

The advice in the Annex to the 1977 *Code of Guidance, supra,* made no mention of the archaic remedy of "distress," although a Ministerial statement in 1978 expressed the hope that it would be used "only as a last resort and with proper regard to the interests of the families concerned" (see *Hansard* (Commons) May 16, 1978, Vol. 950, col. *118*). This remedy (which has not been affected by the Housing Act 1980) has been enjoying something of a renaissance at the hands of some authorities, and deserves separate treatment.

"Distress" is a form of self-help under which the

landlord can take and detain his tenant's goods until the rent arrears are paid, failing which the goods may be sold. The details of this procedure may be found elsewhere (see, *e.g.* A. Arden (1978) L.A.G. Bul. 57); but it is important to note that while private landlords cannot distrain for rent owed by tenants protected by the Rent Act unless they first obtain the leave of the county court (Rent Act 1977, s. 147), a council can institute distress without a court order: it can simply write a "distress warrant" authorising its bailiff to distrain (although the bailiff must be "certificated," *i.e.* authorised to act by a county court judge: Law of Distress Amendment Act 1888, s. 7). Of the authorities using distress which were surveyed by Shelter in 1978, approximately one-third employed private firms of bailiffs, which were "generally not . . . sensitive to welfare considerations" (*In Distress Over Rent* (1978), p. 6; see also *Roof*, January 1978, at p. 8).

This procedure has been described as "more of a deterrent than a means of debt recovery as the resale value of second-hand goods is low and certain items are protected from seizure" (National Consumer Council, *Behind With the Rent* (1976), p. 13). Nevertheless, Shelter discovered that over 100 councils were using the remedy in 1978 (*In Distress Over Rent, op. cit.*); indeed, it has been suggested that "the new fashionability of distraint appears to be an unpredicted and worrying side effect of the Housing (Homeless Persons) Act which some councils see as removing the threat of eviction which was an inhibition to the growth of rent arrears" (S. Schifferes, *Roof*, May 1978, at p. 67): this "short sharp shock" factor may be even more significant following the introduction of statutory security of tenure by the Housing Act 1980.

The abolition of distress was recommended by the Report of the Payne Committee on the *Enforcement of Judgment Debts,* Cmnd. 3909 (1969); and there would at least seem to be little justification for continuing to exempt authorities from the requirement of obtaining a court order before the right is exercised, especially since the unregulated use of distress is surely contrary to the spirit (though not the letter) of the "tenants' charter" in the 1980 Act.

(d) *Harassment of rent defaulters*

Some rather more unorthodox methods of collecting rent arrears have been considered by individual councils, such as the use of "shame vans" which either have a list of all tenants owing more than £40 in rent pasted on the side (*Roof*, July 1977, at p. 105), or are clearly marked "Council Debt Collection Service" (*The Times,* June 22, 1978). These authorities should bear in mind in this context the provisions of section 40 of the Administration of Justice Act 1970: section 40(1) makes it an offence for any person "with the object of coercing another person to pay money claimed from the other as a debt due under a contract" to "harass . . . the other with demands for payment which, in respect of their frequency or the manner or occasion of making any such demand, *or of any threat or publicity by which any demand is accompanied,* are calculated to subject him or members of his family or household to alarm, distress *or humiliation*" (italics supplied).

Notes

[1] See *supra,* p. 123.

[2] A similar provision in the 1957 Housing Act as originally drafted (s. 113(4)) had covered both rents and rebates (see *infra*), and its predecessor in the 1936 Housing Act had been described as imposing "a duty on the authority and not merely [a power]": *per* Danckwerts J. in *Smith* v. *Cardiff Corp.* [1955] 1 All E.R. 113, 117.

[3] See the D.o.E. Report on *The Administration of the Rent Rebate and Rent Allowance Schemes*, 1976, at p. 22; this Report also pointed out (at p. 21) the practical distinction between *rent rebate* schemes and *differential rent* schemes (*i.e.* schemes where the rent itself is adjusted to the tenant's income and needs): " . . . in rent rebate schemes a standard

rent is fixed and is generally related to some kind of concept of what the average tenant pays and deductions are made from it; whereas in differential rent schemes [the] maximum rent, being a full economic rent, may be very much higher."

[4] For an account of the workings of the scheme, see, *e.g.* D. Yates (1972) 36 Conv. (N.S.) 402.

[5] See further D. Yates (1975) 39 Conv. (N.S.) 387.

[6] As at April 1980 the average unrebated council rent was £7.71p per week in England and Wales; the lowest council rents at that time were in Yorkshire and Humberside, where the average was £6.95p per week for a three-bedroom house (see *Housing Rents Statistics at April 1980*, C.I.P.F.A., 1981).

[7] The Minister was able to remind the Opposition that it had stated in the 1977 Green Paper on *Housing Policy* (*op. cit.*, at p. 37) that it intended council rent increases to keep broadly in line with changes in earnings.

[8] See *infra*, pp. 151–3.

[9] See *supra*, pp. 32–4.

[10] See *infra*, pp. 210–11.

[11] See "The Case of the St. Pancras Rents," *The Listener*, May 26, 1960, at p. 919 (quoted by R.A. Parker, *op. cit.*, at p. 11).

[12] See *supra*, pp. 42–3.

[13] See, *e.g.* the case briefly reported in *The Times*, February 14, 1981, where Forbes J. decided that a council's rent increase was invalid because the housing committee had adjourned the matter to another place (because of rowdy behaviour in the public gallery to the council chamber) before reaching its decision, whereas under the council's standing orders the committee could only adjourn the matter to another time, and not to another place.

[14] In this case the Attorney-General's consent was subsequently given: see *The Times*, July 17, 1981.

[15] See note 3, *supra*.

[16] *cp.* the report in *The Times*, April 24, 1981, of a council's decision to raise the rent of a "stately council house . . . set in acres of superb, landscaped gardens, with ponds and fountains," from £350 per annum to £3,500 per annum.

[17] An "economic" rent is the rent at which the dwelling must be let in order to cover the costs of loan repayments, management, repairs and maintenance.

[18] See *supra*, p. 130.

[19] See *supra*, pp. 10–18.

[20] See *infra*, Chap. 7.

[21] See *supra*, p. 142.

Chapter 7

EVICTION

1. *General*

The security of tenure long enjoyed by private sector tenants under successive Rent Acts has never extended to council tenants (see: the Housing Act 1957, s. 158; the Rent Act 1977, ss. 14, 19(5) (*aa*); *cf. Lambeth L.B.C.* v. *Udechuka, The Times*, April 30, 1980, (C.A.)). Instead, "for numerous years past, it had been thought safe and proper to give to local authority landlords a complete discretion with regard to the eviction of public sector tenants, and to rely on them to exercise such discretion fairly and wisely" (*per* Brandon L.J. in *L.B. of Hammersmith & Fulham* v. *Harrison* [1981] 2 All E.R. 588, 597, (C.A.)). Although councils were subject to general administrative law principles[1] in evicting their tenants, the practical burden of proving a breach of these principles was such[1] that the courts exercised very little control over council evictions. Government statistics revealed that before the Housing Act 1980 considerable numbers of possession orders were being granted to "social landlords," *i.e.* local authorites, registered housing associations and new town corporations (*e.g.* it was estimated that no less than 44,190 such orders were made in 1978 alone: *Housing and Construction Statistics*, Vol. 30 (1979) Supp. Table XXXVIII); and several individual "hard cases" were recorded (see, *e.g.*: *Homes Fit For Heroes,* Shelter, 1975, pp. 2–3; A. Harvey (1972) 122 N.L.J. 685, (1974) 124 N.L.J. 541).

By the 1970s, it was becoming increasingly illogical for Parliament to have provided an elaborate system of statutory security for tenants in the fast-diminishing private sector, while it still failed to give security to tenants in the (then) rapidly-expanding public sector. Statutory security for the public sector was eventually conferred by the Housing Act 1980; although according to Brandon L.J. this "was not an urgent matter" (see *Harrison's* case, *supra, loc. cit.*), it is likely to prove a more enduring (and no less important) aspect of the statutory "council tenants' charter" than the controversial "right to buy."

It is therefore necessary separately to consider the new security of tenure enjoyed by secure[2] council tenants under the 1980 Act, and then to turn to the much more limited protection afforded to non-secure council tenants.

2. *Possession Proceedings against Secure Tenants*

Where the tenancy is secure[2] (and it will be recalled that under s. 48 of the 1980 Act a council *licensee* will normally be treated as a secure tenant[3]), then the council can only gain possession by following carefully the prescribed procedure in the 1980 Act. This procedure differs in several important respects from that under the Rent Act 1977: thus we shall see that the 1980 Act does not import the difficult Rent Act distinction between a protected (contractual) tenancy and a statutory tenancy, and instead provides for the artificial continuation of the contractual tenancy until the date when the tenant is due to give up possession in pursuance of the court's possession order; further, although some of the grounds for possession in the 1980 Act are the same as those in the Rent Act, it will be seen that there are several special grounds "tailor-made" for the public sector, and that the definition of "suitable accommodation" in the 1980 Act differs from the definition of "suitable alternative accommodation" in the Rent Act. Thus, as the Court of Appeal emphasised in *Harrison's* case, *supra*, it can be misleading to try and draw too many parallels with the Rent Act regime. In the ensuing discussion, references to the security provisions of the Rent Act will only be made either where they are of direct relevance, or alternatively where they assist by way of contrast in the understanding of the 1980 Act.

(a) *Artificial continuation of the contractual tenancy*

The security of tenure system in the 1980 Act has "abolished . . . the common law principles on which contractual tenancies, both periodical and for a term certain, could be brought or come to an end" (*per* Brandon L.J. in *Harrison's* case, *loc. cit.*).

Where the secure tenancy is *periodic* (*e.g.* weekly), it cannot be brought to an end by the council[4] except by the obtaining of a court order for possession of the dwelling (s. 32(1)), which can only be granted on certain grounds (s. 34, *infra*), whereupon the tenancy ends on the date on which the tenant is due to give up possession in pursuance of the (final[5]) order (s. 32(1)). Note that the tenancy ends on the date when the tenant is to give up possession in *pursuance* of the order, not at the date when he is actually evicted by the bailiffs (if later): in between these two dates, he will in theory be a trespasser,[6] though protected from unlawful eviction by section 3 of the Protection from Eviction Act 1977 (*infra*); and even if, during such period, the council purports to accept further "rent" from the former tenant (as opposed to "mesne profits": *cf.* A. Arden (1979) LAG Bul. 44), it is unlikely that a new tenancy (or even a licence—*cf.* s. 48(1)) will arise unless there is a very clear intention to that effect (see, *e.g.*: *Musto* v. *Otiero* (1974) LAG Bul. 278, (C.A.); *Longrigg, Burrough & Trounson* v. *Smith* (1979) 251 E.G. 847, (C.A.); N. Nardecchia, *Law Society's Gazette*, April 1, 1981, at p. 360).

A secure tenancy which is for a *fixed term* (*e.g.* one year) and comes to an end by *effluxion of time* does not end as such: a periodic tenancy thereupon arises under section 29 (the periods being those of the rent payments of the former fixed-term tenancy); while a fixed-term secure tenancy which is prima facie subject to termination by the council by way of forfeiture cannot in fact be so forfeited: on such a forfeiting event arising, the court cannot order possession on account of that forfeiting event as such, but if apart from the Act it would have ordered possession,[7] it must instead make an order terminating the fixed-term secure tenancy on a date specified in the order (s. 32(1)–(2)), and from that date a periodic tenancy again normally arises under section 29 (*i.e.* the forfeiting event is not itself a ground for possession: a separate statutory ground for possession under the Housing Act must be shown, and on such a ground being established the "section 29" periodic tenancy ends on the date specified for possession in the possesion order, in accordance with the normal rule for periodic secure tenancies, *supra*). It seems clear[8] that the "section 29" periodic tenancy, arising at the expiry of the fixed term or following a court order under section 32(2), is itself secure (see ss. 13(1), 40(10)).

Thus a secure tenancy simply continues on a *contractual* basis until the date fixed by the court for possession, and terminated fixed-term secure tenancies are normally extended automatically as secure periodic tenancies. It follows that it will be a criminal offence under section 1(2) of the Protection from Eviction Act 1977 to evict the tenant, even by peaceful means, before the date fixed by the court for possession, since the tenant will until then be a " 'residential occupier' . . . occupying the premises as a residence . . . under a contract" within section 1(1) of that Act; and even after the date fixed by the court for possession, the former tenant will be protected from eviction, other than at the hands of the court bailiffs, by sections 3 and 8(1) of that Act (*cf. Kyriacou* v. *Pandeli* [1980] C.L.Y. 1648, Shoreditch County Court).

(b) *The procedure for possession*

Under section 86(1) of the Housing Act 1980, the *county court*[9] has jurisdiction over secure tenancies; and if the council takes proceedings in the High Court which could have been taken in the county court, then it is not entitled to recover any costs (s. 86(3)).

The procedure for obtaining possession differs depending on whether the secure tenancy is periodic, or for a fixed term.

(i) Periodic secure tenancies

Instead of serving a notice to quit,[10] the council has to serve a special (untitled) notice under section 33, which is in effect a "notice of intended proceedings": this notice has to specify the ground on which the court will be asked to make an order for possession, and must be in a prescribed form (s. 33(2); see S.I. 1980/1339[11]: the legality of these regulations was established in *Wansbeck D.C.* v. *Charlton, The Times,* February 19, 1981, (C.A.)). The notice must specify the date after which proceedings for possession may be begun, and the date specified must not be earlier than the date on which the tenancy could, apart from the Act, be ended by a notice to quit served on the same date as the notice of intended proceedings (s. 33(3); thus, by virtue of s. 5 of the Protection from Eviction Act 1977, at least four weeks' notice must be given[10]). Service of the notice is governed by section 233 of the Local Government Act 1972, which authorises (*inter alia*) service by post; though if the notice was sent by ordinary post rather than by the registered or recorded delivery service, the tenant could defeat the notice by proving non-receipt: see section 7 of the Interpretation Act 1978. If the tenant has left and the authority is unable to discover his new address after reasonable inquiry, then by section 233(7) of the Local Government Act it can affix the notice conspicuously to some part of the property.

Proceedings must then be begun after the date specified in the notice, but within 12 months of the date so specified (ss. 33(1), 33(3)(*b*) of the 1980 Act). Failure to serve the correct notice, however, means that the court cannot entertain the possession proceedings (s. 33(1)).

(ii) Fixed-term secure tenancies

Where the council seeks possession of property let on a fixed-term secure tenancy while the original term is still on foot (*cf.* s. 29, *supra*), then again a "notice of intended proceedings" must be served[7] under section 33: here the notice has to specify the ground on which the court will be asked to *terminate* the tenancy (s. 33(2)); again it must be in a prescribed form (s. 33(2), S.I. 1980/1339[11]), but this notice does not have to specify the date after which proceedings for possession may be begun (s. 33(4); *cf.* the notice relating to a periodic tenancy, *supra*). The notice has effect also with regard to any periodic tenancy arising under section 29 (*supra*) on the termination of the fixed-term tenancy (s. 33(4)), so that the council may seek, all in the same proceedings, an order which both *terminates* the term certain and requires the tenant to give up *possession* (assuming an appropriate statutory ground can be established). But failure to serve the correct notice precludes the court from entertaining either the termination proceedings or the possession proceedings, as appropriate (s. 33(1)).

(c) *The grounds for possession*

Under section 34, the court cannot make an order for the *possession* of a dwelling let under a secure tenancy (as opposed to an order for the *termination* of a *fixed-term* tenancy, *supra*), except on one or more of the grounds set out in Part I of Schedule 4; and the court cannot make such an order unless the appropriate ground is specified in the notice of intended proceedings (*supra*), although the grounds set out in this notice can be altered or added to with the leave of the court (s. 34(1)).

The grounds fall broadly into two main groupings, *i.e.* (in effect) "tenant's misconduct" grounds or "council's

management" grounds; even where a "council's management" ground applies, the Act does not expressly prohibit
the court from ordering the tenant to pay the council's
costs of the proceedings, although in its discretion the
court will often refuse to make such an order for costs in
these circumstances without special reason.

In order fully to understand the new grounds, however,
it is best to divide them into *three* separate groupings
(among which "tenant's misconduct" grounds and
"council's management" grounds are interspersed), since
the conditions which must be met before the court can
order possession on the various grounds may differ
according to three separate criteria.

(i) Grounds on which the court can only make a
    possession order if it considers it *reasonable* to do so

These grounds largely relate to "tenant's misconduct,"
and it is important to note that where they apply, the court
only has to be satisfied as to the reasonableness of making
the order; it does *not* have to be satisfied that suitable
accommodation will be available to the tenant when he is
evicted (see s. 34(1)–(3), Sched. 4, Pt. I, gds. 1–6). The
council may however be subject to its normal duties under
the Housing (Homeless Persons) Act 1977[12] towards the
displaced tenant and his family (although the extent of
these duties may be diminished by a finding of "intentional" homelessness where appropriate).

The relevant grounds (suitably paraphrased) are:
—Non-payment of rent lawfully due or breach of any
  other (express or implied[13]) obligation of the tenancy: ground 1.

If rent arrears are alleged, they must still be due at the
date when court proceedings are issued (*Bird* v. *Hildage*
[1947] 2 All E.R. 7, (C.A.), where tender of the arrears
before commencement of the proceedings precluded the
court from ordering possession; see also *Johnson-Sneddon*
v. *Harper* (1977) LAG Bul. 114, (C.A.)); and although

possession can be ordered where the tenant tenders the arrears *after* commencement of the proceedings, such an order will rarely be made (*Dellenty* v. *Pellow* [1951] 2 All E.R. 716, (C.A.)). There will be no arrears "lawfully due" where rent is being withheld in circumstances where the tenant is exercising a common law or equitable right of set-off.[14]

—The tenant or any other person residing in the dwelling has caused a nuisance or annoyance to neighbours (not necessarily the adjoining occupiers), or has been convicted of illegal or immoral user of the property: ground 2.

This ground could be used for example against tenants found responsible for racial harassment on council estates (*cf. Racial Harassment on Local Authority Housing Estates,* 1981, Commission for Racial Equality).

—Deterioration of the condition of the dwelling or of the common parts[15] (or of any furniture provided by the council for use in the dwelling or the common parts), due to the fault of the tenant[16] or any other person residing in the dwelling (provided that, where the fault has been on the part of the tenant's sub-lessee or lodger, the tenant has not taken reasonable steps to evict that person): grounds 3–4.

The grounds so far considered (grounds 1–4) have broadly equivalent counterparts in the Rent Act 1977: for a discussion of some of the extensive case-law relating to these Rent Act grounds, most of which will be relevant to secure tenancies, see, *e.g.* A. Arden (1978) LAG Bul. 186, (1979) LAG Bul. 11, 12.

—The council was induced to grant the tenancy by a false statement made knowingly or recklessly by the tenant: ground 5.

This ground[17] has no counterpart in the Rent Act (but *cf.* the offence of knowingly or recklessly making false statements in s. 11(1) of the Housing (Homeless Persons) Act 1977); in theory, tenants can be evicted under ground 5 on account of statements (relating, *e.g.* to the size of their families) made many years previously, but this is of course a "reasonableness" ground, and in any event the statement must have been material to the council's decision to grant the tenancy. In view of this ground, however, an applicant for council housing would now be well advised to exercise his right to require the authority to furnish him with details of the particulars given by him to the authority and recorded by it as relevant to his application (s. 44(6)[18]), so that any misunderstandings can be cleared up forthwith.

> —The tenant, having been a secure tenant of a dwelling on which works have been carried out, has been temporarily accommodated elsewhere during the works on the understanding that he would leave on their completion, and he now refuses to vacate this "temporary" accommodation even though the dwelling which he formerly occupied is ready for his renewed occupation: ground 6.

Although this is in effect a "council's management" ground, it is grouped with the "reasonableness" grounds because, if the works have taken a considerable time, it might not be reasonable to expect the "decanted" tenant to be displaced yet again.

(ii) Grounds on which the court *must* make a possession order if it is satisfied as to *suitable accommodation*

These are mandatory grounds (*i.e.* not depending on reasonableness as such), provided the court is satisfied that suitable accommodation will be available for the tenant when the order takes effect (see s. 34(1)–(4), Sched. 4, Pt. I, gds. 7–9). Only two of these grounds are relevant to councils, namely:

> —Overcrowding, within the meaning of the Housing Act 1957 (ss. 77–80), in such circumstances that the occupier is guilty of an offence: ground 7.

This ground operates as a limitation on the "charter"

rights for secure tenants to take in lodgers[19] and sub-let part of the property.[20]

—The council intends within a reasonable time of gaining possession to demolish or reconstruct the building (or part thereof) comprising the dwelling, or to carry out work thereon, and cannot reasonably do so without obtaining possession of the dwelling: ground 8.

This ground applies where the tenant refuses to vacate in order for the work to be carried out on his dwelling; if he leaves voluntarily, he may be subject to the "reasonableness" ground 6, *supra*, in respect of the property into which he is "decanted."

It is important to note that, unlike the position in the privately rented sector, the availability of suitable alternative accommodation is *not of itself* a ground for possession (*cp.* the Rent Act 1977, s. 98(1)(*a*), which makes the availability of such accommodation a "reasonableness" ground).

For Housing Act purposes, "suitable accommodation" is defined in Part II of Schedule 4: in essence, the available accommodation has to be let either under a secure tenancy within the 1980 Act, or under a protected tenancy within the Rent Act 1977 which is not subject to one of the mandatory Rent Act grounds for possession (to avoid any "out of the frying-pan, into the fire" effect). The accommodation also has to be "reasonably suitable to the needs of the tenant and his family" (*not* his lodgers or sub-lessees), having regard to various listed factors,[21] such as distance from place of work or education, distance from other close family members, and the means[22] and needs (as regards *extent* of accommodation) of the tenant and his family.

Unlike the definition of suitable alternative accommodation in the Rent Act 1977 (see Sched. 15, Pt. IV, para. 5 thereof), under the Housing Act the accommodation can be suitable even though it is not suited to the needs of the tenant and his family as regards its *character*,[23] so that the tenant can in effect be "down-graded." Further, a special rule regarding suitable accommodation applies where possession is sought under the "statutory overcrowding" ground (ground 7, *supra*): here the alternative accommodation can nevertheless be suitable to the needs of *the tenant and his family*, even though it will still be overcrowded by the *space standards* in Schedule 6 of the Housing Act 1957 if all the existing occupiers move to it! Insofar as it is possible to make sense of this Alice-in-Wonderland provision (to be found in Sched. 4, Pt. II, para. 2 of the 1980 Act), it seems to have been designed to enable a council to shift the occupants of a dwelling which is overcrowded due to the presence of lodgers or sub-lessees to smaller accommodation, so that the tenant is in effect compelled to jettison his lodgers or sub-lessees before moving to the new accommodation (the provision only refers to the suitability of the accommodation to the needs of the tenant and his *family*). Yet objection may still be raised as to the unsuitability of the new accommodation on the grounds of (for example) overcrowding due to the *sleeping arrangements* (*i.e.* as opposed to the space standards: *cf.* the Housing Act 1957, s. 77, Sched. 6), or the lack of amenities or services (*cf.* the "multiple occupation" provision in the Housing Act 1961, s. 15).

(iii) Grounds on which the court can only make a possession order if it considers it *reasonable* to do so *and* it is satisfied as to *suitable accommodation*

The criteria for the following grounds (in s. 34(1)–(4) and Sched. 4, Pt. I, gds. 10–13) combine the general requirements of groups (i) and (ii) above.[24] These grounds are broadly concerned with tenants who do not satisfy the "purpose" for which the accommodation was originally provided; they are thus primarily (and in the case of gd. 13, exclusively) concerned with statutory successors[25] of the original tenants. Only three of these grounds are relevant to council landlords, namely:

—The dwelling has unusual features which are designed for a disabled person (not necessarily the tenant himself), there is no longer such a person in residence, and the council requires the dwelling for occupation by such a person: ground 10.

This ground covers dwellings which are either purpose-built for, or adapted for, the disabled.

—The dwelling is one of a group normally let to persons with special needs, a social services or special facility is provided nearby for the occupants, there is no longer a person with those special needs residing in the dwelling, and the council requires it for occupation by such a person: ground 12.

The needs here do not necessarily have to be connected with old age[26]: the ground relates to "sheltered" housing in a wide sense.

—The accommodation afforded by the dwelling is more extensive than is reasonably required by the tenant, the tenancy vested in the tenant on the death of the previous tenant under section 30 (succession to *periodic* secure tenancies[27]) as being a member of the previous tenant's family[28] *other than* the spouse, and the notice of intended proceedings under section 33 (*supra*) was served more than six months but less than twelve months[29] after the date of the previous tenant's death: ground 13.

This "under-occupation" ground is very narrowly defined: it cannot be used against an original tenant,[30] nor against a spouse-successor of an original tenant.

(d) *Adjournment, postponement and suspension*

Where possession proceedings are brought on one or more of the "*reasonableness*" grounds (1–6, *supra*), or "*reasonableness plus suitable accommodation*" grounds (10–13, *supra*), then the court may adjourn the proceedings for such period or periods as it thinks fit (s. 87(1)). Further, if it makes a possession order on any of these grounds, or at any time before the execution of the order, the court may postpone the date of possession, or stay or suspend execution of the order, again for such period or periods as it thinks fit[31] (s. 87(2)). But on any such adjournment, postponement, stay or suspension, the court *must* normally impose conditions regarding the payment by the tenant of arrears of rent (if any) and current[32] rent or mesne profits,[33] and *may* impose such other conditions as it thinks fit (s. 87(3)); on compliance with such conditions, the court may discharge or rescind the order (s. 87(4)).

However, as regards the "*non-reasonableness*" grounds (7–8, *supra*), section 89 in effect provides that where the court makes the possession order, it shall not postpone the giving up of possession (whether by the order or any variation, suspension or stay of execution) to a date later than *fourteen days* after the making of the order (save in cases of exceptional hardship, where possession can be postponed for a maximum of six weeks from the making of the order): section 89(1), (2)(*c*). This new "fourteen days" rule represents a tightening-up of the former "four to six weeks" rule[34] in cases where the landlord had a mandatory ground for possesssion, which had been approved by Lord Denning M.R. in *McPhail* v. *Persons Unknown* [1973] 3 All E.R. 393, 399, (C.A.).

(e) *The right to security of the tenant's spouse*

Section 87 also seeks to ensure that the position of the tenant's spouse is safeguarded where the council obtains a possession order against the tenant, and, in particular, that the spouse's "rights of occupation" under section 1 of the Matrimonial Homes Act 1967[35] are not inadvertently destroyed following expiry of the time fixed for delivery of possession under a possession order made against the tenant alone (*cf.* the private sector case of *Penn* v. *Dunn*

[1970] 2 All E.R. 858, (C.A.)[36]). Thus section 87(5)–(6) provides that where (i) possession proceedings are brought on one or more of the "reasonableness" grounds (1–6, *supra*), or "reasonableness plus suitable accommodation" grounds (10–13, *supra*), and (ii) the tenant's spouse, having rights of occupation under the Matrimonial Homes Act 1967, is then in occupation, and (iii) the tenancy is ended as against the tenant as a result of those proceedings, then the tenant's spouse (so long as he or she remains in occupation) has the same rights to ask the court to adjourn the proceedings, postpone the date of possession, or stay or suspend execution of the order, as he or she would have if those rights of occupation were not affected by the ending of the tenancy.

3. *Possession Proceedings against Non-secure Tenants*

Those council tenants whose tenancies are not secure[37] do not enjoy statutory security of tenure, but they continue to have the (very limited) protection which was available to all council tenants prior to the 1980 Act, primarily by virtue of general administrative law principles. The details of this protection will be found in Chapter 7 of the first edition of this book; what follows is merely an outline of the position.

An authority, in deciding whether to evict a non-secure tenant by virtue of the power of "general management, regulation and control" of council housing vested in it under section 111(1) of the Housing Act 1957, must act "in good faith, taking into account relevant considerations and not irrelevant considerations" (*per* Lord Denning M.R. in *Bristol D.C.* v. *Clark* [1975] 3 All E.R. 976, 980, (C.A.))[38]; failing which, the tenant will have a defence to the possession proceedings.[39] In *Clark's* case, which was concerned with eviction for rent arrears, the court regarded D.o.E. circulars as "relevant considerations" for this purpose; and we have seen in Chapter 6 that there are a considerable number of such circulars dealing with the problems of rent arrears.[40]

The major difficulty presented for tenants by the reasoning in *Clark's* case, however, is that it may well be impossible to prove that the authority has failed to take these "relevant considerations" into account (in the case itself the council was found to have obeyed the relevant guidelines in deciding to evict). A Local Commissioner might be able to do the necessary delving into a council's administrative processes,[41] but he would not be able to do so swiftly enough to provide the tenant with a defence to the possession proceedings.

The virtually insuperable burden of proof which confronts a tenant who seeks to show bad faith or "abuse of power" has become even clearer from two subsequent decisions of the Court of Appeal (*Cannock Chase D.C.* v. *Kelly* [1978] 1 All E.R. 152, *Sevenoaks D.C.* v. *Emmott* (1980) 130 N.L.J. 139[42]); and although the principles from *Clark's* case were later extended to the termination of council licences[43] (*Cleethorpes B.C.* v. *Clarkson* (1978) LAG Bul. 166, (C.A.)), there seems to be no recorded case where a tenant or licensee has actually been successful in blocking the possession proceedings on these administrative law grounds. This "administrative law protection" against arbitrary eviction is therefore worth very little in practice (see also, *e.g.* D.J. Hughes (1977) 127 N.L.J. 1067); and although it extends equally to secure tenants, the protection offered by the 1980 Act is such (particularly where a "reasonableness" ground is in issue) that it will be very unusual for a secure tenant to need to rely on these common law principles.

Assuming the authority's initial decision to evict a non-secure tenant is unassailable, it may nevertheless be possible for the tenant to challenge the eviction process itself. Where the tenancy is periodic, a written notice to quit must first be given, at least four weeks before the date on which it is to take effect, and expiring at the end of a completed period of the tenancy (see the Protection from

Eviction Act 1977, s. 5(1)); the notice must also inform the tenant of the need for a court order before he can lawfully be evicted, and of the availability of advice from a solicitor (if necessary under the legal aid scheme), or from a Citizens' Advice Bureau, Housing Aid Centre, etc. (see the Protection from Eviction Act 1977, s. 5(1)–(2); S.I. 1980/1624).[44] Service of the notice is governed by section 233 of the Local Government Act 1972.[45] Even a technically valid notice to quit may be vitiated by a clearly unlawful purpose underlying it, such as the recovery of an invalid rent increase which is therefore *ultra vires* the authority (see *G.L.C.* v. *Connolly* [1970] 1 All E.R. 870, 875, (C.A.)).

If the tenant refuses to leave after expiry[46] of a proper notice to quit, the authority cannot regain possession without a court order, since it is bound by the unlawful eviction and harassment provisions in Part I of the Protection from Eviction Act 1977 (see particularly ss. 3 and 8(1) thereof). At the hearing, the authority need not prove that it requires the property for housing purposes (*Bristol D.C.* v. *Clark* [1975] 3 All E.R. 976, (C.A.); *cf.* the Housing Act 1957, s. 158). It is entitled to a possession order as of right if the tenant has no viable defence (see: *Sheffield Corp.* v. *Luxford* [1929] 2 K.B. 180, (D.C.); *Bristol C.C.* v. *Rawlins* (1977) 34 P & C.R. 12, (C.A.)); although in rent arrears cases the tenant may be able to persuade the authority to accept a suspended possession order (*i.e.* an order suspended so long as the tenant pays off the arrears by agreed instalments: *cf. Bristol C.C.* v. *Rawlins, supra*). The judge has some discretion in fixing the date for possession or suspending execution of the possession order (see the County Court Rules, Ord. 24, r. 11 and Ord. 25, r. 72); but the giving up of possession cannot normally be postponed for more than 14 days: see section 89(1) of the 1980 Act, discussed *supra*.

Thus the protection against eviction afforded to secure council tenants under the 1980 Act is much clearer and more wide-ranging than the pre-1980 Act protection, although only this latter protection can apply to those tenants who are not secure.

Notes

[1] See *infra*, pp. 162–3.

[2] See Chap. 2, *supra*.

[3] See *supra*, pp. 9–10.

[4] There is no restriction on the *tenant* ending the secure tenancy by surrendering it (see p. 87 *supra*), or serving notice to quit (see p. 34, *supra*); but the Act narrowly defines the ways in which the *council* can unilaterally end the tenancy.

[5] *cf.* s. 87(2), *infra*.

[6] See, *e.g.* Bridge L.J. in *Landau* v. *Sloane* [1980] 2 All E.R. 539, 545, (C.A.): "A trespasser who retains possession after an order for possession has been made against him during a postponement of the execution of the order is, of course, a character well known to the law" (reversed on appeal [1981] 1 All E.R. 705, (H.L.), though not on this point); *cf.* Waller L.J. in *Harrison's* case, *supra*, at p. 601.

[7] The general provisions in s. 146 of the Law of Property Act 1925 relating to restrictions on and relief against forfeiture (except s. 146(4), relating to the protection of sub-lessees) will also apply here: see s. 32(3) of the 1980 Act.

[8] But *cf.* D. Yates [1981] J.S.W.L. 129, 137; 225, 229–230.

[9] For an unenthusiastic appraisal of the effectiveness of the county courts as regards Rent Act security of tenure, from the unrepresented tenant's viewpoint, see M. Cutting (1976) LAG Bul. 101.

[10] See *infra*, pp. 163–4.

[11] The prescribed forms (in the Sched. to these regulations) state that the council must get a court order before the tenant can be evicted, and that he can get advice from a Citizens' Advice Bureau, Housing Aid Centre, Law Centre, or solicitor (if necessary with the help of legal aid, which should be more easily available now that the tenant is more likely to have a viable defence).

[12] See *supra*, p. 46.

[13] See, *e.g.*: s. 35(2), *supra*, p. 25; s. 81(2), *supra*, p. 120.

[14] See *supra*, pp. 109–110.

[15] The condition of the common parts may in an appropriate case be the council's responsibility: see pp. 104–6, *supra*.

[16] The tenant's implied repairing and maintenance obligations are discussed *supra*, at pp. 107–8; breach of the tenant's contractual obligations permits the council also to proceed under gd. 1, *supra*, but for the purposes of gds. 3 and 4 it is not necessary for the deterioration to

amount to such a breach: *cf. Lowe* v. *Lendrum* (1950) 156 E.G. 423, (C.A.).

[17] Which does not cover mere non-disclosure: *cp.* the "Kinsella" saga, reported in *The Guardian*, September 13–14, 20, 27, of 1979.

[18] See *supra*, p. 60.

[19] See *supra*, pp. 24–5.

[20] See *supra*, pp. 25–6; note also the specific reference to overcrowding in s. 36(1) (*supra*, at p. 26).

[21] For a discussion of the factors relating to "suitable alternative accommodation" for Rent Act purposes, much of which is also relevant to the definition in the Housing Act 1980, see A. Arden (1976) LAG Bul. 280, 281–2.

[22] The fact that the alternative accommodation is subject to a higher rent does not *of itself* render it unsuitable: *cf. Cresswell* v. *Hodgson* [1951] 1 All E.R. 710, (C.A.), a Rent Act case.

[23] *cp., e.g.* the Rent Act cases of *Redspring Ltd.* v. *Francis* [1973] 1 All E.R. 640, (C.A.), and *Siddiqui* v. *Rashid* [1980] 3 All E.R. 184, (C.A.).

[24] Thus the "character" of the accommodation, which (as has been seen) is excluded as a factor relating to "suitable accommodation," may nevertheless be considered as relevant to the issue of "reasonableness."

[25] See *supra*, pp. 28–31.

[26] *cp.* the exemption from the "right to buy" of certain old people's dwellings in Sched. 1, Pt. I, para. 4 (*infra*, p. 176).

[27] See *supra*, p. 29–31; thus if the tenant succeeded to the tenancy at common law before October 3, 1980, this ground will not apply.

[28] See *supra*, pp. 29–30.

[29] The prohibition against serving the notice within six months from the death is presumably for reasons of compassion, while the prohibition against serving it after 12 months from the death is no doubt intended to prevent hardship being caused to a successor who has "settled in" (see A. Arden, *The Housing Act 1980,* Current Law Statutes Reprints, notes to Sched. 4, gd.13). If an authority is going to be able to observe these time limits, it must have an efficient system of "diarying ahead."

[30] See *supra*, pp. 86–7.

[31] Postponement of the date of possession could be made indefinite, *e.g.* (as regards gd. 2) "provided no further nuisance occurs" (*cf. Yates* v. *Morris* [1950] 2 All E.R. 577, (C.A.)); and even an absolute possession order can subsequently be replaced by a postponed order at any time before actual execution (*cf. Birtwhistle* v. *Tweedale* (1954) 163 E.G. 4 (C.A.)).

[32] *e.g.* in cases of adjournment of the proceedings, or in respect of the period up until the date fixed for possession (see s. 32(1), *supra*).

[33] *i.e.* for the period between the date fixed for possession and the actual eviction of the tenant (where later): see s. 32(1), *supra*.

[34] It had been argued that even the "four to six weeks" rule was too short: M. Rowland (1976) LAG Bul. 109.

[35] See *supra*, p. 75.

[36] The anomalies of this decision as regards the private sector have now been removed by s. 75(3) of the 1980 Act.

[37] See Chap. 2, *supra*.

[38] These administrative law principles do not apparently apply to evictions by housing associations, even though they may be in receipt of public funds: *Peabody Housing Association Ltd.* v. *Green* [1979] J.S.W.L. 178, (C.A.).

[39] He is not required to raise these "administrative law" points via an action for judicial review in the High Court under R.S.C.O. 53: *Cannock Chase D.C.* v. *Kelly* [1978] 1 All E.R. 152, (C.A.).

[40] See *supra*, pp. 144–5.

[41] There have been some findings of maladministration concerning council evictions: see, *e.g.* Investigations 3917S, 1977, and 1094S, 1978.

[42] Criticised by A. Arden (1980) LAG Bul. 92.

[43] *cp.* the "secure licence" provisions in the H.A. 1980, s. 48 (*supra*, pp. 9–10).

[44] *cp.* the comments on one council's notice to quit (at a time when no such information was prescribed for local authorities) in *Homes Fit For Heroes, op. cit.*, at p. 45: "The notice . . . tells people that they must deliver up possession . . . in 28 days. There is nothing to explain that this is not what the document means, but that it is just the first stage in taking a tenant to court. . . . "

[45] See *supra*, p. 153.

[46] A demand for the payment of *rent* (as opposed to mesne profits) after expiry of a notice to quit, but prior to the granting of a possession order, will only create a new periodic tenancy if there is very clear evidence that this is the intention of the parties: see *supra*, p. 151.

Chapter 8

THE SALE OF COUNCIL HOUSES

1. *General*

The sale of council houses has long been a contentious matter, but the introduction by the Housing Act 1980 of a *right* for sitting council tenants to buy their houses and flats (with very attractive discounts) brought the various issues to a head; an analogy has indeed been drawn between the opposition of many Labour councillors to the "right to buy" and the strength of feeling which led to the famous revolt of councillors in Poplar during the 1920s (see B. Bronterre, *Roof,* January 1981, at p.30).

The topic of council house sales is not one on which supporters of the two major political parties necessarily take up the stances which might be expected (*i.e.* Conservatives favouring sale,[1] and Labour favouring retention): in 1976 Frank Field, a left-winger and formerly Director of both the Child Poverty Action Group and the Low Pay Unit, favoured the sale of council housing as constituting a "direct attack on the cycle of poverty" (*Do we need Council Houses?* C.H.A.S., 1976, p.16); and several Conservative councils have expressed misgivings at the width of the "right to buy" provisions in the 1980 Act (see S. Schifferes, *Roof,* November 1979, at p.184).

The quality of debate concerning the implications of the statutory "right to buy" has been very variable.[2] Public confidence in even the D.o.E.'s grasp of the fundamental issues was somewhat shaken by the department's production of two separate documents on the effects of council house sales, for successive Labour and Conservative governments, which gave very different analyses of the financial effects on local authorities (*The Financial Aspects of Sales of Council Houses,* 1978, indicating

168

long-term losses, and *Appraisal of the Financial Effects of Council House Sales,* 1979, indicating continuing gains: see further B. Kilroy, *Roof,* January 1980, at p.16, A. Murray, *Roof,* January 1981, at p.8).

Some of the wider issues concerning council house sales will now be discussed, albeit briefly.

(a) *The likely take-up of the "right to buy"*

To what extent are council tenants likely to avail themselves of the "right to buy"? It was estimated in 1977 by reference to the General Household Survey that although 68 per cent. of mortgaged accommodation consisted of detached or semi-detached houses, nearly two-thirds of the housing let by local authorities consisted of terraced houses or flats; and it was further suggested by reference to various local surveys that while many council tenants preferred the *idea* of owner-occupation to council renting, relatively few actually wanted to buy the council properties in which they were living, since the "ideal" purchase was generally seen to be that of a begardened semi in a good area: A. Murie, *Roof,* March 1977, at p.46 (some of these arguments had earlier been developed by A. Murie in *The Sale of Council Houses,* C.U.R.S., 1975).

Recent figures on council housing sales at least indicate that few *flats* will be sold: although the 1981 Second Report from the Environment Committee on *Council House Sales* (H.C. Paper 366–1) estimated at para. 161 that sales of dwellings under the "right to buy" would total around 100,000 a year,[3] of the 83,095 dwellings actually sold by councils in 1980 (*i.e.* before "right to buy" purchases began in earnest), only 1,640 flats were disposed of (see the statistics abstracted in *Roof,* July 1981, at p.8).

(b) *Who wins and who loses?*

It is generally assumed that, for a *sitting tenant* who wishes to buy his council dwelling, the exercise of the "right to buy" will prove a very wise investment. Certainly the discount from the market price (discussed later) is a powerful incentive, and although in the short term the buyer will probably have to pay more by way of mortgage instalments[4] (even after tax relief) than he would have paid in rent, before very long his mortgage repayments will diminish in real terms while the rent would have increased considerably.[5]

However, the prospective purchaser should bear in mind that economic recessions may cause, at worst, the loss of his job, or, less bad but still difficult, a change of job to another area and consequently the enforced repayment of some or all of the discount received on the original purchase if he is forced to sell within five years of that purchase.[6] It is also significant that the 1980 Act has no provision enabling tenants who purchase under the "right to buy," but who subsequently find that they cannot cope with the mortgage instalments, to elect as of right to "sell" their properties back to the council and resume their former status as council tenants in the same property. Once the mortgagee (normally the council itself) repossesses the property, permanent accommodation for the former purchaser and his family may have to be made available by the council under the Housing (Homeless Persons) Act 1977 (assuming "priority need"[7] and "unintentionality"[8]), but it would be miraculous indeed if this accommodation turns out to be the same property in respect of which he defaulted as mortgagor.

The position of *prospective council tenants* would appear to be much less rosy as regards the implications of the "right to buy." A sale of a council dwelling does not immediately reduce the council's stock available for reletting (since if the former tenant had not bought the house, he would still be living there). Nevertheless, when that former tenant comes to sell the property (which is likely to be the more desirable type of council dwelling), it will normally have ceased to have any connection with the council's stock, and is unlikely to be within the price-range open to those on waiting lists for council tenancies; whereas if the former tenant had remained such and had vacated the property, it would normally have been available for reletting to someone on the council's waiting list. Bearing in mind the current cuts in council house-building rates, the benefits of the "right to buy" will therefore largely accrue to present, rather than potential, council tenants, and considerable concern regarding the effect of sales on council waiting lists was expressed in the Second Report from the Environment Committee, *op. cit.*, at paras. 28–42.

Turning to the effects of sales on *local authorities*, where an authority provides the mortgage (as is likely to be the case with the majority of "right to buy" purchases), there will be no immediate substantial capital benefit to the authority (unless the purchaser chooses to bear a proportion of the price himself): the authority will obviously not go through the fatuous exercise of paying over as mortgagee its own money to itself as vendor; such mortgages will therefore neither increase the Public Sector Borrowing Requirement nor be debited against the council's Housing Investment Programme allocation, and are in essence "paper" transactions. However, the author-ity will of course receive interest on the mortgage loan, together with periodic repayments of principal[9] (which will increase as the end of the mortgage term approaches), and it will also generally be freed from having to pay the costs of repairing and maintaining the dwelling.[10] Never-theless, the authority will obviously lose the former rent income and any Exchequer subsidy relevant to the dwelling; and although, as noted earlier, the mortgage payments will normally exceed the rent for the first few years, eventually the time will arrive when the mortgage payments are less than the rent would have been (bearing particularly in mind the trend towards hefty increases in council rents). Moreover, even where immediate and substantial capital receipts are forthcoming (*e.g.* where the mortgage is granted by a building society or bank), councils are only allowed to benefit from *half* of such receipts under their Housing Investment Programme allocations for 1981–82. For more information regarding the ways in which a council may lose financially on sales, see A. Murie, *Roof,* May 1977, at p.76.

Quite apart from the general financial implications, authorities in rural areas are in particular danger of losing their better stock through enforced sales. As we shall see, there is some protection for rural authorities in the 1980 Act[11]; but this protection has been criticised for being quite insufficient (see the Second Report from the Environment Committee, *op. cit.*, at paras. 76–84).

What effects will sales have on the *central government*? It will receive, in effect, half of the profits realised by sales, since it will reduce the subsidies due to councils by equivalent amounts. However, where the dwelling is sold and remortgaged several times, the cost of tax relief on the mortgage payments of successive purchasers can soon exceed the Exchequer subsidy formerly payable on the property while it remained part of council stock, since that subsidy would have declined steadily in real terms over the years (see A. Murie, *Roof*, May 1977, at p.79).

(c) *Unwilling councils*

In view of the strength of feeling on the part of many councils against the "right to buy," it is not surprising that several weird and wonderful methods have been devised with a view to frustrating the exercise of this right.[12]

Starting with the "lunatic fringe," one council appears to have threatened potential purchasers that they would find some very undesirable neighbours allocated to the adjoining properties following completion[13]; arguably, such threats could amount to the criminal offence of harassment contrary to section 1(3) of the Protection from Eviction Act 1977, since they are "calculated to interfere with the peace or comfort of the residential occupier or members of his household," and are made "with intent to cause the residential occupier . . . to refrain from exercising any right . . . in respect of the premises."

Other potential claimants have been told that the council will carry out no further repairs on the property if they claim the "right to buy": this clearly cannot be acceptable in law, since (as we shall see) section 16(11) of the 1980 Act provides that where the "right to buy" is exercised, the secure tenancy only ends when the freehold or long lease is actually *granted,* so that the relevant repairing obligations[14] must apply until then. A variation on this theme was to tell tenants who wanted their houses modernised that the work would only be carried out if they agreed to sign a form relinquishing the "right to buy" for the next five years.[15] Now admittedly there is no general provision in the 1980 Act stating that the tenant cannot contract out of the "right to buy," whereas a general provision to this effect is included in section 23 of the Leasehold Reform Act 1967 relating to the enfranchisement rights of certain private sector long-leaseholders. Nevertheless, such contracting out would surely be held contrary to public policy, in the light of the cases establishing that it is not possible to contract out of the Rent Acts (see, *e.g. Barton* v. *Fincham* [1921] 2 K.B. 291, (C.A.), *Brown* v. *Draper* [1944] K.B. 309, (C.A.); see also *Johnson* v. *Moreton* [1978] 3 All E.R. 37, (H.L.), where a similar decision was reached concerning the Agricultural Holdings Act 1948).

The most common complaint against councils levelled by tenants wanting to exercise the "right to buy" seems however to be one of simple delay. We shall see that there do not appear to be any effective *general* loopholes in the "right to buy" provisions (and although there are some *specific* exemptions, these have been quite tightly drafted). We shall further see that in cases of excessive delay the tenant may have his own private remedies, and the Minister can exercise very wide default powers.

Thus pending any change of (central) government,

councils are having to live with the "right to buy,"
however distasteful some may find it.

2. *Sales Under the "Right to Buy"*

Having considered some of the wider implications regarding the sale of council housing, we can now turn to the
detailed legal machinery whereby the "right to buy" has
been conferred. The importance of the "right to buy"
provisions to the government's general housing strategy is
reflected in the fact that the relevant sections of the 1980
Act (ss.1–27) precede even the key definition of a "secure
tenancy" (in s.28), on which the "right to buy" depends.

(a) *Qualifying for the "right to buy"*

(i) The general conditions

The right to buy is conferred by the Housing Act 1980
on certain sitting council (and other public sector) tenants.
It is a right to purchase the *freehold*[16] of the tenant's
"house," or a *long lease* (normally for at least 125 years)
of the tenant's "flat," and there is also the right to a
mortgage from the council covering the whole or part of
the price (s.1(1) and Sched. 2, Pt. III, para. 11). The
definition of "house" in section 3(2) covers detached,
semi-detached and terraced dwellings, but excludes both a
dwelling formed by horizontal division of a building, and a
dwelling of which a material part lies above or below the
remainder of the structure to which it is attached (thus,
e.g. council maisonettes built over a parade of shops
would not be "houses" for this purpose). Any dwelling
which is not a "house" within this definition is treated as a
"flat" (s.3(3)). Land let together with a dwelling is to be
treated as part of the dwelling, unless that land is
agricultural and exceeds two acres (s.50(2) (*b*), incorporated into the right to buy provisions by s.27(1)); thus for
example garages which are some distance from the

dwelling, but which are let (or licensed: s.48(1)) to the tenant, may be included in the "right to buy." Further, the parties can *agree* to include as part of the dwelling *any* other land used for the purpose of that dwelling (s.3(4)).

Only a *secure* tenant[17] can enjoy the right to buy and the right to a mortgage (s.1(1)). The rights can normally only arise after the secure tenant has been such for not less than three years, or for periods totalling not less than three years. But periods spent as a secure tenant of a different public landlord (not necessarily another council),[18] or in a different public sector dwelling, are also normally to be counted (s.1(3)), as is occupation preceding October 3, 1980, which would have been under a secure tenancy if the Housing Act 1980 had then been in force (s.27(3)). In the case of joint tenants, the three years' residence requirement needs only to be satisfied by *one* of the tenants (s.1(4)).

Further, where the secure tenant became such on the death of his or her *spouse,* and at the time of the death they occupied the same property as their only or principal home, then any period during which the dead spouse was a secure tenant must normally be counted towards the current secure tenant's entitlement (s.1(5)); and where the secure tenant became such following the death of his or her *parent* (or otherwise upon the parent ceasing to be a secure tenant, *e.g.* following assignment,[19] or a surrender of the secure tenancy by the parent and the grant by the authority of a new secure tenancy to the child), the authority *may* count certain periods during which, since reaching 16, that child[20] occupied a dwelling of which his or her parent was a secure tenant (s.15).

However, the same "clocking-up" residence period cannot be used for more than one purchase (s.1(6)–(7)).

(ii) The excluded categories

There are certain exceptional cases where the statutory rights *do not arise even where the tenant is a secure tenant who has "clocked-up" the three years' residence requirement*; those relevant to council tenants are as follows:

—Where the landlord does not own the freehold (s.2(3)). The requirement in section 104 of the Housing Act 1957 for Ministerial consent for certain disposals of council property[21] prevents authorities from attracting this exemption by the simple expedient of disposing of their stock on a "sale and lease-back" basis (see also ss.91 and 137 of the 1980 Act[21]). Tenants within council *management* co-operatives[22] can normally enjoy the right to buy, since the landlord will be the council, which will retain the freehold.

—Where the council holds the dwelling other than under Part V of the Housing Act 1957 (*i.e.* other than under its normal housing powers), *unless* the Minister otherwise orders (s.2(5) and Sched.1, Pt. I, para. 1: this exemption would cover properties held by the council under, *e.g.* a local Act or a charitable trust deed).

—Where the dwelling has unusual features which are designed for the physically disabled (Sched. 1, Pt. I, para.3).

—Where the dwelling is one of a *group* usually let to pensioners and a social service or special facilities (*sic*) are provided nearby for the occupants (Sched. 1, Pt. I, para. 4: thus "sheltered" housing—which constitutes about 250,000 council dwellings—is exempt from the right to buy).

—Where the Minister, on application by the council made within six weeks of it receiving a notice claiming the right to buy,[23] considers that the dwelling is designed or specially adapted for pensioners *and* that it is the council's practice to let it only for occupation by pensioners (Sched. 1, Pt. I, para. 5: this exemption is therefore concerned with *individual* old people's dwellings, not forming part of a group within a "sheltered" housing scheme; see also D.o.E.

Circular no. 82/69 on *Housing Standards and Costs—Accommodation Specially Designed for Old People* (1969), especially the "check list" in App. VI). The six weeks' time limit here does not relate very well to the four weeks' period within which a council must normally respond to a tenant's claim to buy (s.5, *infra*): in such a case, the right to buy will have to be denied in the council's response to the tenant, on the assumption that the Minister will uphold the council's view of the relevant circumstances.

Further, the rights, even though they have *arisen*, cannot be *exercised* where a court order for possession has been made under which the tenant is *obliged* to give up possession (as opposed to an order suspended on conditions), or where the potential purchaser or one of them is (in effect) bankrupt (Sched. 1, Pt. II, paras. 1–2); and the council is not bound to complete the transaction if the tenant has incurred at least four weeks' arrears of rent (or other payments due from him as tenant, *e.g.* service charges), which have not been fully paid off (s.16(9)).

(b) *The price*

The purchase price is normally[24] the market value at the time when the tenant serves his initial notice (under s.5, *infra*), *less* the relevant discount (ss.3(5), 6(1)–(2)). The valuation is on a vacant possession basis (thus ignoring the fact that *ex hypothesi* there is a sitting tenant, which would normally depress the price), and on the assumption that neither the tenant nor a member of his family (*cf.* s.50 (3)) wishes to buy (the occupier's willingness to buy would otherwise tend to increase the price): section 6(2)–(4); further, it is necessary to disregard improvements made by, or failure to repair internally by, the tenant and certain other specified persons (s.6(2), (5)).

The discount increases with the period of residence: it is 33 per cent. of the value where the relevant occupation periods (prior to the service of the tenant's initial notice:

s.7(5)) total less than four years, but it rises by one per cent. for each "clocking-up" year thereafter, to a maximum of 50 per cent. (*i.e.* after 20 years' occupation): section 7(1). However, the discount must not exceed £25,000 (s.7(4) and S.I. 1980/1342)[25]; nor must the discount reduce the price below such of the post-March 31, 1974 (*i.e.* post-local government reorganisation) costs of the dwelling (relating to building, improving, etc.) as the Minister determines, so that properties built in recent years and at very high cost may attract little or no discount (s.7(2)–(3): see the Housing (Local Authorities and New Towns) (Cost Floor) Determination 1980, contained in Annex 1 to the Ministerial Letter dated October 2, 1980, which allows the authority's chief financial officer to certify the appropriate costs). If the market value is already below the amount of these costs, there is no discount (s.7(2)).

The relevant "clocking-up" periods for discount purposes are much wider than the eligible periods for basic right to buy purposes (*supra*): thus not only are periods spent as a secure tenant of a different public landlord or in a different public sector dwelling normally to be counted (s.7(6)), but also certain periods of occupation spent in armed forces accommodation (s.7(5)(*b*), 7(6)(*d*)). Further, the tenant can "clock-up" not only his or her *own* periods spent as a secure tenant, but also (subject to certain joint occupation requirements) periods when his or her *spouse or deceased spouse* was *either a secure tenant or the spouse of a secure tenant* (s.7(5)(*a*), 7(6)(*a*)–(*c*)); and where the secure tenant becomes such upon his or her parent ceasing to be a secure tenant, the authority *may* count for discount purposes certain periods during which, since reaching 16, that child[26] occupied a dwelling of which the *parent* was the secure tenant (s.15).

However, a "clocking-up" period of residence cannot be used for more than one purchase (s.7(8)–(9)); and where joint tenants are exercising the right to buy, the discount will be based on the *longest* of their respective periods of tenancy (s.7(7)): thus the respective periods cannot be aggregated in order to push up the discount.

Where a discount is given, stamp duty will be assessed by reference to the *discounted* price rather than the market value, provided that the conveyance or long lease is executed on or after March 23, 1981 (see the Finance Act 1981, s.107); thus where the *discounted* price does not exceed £20,000, no duty is payable.

If the dwelling is further disposed of (by way of conveyance,[27] assignment, or grant of a lease exceeding 21 years other than at a rack rent, but *excluding*[28] disposals in pursuance of an order under section 24 of the Matrimonial Causes Act 1973[29] or under section 2 of the Inheritance (Provision for Family and Dependants) Act 1975 or a vesting in a beneficiary under a will or intestacy[30]), and this "disposal" takes place *within five years from the original conveyance*[27] *or long lease,* then, pursuant to a covenant which the council has to include in the original conveyance or long lease, the former secure tenant *and his successors in title* must repay on demand[31] the discount, or a percentage thereof, on a sliding scale reducing by 20 per cent. for each complete year since the original conveyance or long lease (s.8(1)–(3)). Thus, contrary to the common law rule, this is a positive covenant which can bind successors in title where the discount falls to be repaid.[32]

This liability to repay the discount on a premature disposal only arises on the first relevant (*i.e.* non-exempt) transaction, but the liability is treated as a charge by deed by way of legal mortgage, having priority immediately after any prescribed mortgage granted to enable the tenant to exercise his right to buy (s.8(4)); and the liability is a land charge within section 59 of the Land Registration Act 1925 (s.8(6): thus registration will be by notice or caution, and there is no need for separate registration as a charge or for the issue of a separate charge certificate; it will be seen that the title must always be registered following a right to buy transaction, even if it was not previously registered). For a more detailed discussion of the discount-repayment provisions in section 8, see P. Matthews (1981) 131 N.L.J. 816, *Law Society's Gazette*, October 14, 1981, at p. 1126.

Authorities are *not* generally permitted to insert *pre-emption clauses* covering early disposals (*i.e.* provisions enabling the authority to purchase the property if the owner seeks to sell within a specified period): we shall see that such clauses can now only be inserted in very exceptional circumstances.

(c) *The purchase procedure*

The secure tenant must first serve[33] on the council a written notice, in a prescribed form, claiming the right to buy (ss.5, 22; S.I. 1980/1391). The form is not an "easy read": it is eight pages long, plus 10 pages of notes for guidance as to its completion; in view of the form's complexity, and since the authority would presumably be entitled to reject a form which was incorrect in a material particular, the tenant would be well advised to seek informed guidance before completing it.

The notice can be withdrawn by the tenant "at any time" (s.5(3)). After the notice has been given, then if a new tenant takes over the secure tenancy (*cf.* ss.30, 37), he will be in the same position as if *he* had given the notice himself and had been the secure tenant at the time it was given: thus he must qualify in the normal way, and cannot take over the former tenant's eligibility to buy or discount entitlement as such, but he has a separate right to a mortgage (s.13(1)–(3)).

In the case of joint tenants, the right to buy and the right to a mortgage prima facie belong to all of them jointly, but one or more can exercise the rights with the *agreement* of the others (s.4(1)); thus one joint tenant cannot force the other joint tenant(s) to buy, and where only one (or some) of the joint tenants does purchase by agreement, then (although the *secure tenancy* will end on completion of the purchase under s.16(11)), he (or they) will normally hold the legal estate on trust for himself (or themselves) *and the other joint tenants,* in accordance with the general rule in *Keech* v. *Sandford* (1726) 2 Eq. Cas. Abr. 741 (as interpreted in *Protheroe* v. *Protheroe* [1968] 1 All E.R. 1111, (C.A.); see also the Law of Property Act 1925, s.36(1)).

Further, the secure tenant can require in his section 5 notice that not more than three "members of his family"[34] who are not joint tenants but occupy the dwelling should share the right to buy and the right to a mortgage with him, in which case they are thereafter treated as joint tenants (s.4(2)–(3): in order for non-spouse family members to qualify for inclusion, they must satisfy a 12 months' residence requirement unless the council consents to dispense with this); even an *infant* family member can apparently be included, which might be useful if he is already a high earner, thus swelling the mortgage entitlement (*infra*): in such a case the legal estate must be vested in the adults alone, who will hold it on trust for sale for themselves and the infant (*cf.* s.19(2) of the Law of Property Act 1925). A person who *contributes* financially to the purchase but is *not* added as a joint tenant under this provision may nevertheless acquire an equitable entitlement by virtue of his contribution (even if he is not a family member), which if supported by occupation may have priority as an overriding interest under section 70(1)(*g*) of the Land Registration Act 1925 even over the council's mortgage: *cf. Williams and Glyn's Bank Ltd.* v. *Boland* [1980] 2 All E.R. 408, (H.L.).

Following service of the initial section 5 notice by the tenant, the council has *four weeks* to serve on him a written notice (prescribed by S.I. 1980/1391) admitting or denying (with reasons) the tenant's right (s.5(1)), extendable to eight weeks where for part of the qualifying period the landlord was not the council on which the tenant's notice is served[35] (s.5(1)–(2)). We shall hereafter call this notice from the council the "first response notice."

Once the tenant's right has been established, whether

by the council's acceptance or as a result of a county court's decision (*cf.* s.86(1)–(2)), the council must serve "as soon as practicable" a second notice on the tenant pursuant to section 10, stating the price and the terms, and telling him (*inter alia*) of his right to a mortgage (a form must be included for claiming this), his right to a valuation from the district valuer (*infra*), and his right to defer completion (*infra*). We shall hereafter describe this section 10 notice as the "second response notice."

Within (normally) three months of service of the council's second response notice, the tenant can elect to have the value decided by the district valuer (an officer appointed by the Commissioners of Inland Revenue: *cf.* s.27(2)), whose decision is final (ss.11(1), 86(1)). An authority looking for ways to delay the tenant's claim might be tempted to pitch the price unrealistically high, thus forcing him to refer the matter to the district valuer.

Where the title to the land has not already been registered at H.M. Land Registry, a streamlined conveyancing procedure is prescribed by section 20, under which first registration of the title must be effected even if the dwelling is outside an area within which registration has been prescribed as compulsory under section 120 of the Land Registration Act 1925 (see s.20(1) of the 1980 Act)[36]; in such a case, the council must give the tenant a prescribed certificate (form RB1 for freeholds or form RB2 for leaseholds) as to the title, which the Chief Land Registrar must accept as sufficient evidence for registration purposes (s.20(2)–(4)), although the council will be liable to indemnify the Registrar against subsequent claims (s.20(4); and *cf.* the Land Registration Act 1925, s.83(9)–(10)).

As soon as all relevant matters have been decided, the council must normally make the necessary grant (of the freehold or long lease) to the tenant (unless he has rent arrears of four weeks or more: s.16(9), *supra*); and this duty is enforceable by injunction in the county court (ss.16(1), (10), 86(1)). On the conveyance of the freehold or the grant of the long lease, the secure tenancy ends, but the rights and liabilities of any subtenants are expressly preserved (s.16(11)). If it is the *tenant* who fails to complete, the council may serve a notice requiring him to complete within not less than 28 days (s.16(2)). This completion notice can only be served on the expiration of the relevant time limit (s.16(3)), which depends on whether the tenant has claimed the right to a mortgage, and if so whether he is entitled to defer completion: if no claim to a mortgage has been made, the completion notice can be served, in effect, six months after service of the council's second response notice; the position concerning completion notices where the right to a mortgage is claimed, and where completion is deferred, will be dealt with later. If the tenant fails to comply with the completion notice (and he is deemed by s.16(9) not to comply while rent arrears are outstanding), then his right to buy lapses for one year (s.16(6)); but he is under no further liability, since the transaction is not contractual in nature (see s.5(3)): thus there is no question of either an equitable claim against him for specific performance, or a common law claim for damages in respect of his failure to complete (*cp., e.g. Raineri* v. *Miles* [1980] 2 All E.R. 145, (H.L.), and the Leasehold Reform Act 1967, s.5(3) of which expressly confers "the like rights and remedies as in the case of a contract freely entered into").

The county court has jurisdiction over *any* question concerning the right to buy other than the price, even if no other relief is sought than a bare declaration (s.86(1)–(2)).

(d) *The terms of the purchase other than the price*

(i) General

The 1980 Act contains very detailed provisions concerning the terms of the conveyance or long lease, designed principally to preserve certain rights for (respectively) the council, the former secure tenant, and neighbouring occupiers (see s.17 and Sched. 2; for precedents of standard conveyances of houses or long leases of flats pursuant to the right to buy, see, *e.g.* The Conveyancer and Property Lawyer, *Precedents for the Conveyancer,* Forms 16–38 and 5–73 respectively). A detailed conveyancing critique of the relevant provisions was produced by J.E. Adams in [1981] Conv. 92, 171. What follows is merely an attempt to draw attention to some of the more important terms governing right to buy transactions.

(ii) Long leases of flats

As regards the grant of a long lease of a flat, the ground rent cannot exceed £10 per year (Sched. 2, Pt. III, para. 11(1)), so that it is probably not possible for service charges to be reserved in the form of *rent,* as opposed to a mere covenant to pay the charges.

Special provisions govern liability for the condition of the flat, which are likely to prove very important in practice: unless the county court otherwise orders with the consent of the parties, the *council* retains *liability* for: repairing the structure and exterior of the flat and the building in which it is situated[37]; making good any defect affecting that structure[38]; repairing any other property in respect of which the tenant has rights; maintaining so far as practicable those services to which the tenant is entitled (whether alone or with others)[39], and repairing installations connected with the provision of those services; while the *tenant* covenants to repair and decorate the interior, subject to contrary agreement (Sched. 2, Pt. III, paras. 13–14). Nevertheless, the council may stipulate for the *recovery from the tenant* of a reasonable part of the *costs* of: non-structural repairs; structural repairs where either the defects were notified by the council to the tenant prior ιο the granting of the long lease, or the council did not become aware of them earlier than ten years after that grant; and the maintenance of services and the repair of installations connected with the provision of those services (Sched. 2, Pt.III, paras. 15–17).

Where the tenant pays such a "service charge" in respect of services, repairs, maintenance, etc., then the general provisions in Schedule 19 of the 1980 Act will be relevant, whereby (*inter alia*) the county court can pronounce on the reasonableness of the charges (see Sched. 19, paras. 3, 12 and 14(1)). The service charges initially imposed by some councils are likely to be quite high:in Sheffield, for example, the housing department calculated that a typical two-bedroom flat with district heating, a caretaker, and other services, would attract a charge of £495 per year payable in advance by two instalments (*Sheffield Telegraph,* August 22, 1981).

The imposition of any restriction on the tenant against assignment or subletting is void (Sched. 2, Pt. III, para.15).

(iii) Defects in title

Turning to liabilities which already affect the title, the purchasing secure tenant (whether he is acquiring the freehold or a long lease) is of course bound according to the normal rules by pre-existing *non-financial interests* of third parties such as easements and restrictive covenants (*cf.* Sched. 2, Pt. I, paras. 2–4). However, he will automatically take free of all pre-existing *financial charges* on the council's title (such as mortgages, liens, etc.), save for rentcharges where he is acquiring the freehold (Sched. 2, Pt. IV, paras. 18–19); the council's personal liability regarding the obligations which the charges were designed to secure is of course preserved (see para.18).

(iv) Discount repayment clauses

Where a discount from the price has been given, it will be recalled that the conveyance or long lease *must* contain a covenant binding the tenant and his successors to repay the discount or part thereof on certain premature disposals (s. 8, discussed *supra*).

(v) Disposals in special areas: restrictive covenants and pre-emption clauses

In the case of properties in certain special areas, the conveyance or long lease *may* contain additional stipulations designed to avoid the disappearance of low-priced housing for rent. By section 19, where the dwelling is in a National Park, or an area designated as one of outstanding natural beauty (under s.87 of the National Parks and Access to the Countryside Act 1949), or an area designated by the Minister as a rural area (see S.I. 1980/1375, S.I. 1981/397, S.I. 1981/940), then the conveyance or long lease *may* contain a restrictive covenant on the part of the purchaser that until such time as may be specified by the council there will be no further "disposal" (*i.e.* conveyance, assignment, or grant of a lease for more than 21 years other than at a rack rent, but *excluding* disposals in pursuance of an order under s.24 of the Matrimonial Causes Act 1973[40] or under s.2 of the Inheritance (Provision for Family and Dependants) Act 1975 or a vesting in a beneficiary under a will or intestacy[41]), by either the purchaser or his successors in title, without the written consent of the council (s.19(1)–(2), (8)); but that consent must not be withheld if the disposal is to someone who for the previous three years lived or worked in a region designated by the Minister, which region or part of which region is comprised in the National Park or area concerned (s.19(2)–(3), (12); S.I. 1980/1345, S.I. 1980/ 1375, S.I. 1981/940).

However, with the Minister's consent,[42] then as an alternative to the restrictive covenant in section 19(2), the council may insert a pre-emption clause to the effect that for 10 years the purchaser and his successors shall make no further "disposal" unless he or his successor has first offered to reconvey the dwelling or surrender the long lease to the council for the then market value (reduced by the appropriate figure representing repayment of discount if the disposal takes place during the first five years), and the council has refused the offer or has failed to accept it within one month (s.19(4), (6)–(7)). Only in this very limited situation, therefore, can a pre-emption clause be inserted.

Any disposal in breach of the restrictive covenant or the right of pre-emption is void (s.19(9)). The restrictive covenant is treated as a local land charge, but the Chief Land Registrar must enter the appropriate restriction on the register of title (s.19(10): thus the covenant cannot constitute an overriding interest under s. 70(1)(i) of the Land Registration Act 1925). It is not clear how the right of pre-emption may be protected, since section 19(10) refers back to section 19(2) and not expressly to section 19(4) (which deals with the right of pre-emption): but arguably, since section 19(4) is designed to "replace" section 19(2) where appropriate, the protection specified in section 19(10) is available; and although it was held in *Pritchard* v. *Briggs* [1980] 1 All E.R. 294, (C.A.), that a right of pre-emption does not as such create an interest in land, it appears that this decision cannot affect the enforceability of the right of pre-emption in section 19, since the section expressly makes this binding on successors in title: see *First National Securities Ltd.* v. *Chiltern D.C.* [1975] 2 All E.R. 766, and *Hansard* (Commons) April 3, 1980, Vol.982, col. *338.*

(vi) Conveyancing costs

Finally as regards the terms of the purchase, the secure tenant cannot be forced to pay the council's costs of the conveyance or long lease (s.21(1)); but he can be required to pay the council's costs of providing a *mortgage,* so long as these costs do not exceed £50 (s.21(2); S.I. 1980/1390).

(e) *The right to a mortgage*

We have seen that a secure council tenant who has the right to buy, also has the right to a mortgage from the council (s.1(1)); this right, the details of which will now be examined, does *not* depend on a prior building society refusal (*cp.* the Tenants' Rights, etc. (Scotland) Act 1980, s.5(2)(*b*)(iv)).

(i) The amount

The amount of the mortgage will basically be the purchase price, plus the council's costs of providing the mortgage up to a maximum of £50 (a figure which many authorities consider to be inadequate), together with such of the secure tenant's costs which the council agrees to pay for him, if any (ss.9(1), 21(2); S.I. 1980/1390). But there is *no obligation* on the council to provide a mortgage exceeding a specified multiple of the secure tenant's "available annual income" (or of the combined incomes of joint purchasers: ss.4(1)–(3), 9(3)), as prescribed by the Minister (s.9(2)–(5)).

The relevant regulations (in S.I. 1980/1423) include within the term "annual income" not merely income from employment or business, but also long-term State benefits (*e.g.* retirement benefits, invalidity benefits, widow's benefits, and disability benefits), although short-term State benefits are excluded (such as unemployment or sickness benefits, supplementary benefit, and family income supplement). From the "annual income," certain prescribed deductions have to be made for long-term commitments (in the form of maintenance payments and payments under credit agreements or court orders), in order to arrive at the "*available* annual income." Having ascertained this figure, the prescribed multiple for the "principal earner" depends on his age when the initial section 5 notice is served: the multiple is 2.5 if he is then under 60, 2.0 if he is then between 60 and 64, and 1.0 if he is then 65 or over; for the other purchasers who are the non-principal earners (assuming a joint purchase), the multiple for their "available annual incomes" will be 1.0. It can be seen that those approaching or above retiring age will get a much better deal from the council than they could normally expect from a building society or bank: a council tenant aged 60 with a bad record of rent payments and terminal cancer can demand a mortgage from the authority amounting to twice his "available annual income." Yet the Minister stated that the prescribed multiple would be based on "normal commercial practice"! (see *Hansard* (Commons) January 15, 1980, Vol. 976, col. 1447).

(ii) The mortgage procedure

The secure tenant must normally claim the right to a mortgage by serving written notice on the council in a prescribed form (which is six pages long, with four additional pages of explanatory material), not later than three months from the council's second response notice under section 10 (*supra*): see section 12(1), (3), and S.I. 1980/1465; but the council must, on reasonable grounds being shown, extend this period, failing which the county court can do so (s.12(2)). "As soon as practicable" after service of this notice by the tenant, the council must give him notice of the amount of the mortgage, how this figure has been arrived at, and the terms of the mortgage (s.12(4)); the council must further include with this notice a form whereby the tenant can claim to defer completion (*infra*), and must inform him of his right, on deferring completion, to serve a new notice claiming a mortgage (*infra*): section 12(5).

If the tenant, having claimed a mortgage, is not entitled to defer completion (*infra*), the council can serve a completion notice (*supra*) after three months have passed since its notice under section 12(4) (*supra*) was served: see section 16(3).

Where the tenant claims a mortgage and the amount to

which he is entitled is *less* than the aggregate of the price and the council's allowable mortgage costs (*supra*), he may defer completion if within three months (extendable by the council or the county court) of service of the council's notice under section 12(4) (*supra*), he serves notice on the council claiming to defer completion and deposits £100 (s.16(4)–(5)). He may then, at any time before service of a completion notice on him (*infra*), serve a further section 12(1) notice claiming a mortgage, which could result in a higher mortgage being offered, for example where he has since changed to a better-paid job (s.16(8)); the "information" provisions in section 12(4) (*supra*) will then apply again, though apparently he cannot defer completion a *second* time, since section 12(5) (*supra*) does not on this occasion apply (see s.16(8)).

Where completion is thus deferred, the council can only serve a completion notice on the tenant once two years have elapsed from the tenant's initial section 5 notice claiming the right to buy, or, *if later,* three months after service of any notice from the council under section 12(4)(*supra*): section 16(3). Further, it is important to appreciate that the price remains frozen throughout at the valuation figure as at service of the tenant's original section 5 notice (ss.3(5), 6(1)), which can constitute a real bargain for the tenant *if* house prices are rising. Failure by the tenant to comply with such a completion notice, however, causes a lapse of the right to buy for one year (s.16(6)), although the £100 "deposit" must be returned to him (s.16(7)(*b*)). If the deferred transaction is duly completed, then the £100 is treated as having been paid towards the price (s.16(7)(*a*)).

(iii) The terms of the mortgage other than the amount

The length of the mortgage term must normally be 25 years, or at the mortgagor's option a shorter period, but it may be subsequently extended by the council (s.18). Repayment must be made by way of instalments of capital and interest combined (s.18). The rate of interest must (in effect) be the *higher* of the cost of the council's own borrowing plus ¼ per cent., or the rate recommended by the Building Societies' Association (s.110(3)–(6)); since council mortgagors could therefore be paying *more* than mortgagors of building societies, this provides some incentive for a secure tenant to seek a mortgage from the private sector in preference to exercising his right to demand one from the council. There are detailed provisions for adjusting the rate of interest (s.110(3), (6)–(9)): note particularly that under section 110(9) the authority must in effect reduce the periodic payments where the interest rate itself is reduced, but if the interest rate is increased, the authority can extend the mortgage term under section 18 instead of varying the periodic payments.

Although the Act does not provide expressly for the imposition by council mortgagees of restrictions on the letting of the property by the mortgagor, such as are common in building society mortgage deeds (*cf.* the Law of Property Act 1925, s.99(13)), the parties are nevertheless permitted to agree upon the inclusion of such a term, failing which the county court can require its insertion (s.18; *cp.* the embargo on impediments to subletting contained in Sched. 2, Pt. III, para. 15, *supra,* which only relates to a long lease granted under the right to buy and not to any mortgage needed for its acquisition).

(f) *Enforcing the right to buy and the right to a mortgage*

The Act specifically provides that the duty of the council to *complete* the transaction (*i.e.* after the right to buy has been established) is enforceable by injunction (s.16(10)), and that the county court has general jurisdiction over all right to buy matters (other than the price: *cf.* s.11(1)), including the power to make a bare declaration (s.86(1)–(2)). We have seen that the tenant's rights stem from the statute and not from any contract as such (although a change of public landlord after the tenant has exercised the right to buy cannot adversely affect the tenant, despite the absence of any provision in the Housing Act for registering anything resembling an "estate contract" under the Land Charges Act 1972 or the Land Registration Act 1925: see s.14 of the 1980 Act). Nevertheless, the tenant should be able to enforce the right to buy and right to a mortgage (which are duties owed by the council to him as an *individual*) by way of a tortious action for breach of statutory duty, and thereby obtain damages in an appropriate case (*cf. Thornton* v. *Kirklees M.B.C.* [1979] 2 All E.R. 349, (C.A.), holding that such an action lay at the hands of the individual against an authority in breach of the Housing (Homeless Persons) Act 1977); although the Housing Act (unlike, *e.g.* the Housing (Homeless Persons Act) specifically provides for Ministerial intervention (*infra*), this would not exclude other remedies, since section 86 expressly contemplates their availability (*cp.*: *L.B. of Southwark* v. *Williams* [1971] 2 All E.R. 175, (C.A.); *Wyatt* v. *L.B. of Hillingdon* [1979] J.S.W.L. 109, (C.A.); *Meade* v. *Haringey B.C.* [1979] 2 All E.R. 1016, (C.A.)).

The aggrieved tenant may perhaps have an alternative remedy by way of mandamus in the High Court, via a claim for judicial review under the Rules of the Supreme Court, Ord. 53 (in such a case, the prohibition in s.86(3) on the recovery of any costs where the proceedings "could have [been] taken in the county court" would not apply, since mandamus is not obtainable in the county court).

Quite apart from any individual remedies which may be open to the secure tenant, the Minister has very wide powers of intervention where it appears to him that "tenants generally, or a tenant or tenants of a particular landlord, or tenants of a description of landlords have or may have difficulty in exercising the right to buy effectively and expeditiously" (s.23). These powers (which relate) to the right to a mortgage as well as the right to buy: s.23(3), (11)) can culminate in the Minister's execution of a "vesting order" conveying the freehold or long lease to the tenant, and the conveyance or lease has effect as if it had been duly executed by the council (s.24); the Minister can recover all his costs from the council, if necessary by withholding money otherwise due to it, for example by way of subsidy (s.23(9)–(10)). Further, the Minister can order the council to produce documents or supply information, and can even order *individual officers* of the council to do so "without instructions from [the council]" (s.23(5): failure by the officer to carry out such an order would give the Minister the right to obtain an order of mandamus from the High Court against that officer, and could ultimately lead to his imprisonment for contempt of court).

An individual tenant can ask the Minister to intervene by initially contacting the appropriate Regional Office of the D.o.E. However, the Minister has stated that he regards sections 23 and 24 as "reserve" powers, which he will only use against councils guilty of "illegal behaviour or deliberate delaying tactics" (*Hansard* (Commons) January 15, 1980, Vol. 976, col. 1447). Nevertheless, in 1981 he proceeded against Norwich City Council under section 23, and the council's attempt to quash his decision by seeking an order of certiorari was unsuccessful: see *R.* v. *Secretary of State for the Environment, ex p. Norwich C.C., The Times,* February 10, 1982, (C.A.).

Where individual councillors have deliberately obstructed the right to buy, the aggrieved tenant should bear in mind that the district auditor may be able to authorise the levy of a surcharge upon them in respect of any "loss . . . or deficiency" suffered by the authority due to their "wilful misconduct," pursuant to section 161(4) of the Local Government Act 1972 (*cf. Asher* v. *Lacey* [1973] 3 All E.R. 1008, (D.C.)); the tenant in his capacity of local government elector can make the initial objection to the district auditor under section 159(3) of the Local Government Act. However, whether the suppression of council house sales in fact involves an authority in a "loss . . . or deficiency" raises some controversial issues.[43]

3. *Sales Outside the "Right to Buy"*

(a) *General ministerial consents to sales*

Council tenants who are excluded from the right to buy (either because they are not secure tenants[44] or because they fall within one of the categories which are specifically excluded from the right to buy[45]), and those who are not council tenants but who wish to buy council dwellings, may be able to do so through the exercise by councils of their powers of disposal contained in the new section 104 of the Housing Act 1957, as substituted by section 91 of the 1980 Act.

Ministerial consent is required for all disposals, *save for* sales under the right to buy, and lettings on secure tenancies or on what would be secure tenancies if they did not fall within one of the exemptions in Schedule 3 to the 1980 Act[46] (other than the "long tenancy" exemption in para. 1 of Sched. 3)[47]: see sections 104(1)–(3) and 104A of the 1957 Act. However, general consents have been given by way of a Ministerial Letter dated June 2, 1981 (on *Sales of Council Houses and Flats and Disposal of Housing Land*), permitting councils to sell *vacant* houses and flats at discounts of up to 30 per cent. to specified priority groups of buyers, including homeless persons, first-time buyers, and job movers (Annex A, General Consent B(2), (5), and App. 2); this Ministerial Letter also permits councils to sell dwellings to most *sitting council tenants* (even though they are excluded from the right to buy), with similar discounts to those available under the right to buy (*op. cit.*, Annex A, General Consent B(1), (4), and App. 1). Further, consent is given to sales, *other than through the procedure prescribed in sections 1–27 of the 1980 Act* (*supra*), to tenants *with the right to buy, provided* that the terms offered are at least as good as those the tenant would get if he exercised the right to buy (*op. cit.*, Annex A, General Consents A and C); and with the *consent* of a secure tenant *who has the right to buy,* the authority may even *transfer his entitlement to discount* from a *flat or prefab* of which he is secure tenant to a *vacant* dwelling which he prefers to buy instead, though he is of course entitled to insist on purchasing his present dwelling if he wises (*op. cit.*, Annex A, General Consent B(6)).

Provisions for repayment of discount[48] (where appropriate) *must* be inserted in the deed (see s.104B of the 1957 Act and the 1981 Ministerial Letter, *op. cit.*, Annex A, General Consent B(4)–(5)). Restrictive covenants or pre-emption clauses relating to further disposals *may* be inserted where the dwelling is in a National Park, area of outstanding natural beauty, or designated rural area (see ss.104(6)(*b*), 104C of the 1957 Act, and the 1981 Ministerial Letter, *op. cit.*, Annex A, General Consent B(12)); and pre-emption clauses *may* also be inserted where certain dwellings designed for the elderly or the disabled are sold (see s.104(6)(*b*) of the 1957 Act and the 1981 Ministerial Letter, *op. cit.*, Annex A, General Consent B(13)).

A disposal by an authority without the requisite consent and made after July 18, 1980 is *void,* unless it was made to an individual (or to two or more individuals) and did not extend to any other dwelling (see the 1980 Act, s.137); disposals without consent made on or before this date are treated as valid in favour of a person claiming under the council, by section 128(2) of the Local Government Act 1972.

(b) *Special purchase schemes*

(i) "Build for sale" schemes

Section 93 of the 1980 Act makes clear that the power of councils to *acquire* land for the provision of housing accommodation (under s.96 of the Housing Act 1957) "includes power to do so for the purpose of *disposing* of [dwellings] . . . to be erected . . . on the land or of *disposing* of the land to a person who intends to provide housing accommodation on it" (italics supplied). This makes clear that authorities can themselves "acquire and build for sale" (there was previously some doubt as to the legality of this, but a variety of possible "build for sale" schemes for councils had been set out in a 1977 D.o.E. handbook on *Local Authorities and Building for Sale*). Section 93 also in effect allows authorities to sell their land to private developers for the erection of "starter homes," on which council tenants and those on the general waiting list could perhaps be given first option (see also the 1981 Ministerial Letter, *op. cit.*, Annex A, General Consent F(1)); further, authorities can enter into "partnership" arrangements with builders under which the builder is given a *licence*[49] to erect "starter homes" on council land, the freehold of which can later be transferred by the council to the individual purchasers: the 1981 Ministerial Letter was anxious to encourage such schemes, with a view to subsequent sales to purchasers at the maximum allowable discounts (*op.cit.*, Annex B, para. 7(iv)).

(ii) "Improvement and sale" schemes

Section 93 of the 1980 Act also allows councils to acquire land for the purpose of disposing of dwellings already erected on it; and vacant council dwellings in need of repair, improvement or conversion may be sold to private individuals or builders who undertake to repair, improve or convert them for sale into owner-occupation (see the 1981 Ministerial Letter, *op. cit.,* Annex A, General Consent B(3)). In addition, where land with dwellings already on it is acquired by a council with a view to repairing, improving or converting the dwellings and thereafter selling them (*i.e.* pursuant to an "AIMS" scheme—Acquisition for Improvement and Sale), or where land with dwellings on it is already owned by a council which now wishes to repair, improve or convert the dwellings for sale (*i.e.* pursuant to an "IFS" scheme— Improvement for Sale),[50] then under section 108 of the 1980 Act[50] the Minister can make contributions to the council's net cost of operating the scheme (*i.e.* after deducting the resale price received).

(iii) "Equity–sharing" schemes

Another method whereby a council may assist someone (particularly a first-time buyer) to purchase one of its properties, is by way of an "equity-sharing" scheme (sometimes called a "half-and-half" or "shared owner-ship" scheme). These schemes allow the buyer to reduce his mortgage commitments by paying a combina-tion of mortgage instalments and rent. The usual arrange-ment is that the purchaser (who is not necessarily a sitting tenant) buys a long lease of the property with the aid of a council mortgage (*infra*), for a premium which initially represents (in general) half the market value of the property (though the share can be less than half), and he also pays half (or any other appropriate portion) of the usual council rent for the property (subject to a deduction where relevant to reflect his greater repairing responsibili-ties); he is further given an option to purchase the freehold at any time for half (or any other appropriate portion) of the current market value. Thus the title "equity-sharing" is misleading, since the authority retains the whole of the freehold until the purchaser chooses to acquire it (see D. Hughes, *Roof,* November 1976, at p. 164). For an account of the pioneering Birmingham scheme, see *Housing Policy, op. cit.*, at p. 104.

The legality of the grant by an authority of the necessary option to purchase has been confirmed by the new section 104(9) of the Housing Act 1957 (inserted by s.91(1) of the 1980 Act), and, as regards options granted before August 8, 1980, by section 94 of the 1980 Act (previously the law had been in doubt: see, *e.g. Hansard*

(Commons) July 28, 1977, Vol. 936, col. *616*, and
D. Hughes, *Roof*, September 1978, at p. 132). Those buying
under equity-sharing schemes cannot be secure tenants
(see the 1980 Act, Sched. 3, para. 1); and where such a
scheme is entered into with a council on or after August 8,
1980, it will normally be outside the terms of the
Leasehold Reform Act 1967, so that enfranchisement
under that Act will not be possible (see the 1980 Act,
s.140). Specific consent for equity-sharing schemes is
included in the 1981 Ministerial Letter, where the schemes
are described as "shared ownership sales" (*op. cit.*,
Annex A, General Consent D: *inter alia,* this permits
discounts, the selling of several successive "shares" of the
equity—called "staircasing," and the insertion of pre-
emption clauses). A model equity-sharing scheme and
model clauses for adoption were issued by Ministerial
Letters dated October 15, 1980 and February 6, 1981,
respectively: this scheme and these model clauses have
now been incorporated into the 1981 consent (*op. cit.*,
Annex A, General Consent D (12)).

Nevertheless, despite these recent developments, the
schemes still possess more than their fair share of legal
problems (*cf., e.g.* D. Hughes, *Roof*, January 1977, at p.
19, C. Wolmar, *Roof*, September 1979, at p. 146). A
"low-start" mortgage scheme (*infra*) attached to a "normal" purchase is a much simpler method of encouraging
low-income owner occupation than equity-sharing; and in
any event the "half-rent" arrangement no longer appears
quite such a bargain, given the rent increases planned by
the Minister.[51]

(iv) The slow development of special purchase schemes

Despite these various special methods whereby councils
can encourage low-cost home ownership, they do not
appear to have been greatly used: by January 1981, out of
approximately 365 English housing authorities, 54 had
sold land to private developers for "starter homes," 93

had licensed builders to erect on council land "starter homes" for sale, 42 had modernised properties with a view to sale to first-time buyers, and only 20 had introduced equity-sharing schemes[52] (see *The Times,* January 13, 1981).

(c) *Special mortgage schemes*

Quite apart from the schemes for sale of council properties just considered, councils possess specific statutory powers to grant mortgages in very flexible ways (in addition to the *general* power to allow the price or part thereof to be secured by mortgage, contained in s.104(4) of the Housing Act 1957). Thus under the Housing Act 1980 (s.110(11)–(12)) councils may, for a period of up to five years from the date of the mortgage, charge a lower rate of interest than normal,[53] or waive payments of interest entirely, or dispense with repayments of capital, provided that the mortgagor has acquired a house "in need of repair or improvement," the scheme is approved by the Minister, and the mortgagor has agreed to carry out specified works of repair or improvement within a stipulated period. Such arrangements are popularly called "homesteading" schemes (see further D.o.E. Circular no. 20/80 on *Sale of Unimproved Homes for Improvement by Purchaser—'Homesteading'* (1980), paras. 25–27 and Annex C).

Authorities have separate and rather more general powers to grant "low-start" mortgages under section 43(3) (*c*) of the Housing (Financial Provisions) Act 1958 (as amended in particular by s.37(4) of the Local Government Act 1974), which permits, *inter alia*:

(i) the granting of mortgages providing for lower than normal[53] repayments in the early years of the mortgage term, by reducing the rate of repayment of capital and/or deferring payment of part of the normal rate of interest (which will be particularly helpful for young first-time buyers); and

(ii) the making of maturity loans, under which interest only is payable during the life of the loan and its capital is repaid in a lump sum on termination (which will be particularly helpful for older purchasers who do not intend to move again): see D.o.E. Circular no. 67/74 on *Local Authority Advances for House Purchase* (1974), para. 7. Such 1958 Act schemes no longer have to be submitted to the Minister for approval (see the Housing Act 1980, Sched. 26).

It may be noted here that a council mortgagee can have an additional remedy on the mortgagor's default which is not possessed by other mortgagees, where a council property was purchased by the mortgagor *before* August 8, 1980, and a right of pre-emption was included in the purchase deed (*i.e.* pursuant to the old s.104(3) of the Housing Act 1957): in such a case, once the council has become entitled to exercise the mortgagee's power of sale, then under sections 112 and 113 of the Housing Act 1980 it may, with the leave of the county court, vest the property in itself pursuant to the pre-emption clause and thereby extinguish the mortgage. It had previously been held that the right of pre-emption did not give a council any greater power of sale as mortgagee than that conferred on ordinary mortgagees by section 101 of the Law of Property Act 1925, so that a "sale to itself" was a nullity: *Williams* v. *Wellingborough B.C.* [1975] 3 All E.R. 462, (C.A.). Sections 112 and 113 do not extend to purchases of council properties on or after August 8, 1980, whether or not under the right to buy, but in any event we have noted that rights of pre-emption can now only rarely be inserted (see the 1980 Act, ss.19(4), 104(5)–(6), and the 1981 Ministerial Letter, *op.cit.*).

(d) *Conveyancing machinery*

The legal formalities for a non-right to buy purchase will not generally differ from those of a normal conveyancing transaction, but certain special features merit brief consideration here.

(i) The contract

The normal conveyancing practice is of course for the early negotiations between the parties to be conducted "subject to contract," so that neither party will be bound to proceed until formal contracts are exchanged (see, *e.g.* J. T. Farrand, *Contract and Conveyance, op. cit.,* Chapter 2). However, this "no liability until exchange" principle is not a universal legal rule, and the Court of Appeal has managed to dispense with it, and to hold that a binding contract had been formed at an earlier stage, in a case where a council house was being sold to the sitting tenant: *Storer* v. *Manchester City Council* [1974] 3 All E.R. 824. Here the Town Clerk had sent out a simple form of agreement to the prospective purchaser, together with a letter stating that on him signing and returning the agreement, the Town Clerk would send him the agreement signed on behalf of the Corporation "in exchange"; it was decided that the contract had been concluded once the tenant had accepted the council's "offer" by signing and returning the agreement, despite the absence of any traditional "exchange," so that the council could not escape from carrying out the sale.

The resolution of such disputes can often turn on fine points of construction, as indicated by the subsequent House of Lords decision in *Gibson* v. *Manchester City Council* [1979] 1 All E.R. 972. Here again the council decided to call off the "negotiations" before formal exchange, but this time the tenant failed to establish a binding contract: the negotiations were not as far advanced as in *Storer's* case, and the judgments were able to fall back on the traditional contract law distinction between an offer and a mere invitation to treat. It will be recalled that where the right to buy is involved, there is no contractual element at all.[54]

A contract for sale to a sitting tenant will not normally operate to end the tenancy, whether by surrender or otherwise, so that he will remain liable for rent until the date when the sale is completed, or such other date as may be specified in the contract: see *Doe* d. *Gray* v. *Stanion* (1836) 1 M. & W. 695, *Nightingale* v. *Courtney* [1954] 1 All E.R. 362, (C.A.); we have seen that the situation for right to buy cases is governed by section 16(11) of the 1980 Act.[55]

(ii) Investigation of title

It is quite common, where a council house with an unregistered title is being sold, for the authority to insist on a clause in the contract providing that there shall be no abstract or investigation of title (see, *e.g.* the contract in *Storer's* case, *supra*). Such clauses (which are comparatively unusual in private sales) will not however absolve the authority from the duty to convey free from undisclosed incumbrances of which it either knows or ought to know (see, *e.g. Goold* v. *Birmingham, Dudley and District Bank* (1888) 58 L.T. 560, *Becker* v. *Partridge* [1966] 2 All E.R. 266, (C.A.)).

Where the title to the property is unregistered but the property is in an area of compulsory registration, then the council may be prepared to offer a certificate as to the title containing a statement of all incumbrances affecting it, in a form agreed with the Land Registry, thus easing the task of the purchaser's solicitor in applying for first registration: see the Land Registry's practice note on *First Registration of Title—Purchasers from Local Authorities*, dated December 10, 1974, and compare the special provisions relating to the right to buy in section 20 of the 1980 Act.[56]

(iii) The conveyance or transfer

The contract will usually provide that the deed of conveyance or transfer (and mortgage where appropriate) must be drawn up in the standard form favoured by the vendor-authority; we have seen that for right to buy cases, Schedule 2 to the 1980 Act contains detailed provisions governing the content of the deed.[57]

Where a discount from the price has been given, a covenant governing repayment of all or part of the discount on premature disposal will have to be inserted pursuant to section 104B of the Housing Act 1957.[58]

(iv) Removal and conveyancing costs

Where the tenant is buying a council house other than the one which he occupies, the authority may pay his removal expenses; and if the property in question has never been let and was built expressly for sale or letting, the authority may also pay any other expenses (*e.g.* conveyancing fees) incurred in connection with the purchase (other than the price!): see section 93(1)–(2) of the Housing Finance Act 1972. Section 93 does not apply to sales to sitting tenants of the dwellings occupied by them; and we have seen that conveyancing costs where the tenant exercises the right to buy are dealt with by section 21 of the 1980 Act.[59]

Notes

[1] The then leader of the G.L.C. Conservative opposition described council house sales in 1976 as "a weapon against the tide of Marxism and Socialism": reported in *Roof,* November 1976, at p.161.

[2] The sale of council housing has even featured in a strip cartoon in *Tracy*, a comic for girls: this resulted in a complaint to the Press Council: see *Roof,* September 1980, at p.135. For general discussions concerning the effects of council house sales, see, *e.g.* the 1977 Green Paper on *Housing Policy,* Cmnd. 6851, at p.106; A. Friend, *A Giant Step Backwards,* C.H.A.S. Occasional Paper, No.5, 1980; H. Aughton, *Housing Finance—A basic guide,* (Shelter, 1981), pp.20–22.

[3] If this rate is achieved, after 10 years nearly one-third of the present "traditional" council housing stock (*i.e.* houses, rather than flats or old

people's dwellings, etc.) will have been sold: see the Second Report from the Environment Committee, *op.cit.*, at para. 25.

[4] For a discussion of the interest rate where the mortgage is obtained from the council, see *infra*, p. 191.

[5] See *supra*, pp. 131–2.

[6] See *infra*, pp. 179–80.

[7] See s.2 of the 1977 Act; in the absence of dependent children, it is unlikely that a priority need could be established, since repossession is probably not the sort of "emergency" contemplated by s.2(1)(*b*), and financial hardship may well not be considered "vulnerability" within s.2(1)(*c*).

[8] See s.17 of the 1977 Act, and the *Code of Guidance* to this Act, D.o.E., 1977, para. 2.15; however, there have been some very "hard" cases on intentional homelessness: see, *e.g. De Falco* v. *Crawley B.C.* [1980] 1 All E.R. 913, (C.A.), *Din* v. *L.B. of Wandsworth*, [1981] 3 All E.R. 881, (H.L.).

[9] *See infra*, pp. 190–1.

[10] But the position regarding the incidence of repairing costs where a long lease of a *flat* is purchased can be complicated: see *infra*, pp. 184–5.

[11] *Infra*, pp. 186–7.

[12] Numerous "delaying tactics" were suggested in *The Great Sales Robbery* (S.C.A.T. Publications, 1980), pp. 25–26.

[13] See *Hansard* (Commons) March 4, 1981, Vol. 1000, col. 269.

[14] See *supra*, pp. 98–105.

[15] See *The Times*, October 28, 1980, October 26, 1981.

[16] There is no *right* to buy a *part*-share of a council house under an equity-sharing scheme (*infra*, pp. 197–8).

[17] For a detailed explanation of who can be secure tenants, see Chap. 2.

[18] Thus, *e.g.* tenancies from certain housing associations, or from the Housing Corporation, will qualify: ss.28(2), (4); but *cf.* s.2(2).

[19] See s.37(1), discussed *supra*, pp. 27–8.

[20] As widely defined in s.50(3): see *supra*, p. 30.

[21] See *infra*, pp. 194–5.

[22] See *infra*, p. 208.

[23] See *infra*, p. 180.

[24] But s.3(5) provides for valuation as at August 8, 1980, where the tenant's initial notice was served not later than April 3, 1981.

[25] Were it not for this provision, the discount for some properties in the London area could well currently exceed £25,000: for the position regarding the G.L.C.'s Barbican estate, see D. Summers, *Roof,* November 1980, at p. 166.

[26] See note 20, *supra.*

[27] [*Sic*]: subsequent disposals of the freehold will in fact be by way of *transfer*, since the title will have been registered (*infra*); *cf.* J. T. Farrand, *Contract and Conveyance* (3rd ed., 1980), pp. 214–217.

[28] An exempt disposal does not wipe off the liability to repay discount as such, which continues to bind successive owners for the remainder of the five-years' period.

[29] See *supra*, pp. 78, 81; a disposal in pursuance merely of a separation agreement would *not* be exempt.

[30] Thus it may sometimes be preferable for the relevant beneficiary under the deceased's estate to take the dwelling *in specie* and pay the deceased's debts or legacies himself where appropriate, rather than for the personal representatives to *sell* the dwelling within the relevant five-years' period in order to pay those debts or legacies: see T. M. Aldridge, *The Housing Act 1980*, (1980), p. 37.

[31] Although the obligation is only to repay the appropriate portion of the discount *on demand,* the Minister contemplated that it would *have* to be repaid on *any* relevant disposal within the five-years' period: see H.C. Standing Committee F on the Housing Bill, February 12, 1980, cols. 273–276. It has been pointed out that if this is correct, it "suggests that a local authority omitting to make the demand other than for good cause might find themselves liable to the surcharge provisions of the Local Government Act 1972, Pt. VIII" (A. Arden, *The Housing Act 1980,* Current Law Statutes Reprints, notes to s.8; see also *infra*, p. 193); the concept of "good cause" here is likely to be somewhat restricted in the case of many Labour-controlled authorities.

[32] *cp. e.g. Austerberry* v. *Oldham Corp.* (1885) 29 Ch.D. 750, (C.A.). Where appropriate, therefore, a purchaser must ensure prior to completion that his vendor will pay off the charge.

[33] For the methods of service, see s.22(2) of the 1980 Act, and the Local Government Act 1972, s.231(1); see also P. Liell, *Council Houses and the Housing Act 1980*, (1981), Chap. 8, concluding that "[p]ersonal service . . . is the surest and best method" (at p. 110).

[34] See *supra,* pp. 29–30.

[35] In such a case the council may need extra time to check the alleged prior tenancies, but it may instead simply accept the tenant's statutory declaration as "sufficient evidence" of those tenancies: see s.25.

[36] Solicitors acting either for the "right to buy" purchaser or his successors in title where the property is not within an area of compulsory registration must be alive to this point, since failure to register renders the transaction void as regards the legal estate after two months from the date of the deed (under s.123 of the Land Registration Act 1925); however, if the right to buy is being exercised with the aid of a council mortgage, the authority may be expected to ensure registration of the title; and even if the council is not the mortgagee, the first purchaser's solicitor should realise the need for registration from the special certificate whereby title is deduced (see s.20(2)–(3), *infra*): see further T.M. Aldridge, *op. cit.*, at pp. 126–127.

[37] This avoids the problems presented by *Campden Hill Towers Ltd.* v. *Gardner* [1977] 1 All E.R. 739, (C.A): see *supra*, pp. 99–100.

[38] Thus clearly imposing liabiliy for "inherent defects": *cp. Ravenseft Properties Ltd.* v. *Davstone (Holdings) Ltd.* [1979] 1 All E.R. 929: see *supra,* p. 101.

[39] Such as lifts: *cp. Liverpool C.C.* v. *Irwin* [1976] 2 All E.R. 39, (H.L.): see *supra,* p. 105; subject to contrary agreement, where the tenant enjoyed the use, during the secure tenancy, of any premises, facilities or services in common with others, the long lease must include such rights: Sched. 2, Pt. III, para. 12.

[40] See note 29, *supra.*

[41] See note 30, *supra.*

[42] This has been given in general terms by a Ministerial Letter dated September 22, 1980, para. 28.

[43] See *supra,* pp. 171–2.

[44] See *supra,* pp. 10–18.

[45] See *supra,* pp. 175–7.

[46] See *supra,* pp. 16–18.

[47] See *supra,* pp. 13–14.

[48] Similar to those required in right to buy cases: see *supra,* pp. 179–80.

[49] The grant of such a licence does not constitute a "disposal" for the purpose of either s.93 of the Housing Act 1980 or s.104 of the Housing Act 1957: see the Ministerial Letter dated September 2, 1980, para. 12, and the 1981 Ministerial Letter, *op.cit.,* Annex A, General Consent B(8), (16).

[50] See further D.o.E. Circular no.20/80 on *Local Authority Improvement for Sale Scheme* (1980), paras. 3–24 and Annex A.

[51] See *supra,* pp. 131–2.

[52] Of the 83,095 council dwellings sold in 1980, only 860 were sold under equity-sharing schemes: see *Roof,* July 1981, at p. 8.

[53] For the "normal" interest rate under s.110 of the 1980 Act (which covers not just right to buy mortgages), see *supra,* p. 191.

[54] See *supra,* p. 183.

[55] *Supra,* pp. 182–3.

[56] See *supra,* p. 182.

[57] *Supra,* pp. 183–5.

[58] See *supra,* p. 195.

[59] *Supra,* p. 187.

Chapter 9

TENANT INVOLVEMENT AND HOUSING CO-OPERATIVES

1. *Degrees of Tenant Involvement*

In 1977, the D.o.E. produced a handbook on systems for tenant involvement in housing management, in which reference was made to what many people believed was "a crisis of confidence in council housing management," resulting from a lack of mutual understanding between tenants and councils (*Getting tenants involved*, p. 3). This handbook emphasised that "the involvement of council tenants in their housing management is no passing fad" (*op. cit.*, at p. 6); indeed, several of the problems discussed earlier in this book (relating, *e.g.* to allocations and transfers, tenancy conditions, and repairs) might be alleviated, or at least better understood, by progressively increased tenant involvement.

We have already seen that several *individual* rights have been conferred on secure tenants by the Housing Act 1980; however, the Act does little in relation to the *collective* rights of tenants, which is seen by some as a major omission: thus the Labour party, "tak[ing] an analogy from another field," has pointed out: "We do not see the individual rights of workers under employment protection legislation as any substitute for industrial democracy, or as lessening the need for collective organisation through trade unions" (*A Future For Public Housing*, 1981, p. 30).

Collective tenant involvement can take many forms: there is a broad division between tenant *participation* schemes, enabling tenants to *share* decision-making with the council, and tenant *co-operative* schemes, which enable tenants actually to *control* certain areas of decision-making themselves. Both such schemes of *collective* involvement must be distinguished from the *individual* equity-sharing schemes discussed in the previous chapter.

A more sophisticated four-fold division of schemes for collective tenant involvement emerged from D.o.E. Circular no. 8/76 on *Housing Co-operatives* (1976), para. 5, and the seminal Final Report of the Working Party on *Housing Co-operatives* (1975), p. 4 (this Working Party was chaired by Mr. Harold Campbell, and is hereafter referred to as the "Campbell Report"). First, at the lowest level, tenants may simply have the right to be consulted before the council makes certain management decisions. Secondly, there may be a "management co-operative" in which the tenants, although they do not collectively hold any interest in the property, are given collective responsibility for some (or all) of the management decisions. Thirdly, the tenants may in effect collectively take over the property itself if the council is prepared to lease it to them as a "non-equity co-operative": here the tenants as a body will collectively hold the group of houses or flats which they individually occupy, but they will not have any personal stake in the equity, save that they may be given a stake limited to a share repayable on leaving at its original "par" value. Fourthly, there may be a "co-ownership society," which is similar to the third scheme in that the residents collectively hold and manage the property on a leasehold basis, but differs from it in that each tenant shares in the equity through an entitlement to a payment on leaving (representing, *e.g.* his contribution to paying off the group mortgage or his share of the gain in the value of his dwelling), which exceeds the "par" value of his share.

Co-operative enterprises do of course extend beyond housing to many other activities, such as food retailing (for some of the early history of general co-operative ventures in Britain, see H. Campbell, *Roof*, May 1979, at p. 104). Modern co-operative developments in the housing field have tended to be concentrated overseas, particularly in Scandinavia (see, *e.g.* C. Ward, *Tenants Take Over* (1974), Chapter 7). However, the Campbell Report aroused fresh interest in housing co-operatives, and in 1976 the Housing Corporation set up a separate body called the Co-operative Housing Agency, to provide guidance and financial support for such schemes. The Campbell Report considered that for council estates there could be "a range of practical experiments . . . varying from minority tenant participation to full co-operative ownership and control" (*op. cit.*, at p. 12). However, the Co-operative Housing Agency closed down in November 1978 (when some of its functions were taken over by an internal department of the Housing Corporation); and despite the impetus given by the Campbell Report, co-operatives have failed properly to develop as a new form of tenure: the principal reasons for this failure appear to be the excessive bureaucracy and legal complications with which co-operatives are still bedevilled, together with the unwillingness of many tenants to devote the necessary time to the running of the schemes.

We shall now look in greater detail at the main ways in which council tenants[1] can become collectively involved with the running of their estates.

2. *General Involvement in the Authority's Management Functions*

At its most basic level, tenant involvement can take the form of the right to be *consulted* before the council reaches its decisions. The D.o.E. handbook on *Getting tenants involved* gave general advice to authorities concerning systems whereby tenants could share housing management decisions with council members and officers, including the co-option of tenants (if necessary with full voting rights) on to council committees and sub-committees pursuant to section 102 of the Local Government Act 1972 (*op. cit.*, at pp. 10–13), and the involvement of tenants in special *ad hoc* consultative committees or in regular discussion meetings (*op. cit.*, at pp. 13–14); see also *Tenant participation in council housing management*, H.D.D. Occasional Paper 2/77, D.o.E., 1977. It was estimated that in 1978–79, nearly 60 per cent. of local authorities had some sort of tenant participation scheme (see *The 1980 Annual Review: Local Authority Housing Management Statistics*, Institute of Housing, p. 17).

There were quite detailed provisions in the Labour government's 1979 Housing Bill for imposing uniform schemes of tenant consultation, under which each local authority would have been under a duty to set up a statutory *Tenants' Committee* for its *entire stock*; this statutory committee was to be "broadly representative of those who are [its] secure tenants," and the authority would have been obliged to consult it about matters of "housing management" such as variations in rent or in the other terms of secure tenancies (see cll. 20–21 and Sched. 3, Pt. I of the 1979 Bill). Authorities would also have been obliged under this Bill to establish quite separate consultative arrangements with "representative bodies" at *local* level, concerning changes restricted to particular neighbourhoods or estates (see cl. 22 and Sched. 3, Pt. II).

The consultation provisions relating to secure tenants in sections 42–43 of the 1980 Act are however rather lukewarm[2] by comparison: rents and other charges are excluded from the consultation process, and no detailed consultation mechanism is prescribed.

Consultation duties only arise under the 1980 Act if the matter is one of "housing management", *i.e.* if *in the opinion of the local authority*: (i) it relates to the management,[3] maintenance, improvement or demolition of dwellings let on secure tenancies, or relates to the provision of services or amenities relating to such dwellings (being services or amenities provided by the authority in its capacity as landlord, rather than those provided by it for the local inhabitants generally); and (ii) it represents a *new programme* of maintenance, improvement or demolition, or a *change in the practice or policy* of the authority;

and (iii) it is likely substantially to affect its secure tenants as a whole or a "group" of them: (s. 42(2), (5): a "group" of secure tenants is somewhat obscurely defined in s. 42(4) by reference to the tenants forming a "distinct social group," or occupying a "distinct class" of dwellings). However, a matter is expressly stated *not* to be one of "housing management" if it relates to the *rent* payable under any secure tenancy, or to any charge for services or facilities provided by the authority (s. 42(3): thus there are no consultation rights for tenants regarding those matters which perhaps most affect them as a whole in the present economic and political climate!).

With regard to "matters of housing management," every council must have established by October 3, 1981, and must thereafter maintain, such arrangements *as it considers appropriate* to enable those of its secure tenants who are likely to be substantially affected by these matters to be informed of the proposals and to comment on them within a specified period (s. 43(1)). Before coming to any decision on such matters, the council must consider any representations made to it in accordance with these arrangements (s. 43(2)). Further, every council must publish details of its consultation arrangements; a copy of the relevant information must be available for free inspection, and must be supplied to any member of the public requesting it on payment of a reasonable fee (s. 43(3)).

These duties are hardly onerous, and there is not even a duty to consult a tenants' association[4] as such, but merely to consult such body as the council itself forms (*cp.* the specific provisions relating to the role of "recognised tenants' associations" in the assessment of service charges for flats, contained in Sched. 19 of the 1980 Act, especially in para. 20: these provisions in Sched. 19 do not cover secure council tenancies—see para. 14(1)). However, the duties in section 43 would seem to be enforceable by injunction for breach of statutory duty in the county court (*cf.* s. 86(1)), perhaps by way of a representative action under the County Court Rules, Ord. 5, r. 8 (see A. Arden (1981) LAG Bul. 38); presumably an action in the High Court for mandamus (*via* judicial review under R.S.C. Ord. 53) would also lie.

3. *Management Co-operatives and Non-equity Co-operatives*

In a "management co-operative," control but not ownership is vested in the co-operative (which usually receives funds from the housing department, to be spent at the discretion of the co-operative on specified activities such as estate maintenance); whereas in a "non-equity co-operative," both control and ownership (on a leasehold basis) are vested in the co-operative, although each member can receive (at the most) the par value of his shareholding (which may be as little as £1), the rest of the equity remaining in the hands of the co-operative itself.

Special provisions have been made for co-operatives on council estates by Schedule 20 of the Housing Act 1980 (which supersedes the provisions in Sched. 1, para. 9 of the Housing Rents and Subsidies Act 1975[5]). Schedule 20 provides that where a local authority has made a "housing co-operative agreement" with a "housing co-operative" (*i.e.* a society, company or body of trustees approved by the Minister), whereby, with the Minister's approval,[6] the co-operative exercises any of the authority's powers and performs any of the authority's duties relating to its housing, then neither the agreement itself nor any letting of land in pursuance of it shall cause any relevant housing subsidy to be reduced, discontinued or recouped. These provisions cover not merely management co-operatives, but also non-equity co-operatives where the land is let to the co-operative by the authority (para. 5); but they do *not* generally cover co-ownership societies, unless the Minister otherwise stipulates (para. 2(2)–(3)).

It may be recalled that where the landlord's interest belongs to a "housing co-operative" and the property is comprised in a "housing co-operative agreement" within Schedule 20 (*i.e.* it is in effect a non-equity co-operative), then the tenancies of the individual occupiers can be "secure," since the "landlord condition" will be satisfied (see s. 28(2) (*c*)[7]; but *cf.* s. 49, which exempts from security those tenancies under which the landlord co-operative is a fully mutual housing association—*i.e.* one whose rules restrict membership to tenants and prospective tenants of the association and prevent non-members from taking tenancies—and is registered both with the Housing Corporation under the Housing Act 1974 and with the registrar of friendly societies under the Industrial and Provident Societies Act 1965). Tenants of housing management co-operatives will be "secure" because their immediate landlord will still be the council itself (s. 28(2), (4) (*a*)).

Management co-operatives and non-equity co-operatives can be formed not only on existing council estates, but also on newly-built estates specifically designed for co-operatives, and even in relation to private housing which has been bought by the authority under its municipalisation programme or at the request of the private sector tenants: see the Campbell Report, *op. cit.,* at p. 8. However, this Report also suggested that council housing co-operatives should initially be based on new developments, or at least on carefully selected estates of up to 100 units (*op. cit.,* at p. 12); and Circular 8/76 pointed out that although co-operatives "could be established successfully in either flats or houses," they "may work better where the property is contiguous (*e.g.* a block of flats, a whole street, or a whole estate)": *op. cit.,* Annex A, para. 1. Management co-operatives for council properties have already been set up in several areas, for example the London Borough of Islington, Liverpool, and Glasgow (the Summerston project): see further C. Wolmar, *Roof,* November 1980, at p. 178.

With regard to rent levels, in management co-operatives the rent will still be paid to the authority, so that the normal rules regarding council rent-fixing will apply,[8] and Circular 8/76 suggested that authorities would probably wish to continue to charge rents "similar to those elsewhere on [their] estates" (*op. cit.*, Annex B, para. 6); but the Circular pointed out that authorities cannot normally exercise direct control over the rent levels of non-equity co-operatives (*op. cit.*, Annex B, para. 7). Tenants in council management co-operatives may claim rent rebates on satisfying the normal requirements,[9] while tenants in non-equity co-operatives can claim rent allowances where appropriate (see the new s.19 (5) (*f*) of the Housing Finance Act 1972, introduced by Sched. 15, para. 3 of the Housing Act 1980).

4. *Co-ownership Societies*

We have noted that a "co-ownership society" is similar to a non-equity co-operative in that the residents collectively hold and manage the property, but that it differs from a non-equity co-operative in that each member has a substantial individual share in the equity. The Campbell Report recommended that co-ownership schemes should be introduced in the local authority sector, and considered various ways in which this could be achieved (*op. cit.*, at pp. 44, 50–51). Nevertheless, we have seen that the provisions in Schedule 20 of the 1980 Act relating to "housing co-operative agreements" do *not* generally cover co-ownership societies (which are described in the Schedule as "shared ownership" schemes, and are defined as arrangements where a lease of the individual dwelling is granted on payment of a premium calculated by reference to a percentage of the value of the dwelling or of the cost of providing it, or under which the tenant or his personal representatives will or may be entitled to a sum calculated by reference directly or indirectly to the value of the dwelling), *unless* the Minister otherwise stipulates: Schedule 20, para. 2(2)–(3).

In any event, the introduction of co-ownership schemes for council estates could result in many lower-paid council tenants being unable to meet the higher costs involved[10]; while higher-paid council tenants may be more attracted to the individual "right to buy" discussed in the previous chapter than by proposals for establishing co-ownership schemes.

5. *Conclusions*

Although the director of the Co-operative Housing Agency saw this agency as being "a catalyst for great expansion" in 1976 (*The Times*, December 7, 1976), it is significant that the agency closed down within two years. As noted above, co-operatives have failed to "take off" as a new form of tenure, due partly to excessive administrative and legal complications, and also to a general reluctance amongst tenants to devote their leisure hours to management activities. With regard to council estates in particular, there has been considerable opposition to co-operatives from trade unions representing local authority building workers or "white collar" officers,[11] and many of the articulate and better-paid council tenants who might have been expected to press for the introduction of the various co-operative schemes have doubtless found the individual "right to buy" conferred by the 1980 Act a more attractive outlet for their energies (indeed, even where management co-operatives have already been set up on council estates, most of the residents will normally have the right to buy). At a more general level, the National Consumer Council has pointed out that "[i]nvolvement, participation, consultation [and] representation . . . are all fairly new words in the vocabulary of tenants, councillors and local authority officers" (*op. cit.*, at p. 124)[12]; and the Campbell Report itself was sufficiently realistic to recognise that "the unusual strength of the local authority tradition in this country and the scale of provision of municipal housing" had hitherto been major obstacles to the spread of co-operative housing (*op. cit.*, at p. 7). To a large extent these obstacles remain, and while imaginative schemes of tenant *participation* can do much to remove the "crisis of confidence in council housing management" referred to by the D.o.E. (*Getting tenants involved, op. cit.*, at p. 3), schemes for tenant *co-operatives* are unlikely to prove widespread on council housing estates in the foreseeable future.

Notes

[1] For a more general account of housing co-operatives prior to the 1980 Act, see I. Young and F. Anderson (1979) LAG Bul. 110, 136.

[2] *cp.* John Ward of the National Consumer Council: "Ultimately, this could turn out to be the most important piece of the whole Act. But a radical change in attitude among some councillors and housing officials will be necessary first—and also among some tenants" (reported in *Sheffield's Property Telegraph*, August 15, 1981).

[3] "Management" would include such matters as allocations, the keeping of pets, and the playing of ball games (see H.C. Standing Committee F on the Housing Bill, March 6, 1980, col. 898).

[4] Nevertheless, tenants' associations are not necessarily very representative bodies: the National Consumer Council has estimated that only about 5 to 8 per cent. of council tenants belong to tenants' associations: *Soonest mended* (1979), pp. 42–43.

[5] However, any approvals given for the purposes of Sched. 1, para. 9 of the 1975 Act have effect as if given under Sched. 20 of the 1980 Act: see Sched. 25, Pt. II, para. 74 of the 1980 Act.

[6] This may be given by the Minister in general terms, *e.g.* to all local authorities (Sched. 20, para. 4).

[7] Discussed *supra*, p. 11; Rent Act protection is excluded by s. 16 of the Rent Act 1977, as amended by Sched. 25, Pt. I, para. 34 of the 1980 Act.

[8] See Chap 6.

[9] See *supra*, p. 141.

[10] The provisions of the Rent Act 1977 can apply to such co-ownership schemes as between the co-operative and the individual tenants (unless the scheme is excluded by s. 15 of the 1977 Act), which can give rise to considerable difficulties for a rent officer called upon to fix "fair rents" for the individual dwellings: *cf.* R. Franey, *Roof*, November 1977, at p. 165.

[11] See the Campbell Report, *op. cit.*, at p. 23.

[12] One housing manager described housing co-operatives as a "potty idea": recorded by M. Grant in *Local Authority Housing: Law Policy and Practice in Hampshire*, Hampshire L.A.G., 1976, p. 26.

INDEX